Father's Touch

Millennial Mind Publishing
An imprint of American Book Publishing
325 East 2400 South, Salt Lake City, Utah 84115
www.american-book.com
Printed in the United States of America on acid-free paper.

Father's Touch

Designed by Jana Rade, design@american-book.com

Publisher's Note: *This publication is designed to provide accurate and authoritative information in regard to the subject matter covered. It is sold or distributed with the understanding that the publisher and author is not engaged in rendering legal, accounting, or other professional service. If legal advice or other expert assistance is required, the services of a competent professional person in a consultation capacity should be sought.*

Library of Congress Cataloging-in-Publication Data is available upon request.

ISBN 1-58982-112-2

D'Haene, Donald, Father's Touch

Special Sales

These books are available at special discounts for bulk purchases. Special editions, including personalized covers, excerpts of existing books, and corporate imprints, can be created in large quantities for special needs. For more information e-mail orders@american-book.com or call 1-800-296-1248.

Father's Touch

Donald D'Haene

Dedication

For Erik, Marina, Ronny
My young half-sister and three half-brothers
Mother
Fellow survivors
And silent victims past and present
Unable to find their way out of their darkness

Introduction

"There is nothing more helpless than a human child."

What happens to the soul of a child who is held prisoner in childhood and manipulated to the extent that normal is weird? Following the murder of that soul by unaccountable and unrecountable acts, how does one champion that child? How does one create a haven or a harbour for that soul? These questions, and their answers, provide grist for the therapy mill that is part of the process of healing for adults who were held captive and abused as children.

As an adult who is thriving now following years of abuse as a child, Donald D'Haene provides a personal perspective on his years as an abused boy. As a therapist who has worked with adult survivors of childhood sexual abuse for a number of years, I recognize the importance of telling your story—for yourself, and for others. With his account, Donald allows us to get as close as possible to the experience of being sexually abused, without actually being a victim.

Why is history important for us? Beyond the importance for Donald, his personal account helps to create awareness that abuse happens. With this awareness, all of us can take more responsibility in stopping abuse. It does take a village to raise a healthy child.

Perhaps even more important, Donald's accounting is a source of inspiration for other adults who are feeling isolated and ashamed of being sexually abused as children. His testimony and ultimate journey through healing says that there is hope—not without hardship or distraction—but hope none the less for those whose souls have been so tortured then. There is a NOW!

JOHN R. FIELD, B.A., M. Sc.

Author's Note

With my siblings' blessing, I share with you our autobiographical story. I thank them for their courage and faith.

I began writing a personal diary in 1981. Dated quotes from my diary are used to highlight feelings and emotions which are particular to that period in my life. As well my narrative is sporadically interrupted by italicised memories and experiences in the voice of 'Other Donald'.

Excerpts from newspaper reports, court transcripts and statements, and journal entries are reproduced with the original Canadian spelling.

Certain names have been changed to protect their identities.

I hope the following account will provide insight into the crime of sexual abuse and its effects on children. Education and awareness empowers victims and weakens predators. If one victim, after reading this book, realizes he is not alone, not to blame, and has nothing to be ashamed of, its composition will have been worthwhile.

This book is for survivors of sexual abuse: our numbers are legion.

Chapter One

Nothing looks the same.

Pastoral images glide by my window as we continue our journey. A rabbit emerges from a distant cloud, and my daydream quells my anxiety. Queer how a grown man can float back to the familiarity of a treasured childhood memory. One of my favorite pastimes as a youngster was lying in the tall grass, watching the world go around. Actually, I knew the clouds moved across my stillness, but this game allowed me to go to anywhere I wanted, any place but here.

Why would I expect anything to look the same? I haven't set eyes on my childhood residences for more than two decades. Yet this absence doesn't diminish the importance of my return or the discomfort it causes me. I've raised a thousand excuses why I shouldn't visit the past. Many of them originated with well-meaning friends and acquaintances.

"Forget the past. Look ahead, not behind. With time you'll forget."

But is it possible to forget the past? And if so, is forgetting the healthiest course?

I have recollections of events, of dreams that never lie, of written evidence that the past did indeed occur. For the most part, I experience my past through a series of flashbacks, phenomena that occur frequently. They permeate all facets of my life: a walk in the country, a sound, a smell, or a voice triggering the movie reels in my mind. Instantly, and without warning, I'm returned into a familiar incident or scene, back to a time and place far away. Lasting anywhere from seconds, minutes, to even an hour, flashbacks can be interrupted by present-day activity, yet resumed without breaking their rhythms. I have learned to control their duration by creating diversions.

Because I am not connected to their reality, they seem foreign to me—as though I am experiencing someone else's memories. At times, these flashbacks paralyze, shock, frighten, or sadden me. Sometimes they make me laugh. Only a trained and knowing eye can see through my controlled exterior. The Donald I was in my life with Father is alien to me and alive only in my flashbacks. The world surrounding me assumes any public disclosure translates into a personal reality. However, in my case nothing could be further from the truth. The more I speak or write about my family history, the more unreal it becomes. Those listening to or reading my words may well experience an emotional response to my story I can only envy.

And so my companion's spontaneous insistence that we travel back to the past to make my memories real, takes me by such surprise I consent. I respond before I can muster an objection. While the quest is frightening to say the least, the attraction of the unknown beckons me. It is now or never.

Maurice is driving so I can absorb the sights and sounds of our trip. I would prefer the distractions of driving but he insists. It seems I have barely blinked and we are literally traveling down memory lane, in this case, just south of a small, quaint village named Belmont.

I know this will not be a dull trip for either of us, considering I lived in fourteen houses, attended seven schools and five houses of worship all before I reached my sixteenth birthday. Most were located within a forty-kilometer radius of Aylmer, a town in the southwest of Ontario, population 5,000. Some dwellings were pleasant eno ugh as I recall, while others were nothing more than glorified shacks. None were homes. Each was my father's house—a statement that seems part of a dream to me now, an acknowledgement I had a past, a reality that flows between dream and imagination.

Other than the numbing hum of the engine, our silence is broken only by the occasional directions I provide my companion.

"Turn right, Maurice...go straight...veer left. Wait! Slow down a bit. Something looks familiar."

At first I don't fully recognize this place, and yet it compels me to question if I've been here before. Twenty-five years of renovations nearly disguise it. Signals from certain structures—a house on top of a hill, the barn, a silo, and a chicken coop—tell me to not pass by without a second glance. As I view the surroundings, I wonder why neighboring homesteads appear smaller than they used to. Not that they're tinier now, they just seemed to be, well, bigger in my childhood. Does every child magnify his perceptions ten-fold?

"Go up to the next road...and...turn around."

Sensing my discomfort, Maurice obeys without hesitation—heading east on Concession 7.

I glance in the side view mirror. Reading its small print leaves me cold: *Objects are closer than they appear.*

"I'm pretty sure that *was* it." *Is he really here?*

I become lightheaded and my stomach rebels.

Maurice eases my car onto the gravel shoulder, a few meters from the lane leading to the house.

I open the door slowly. I deliberately focus on the physical—the sound of every cam, latch, and lever. I extend one leg over the edge and downward. Heel, arch, and tip. My sole touches the ground. *He is here.*

A brisk March wind repels the steady flow of warmth from the dashboard, causing the beads of sweat on my forehead to evaporate. *I can feel him.*

My mind becomes still, my breathing shallow. Ears no longer hear. Concentrated beats cluster in my throat. My body throbs with each wave rolling over me, control eclipsed by celluloid reels. A montage of black-and-white home movies plays across my screen. Silently, they flicker, dancing within my disconnected self.

I can see him.

Dust particles float in a sunlit stream through the window, hitting the floor, disappearing. I wonder where they go once they vanish from sight. I try to catch them as they fall, following their flight to the wooden floor beneath me. The blazing sun burns through the windowpanes. The floorboards are particularly warm. The humidity in this tiny room is suffocating. I am enveloped in the heat.

This is his room.

"Where were you?"

"What?"

"I said, 'Donald', but you were on another planet!"

"Just for a moment, I *really* remembered. See those trees right there?" I point to the foremost parcel of property. "Daniel planted some of those, right from seedlings."

"Your father did leave his mark, didn't he?" *Today, we're going to play a new game.*

"Even though it sure looks different, this is the right place. This is *his* place."

Gone are the unfinished coats of pink and green painted siding, replaced by horizontal rows of rich dark-stained wooden clapboards. Windows, probably the double-insulated kind, have replaced the thin glass panes better suited for the sunshine states. The house on the hill looks more like a fortress than ever, as evergreens and maple trees buttress its privacy.

"Listen, Maurice." *Play quietly, 'cause you do not want to get your Papa angry.*

"I don't hear anything."

"That's what I mean. It's so quiet. Unbearably quiet. When we were kids, we'd hear faint noises from the farms around here—a tractor plowing, cows mooing—they'd echo in our silo."

And each winter, I tell him, only an old kitchen cook stove was expected to warm the entire house. I can still hear the wood crackling in the frozen silence. And, there were times I would get so excited listening for the mailman driving up the road, I'd run down the lane trying to beat him to the mailbox. Sometimes I'd even win.

Although I keep busy describing harmless memories, the emotional struggle continues. *You're my favorite.*

"Donald, you'll be okay. You're not alone anymore." Maurice's soothing words are challenged by a bark. The resident dog making his presence known brings us back to reality.

"He doesn't look too friendly, Maurice."

"Ah, bet his bark is worse than his bite, but the owners might be wondering what we're up to. Let's get outta here."

As we travel down the country road, the house on the hill recedes in my memory and with it, I pray, any trace of my father.

But one quick last glance in the mirror couldn't hurt, could it?

"Quit sitting there wasting your time!" Papa bellows.

I love all my animals. I spend long afternoons in the chicken coop studying the hens. I watch them as their chicks hatch, fighting their way out of their darkness. The mama hens protect their young. Suddenly a juvenile rooster is attacked by the larger Rhode Island Red. Provoked, he battles gallantly—and wins! Mesmerized, I cheer the little rooster in his victory. All of my friends have a name that complements their personalities—Duke, Snowy, Bruno. I love them because they don't hurt me.

"Come on Donald, let's feed the rabbits. I've already picked the lettuce," Papa continues. "You love those fluffy bunnies, don't you? Do you want a new one?"

Is a new rabbit worth it? I wonder.

Chapter Two

One of my childhoods was happy.

My first memories flicker like old home movies with sound: inside our house, a sofa with three torn cushions and one broken leg faces an aging television with rabbit ears on top. The TV is turned to an afternoon soap opera. Pages from picture books fill their wooden frames, hanging unevenly on walls of discolored paper. Everything is brown and broken but clean. Outside, the family dog is barking at black birds. My older brother, Ronny, and my baby sister, Marina, are playing in a pile of leaves nearby.

I never played my siblings' games, but I didn't mind watching them or refereeing their fights.

I was never lonely.

This is his room. Bored with the rays of light, I notice a broken doll on the floor. My attention is diverted for the time being. The doll's legs are separated from her hips so I try to fit the doll together so she can walk.

Mama, always adorned with her ten-year-old, gold-colored earrings and a plain white apron, was usually in the kitchen citing biblical verses. "The Lord is my shepherd….And you will know de trut', and de trut' will set you free….God is love." A Bible, apron, and earrings. These were the indelible symbols that marked Mother's simple life. Her daily routine involved cooking, cleaning, and studying scripture—everything she did revolved around her devotion to her children and her faith in God. Although the Lord was very important in her life, Mama constantly reminded us that her children meant everything to her.

Papa, on the other hand, was a remote figure. He never interacted with us. His attention was always directed elsewhere: a book or magazine, a letter he was writing, or a visitor to be engaged in philosophical discussion. Languages and matters of faith especially intrigued him—anything that challenged him intellectually. We children did not fall into those categories. Once in a while he would break from reading to chase us and rub his unshaven whiskers on our cheeks. We hated that. It hurt our skin. He did it to Mama and even she seemed to only tolerate it.

Papa worked a rotation of three different shifts at a factory, so he usually slept during the day. Mama would caution: "Play quietly, cause you do not want to get your Papa angry. He needs his sleep."

When Ronny and Marina made noise, they were disciplined. I wanted to be a good boy. I didn't want to get spanked or cause any trouble. I did what Mama and Papa told me to do.

Papa kept an album of his younger days in the top drawer of his dresser. I found my father's youth fascinating. I felt disappointed there were no pictures of mother as a young girl, but I'd study the photos of my parents' courtship for hours upon hours. I could see my mother's likeness in these old black and white photos, but my father seemed a completely different person. He'd become so much larger, with broad shoulders and large hands. And his hair had been blond but now it had grown dark. I wondered why had it changed.

Family life revolved around worshipping God as members of Jehovah's Witnesses, a religious sect renowned as much for its inflexible moral standards as for its proselytizing and controversial doctrines. Thrice weekly attendance was required at its house of worship, the Kingdom Hall, by every member of my family.

One of my earliest memories was of Mama explaining her faith by the use of picture books.

"See dese sheep here wit' de shepherd? Dere are only a few people in de whole world dat know de trut', Donald. Most of de people worship Satan but dey don't know dey do. Dey are de goats! De shepherd, Jesus, separates de sheep from de goats. Do you understand?"

"I think so."

"Do you know how fortunate you are dat you know de true God?"

"Oh yes, Mama."

"Now you must do what God wants you to do. He helps his people, especially de Elders at de hall, to know what he expects from dem. Dey tell us what we're supposed to do wit' de help from de Bible. Dat is why you must listen to your *vader* and *moeder*. We know de trut'."

"Okay, Mama."

My mother had told me the story of her getting The Truth, her truth, so often I knew it by heart. It became Mother's version of a bedtime story. I'm sure it was her way of convincing me we had the one true religion. Her early instruction proved successful.

My father never told me directly how he became a Jehovah's Witness, but it was a tale I overheard. He frequently repeated his account of discovery to guests and acquaintances. Papa pored over books explaining his faith and had acquired an extensive collection of religious material.

"Come on…breakfast is ready. We have to go to de service soon, too." A voice summons us, steeped in a familiar Flemish accent. "Ronny, Donald, Marina—de time is laat! My goodness, you children do not know how fortunate you are to grow up always knowing 'De Trut'."

"All right, already, we know it's late," says Ronny.

"Thank you, Mama, for 'D e T r u t'!" I add, mimicking Mama's struggle with the word 'truth.'

We're so attuned to our mother's broken English, we all understand what she means. Once in a while, we make fun of her foreign accent.

"Hey, do not laugh at your *moeder*."

But she lets us anyway.

"Mama, repeat after me…I think that the thief is thirteen, thank you."

"I t'ink dat de t'ief is dirteen, t'ank you."

We all break down laughing, especially Mama. She's such a good sport about our teasing. We have good times with her. She always makes us smile.

We might talk back to Mama, as kids sometimes do, but we never, ever, talk back to Papa.

As we gulp down our sweet pancakes with butter generously spread on top, I watch Mama intently.

Mother's white skin and teeth contrast sharply with her auburn hair full of big pink rollers. When she speaks, she talks loudly and gestures frequently, with robust hand motions. She is tall and big. There is never a question as to the meaning of her words or their intent. She seems so happy taking care of us.

Mealtime is not a family occasion, for Mama never sits down and eats with us. She always stands in the kitchen and eats after we are finished, usually in the cold pantry over the deep freezer. Papa doesn't eat with us either, unless we kids take our plates and sit in front of the television and he happens to be there too.

"Get ready for the meeting," Papa commands from his upstairs bedroom. "Your mother already told you once. Wife, send Donald up with my breakfast."

The rules for us do not apply to Papa.

This morning Father is still in bed, having overslept. After I bring the plate of food into his room, I notice Marina's broken doll on the floor. I try to put the doll's legs back in place.

"Pick up the stick, Donald."
Obediently, I bring over one of the doll's legs.
"Here, Papa!"
"Not that stick! Drop that on the floor and come here."
"What stick?"
"Here, I'll show you." Suddenly, he removes his blanket and I see a big person's naked body for the first time.
"See, this stick—this stick right here," he says pointing to it.
"That is a stick?"
"Yes, a different kind of stick." He lifts me up onto the bed. "We're going to play a new game. You like games, don't you?"

Our Sunday morning ritual is familiar to us: rushing through breakfast, running around the bedroom, getting Mama to put on our Sunday best clothes. Mama then fills a briefcase with the biblical literature we will study and preach with today: the latest *Watchtower* and *Awake* issues, a *New World Translation of The Bible*, and a few study books.

Even though it is the only time all of us are together, Papa still does not talk to us. We never stop and ask each other, "Do you feel like going today?" It's understood that Papa expects us to go, and we've been taught never to question him. Papa knows what God expects of us.

"Take the stick and wrap your little hand around it like this. Isn't it nice and soft? Doesn't it feel warm?" The stick is warm and too rubbery to be a stick. *"Then you push up and down, up and down until I tell you to stop."*

"What do you mean?"

"Like this." He wraps his hand around it and shows me the motions.

"Okay, Okay! Let me try." I wrap my small hand around his stick.

"This is fun, isn't it?"

"Donald, get down here already," Mama yells from the kitchen.

"Okay, Mama."

Sometimes it is difficult to please both Papa and Mama at the same time.

"Keep going. We have to go to the hall soon!"

"I can't!" I pull my hand away.

"I'll show you how to finish the game. Someday you'll be able to play the game with your own stick. Won't that be fun?"

I nod my head, wondering what day he is talking about. Tomorrow? Rapidly he makes the up and down movement until white cream spurts out into white tissue.

"Oh, that feels so good!"

I look forward to future games and the time when I can feel good too.

"Now this is OUR game. No one else has to know about it. This is our little secret so don't tell anyone! You want to play games again, don't you Donald?"

"Yes, Papa!"

"From house to house, from door to door, Jehovah's name we praise," I sing along with fellow Witnesses. These words are not foreign to me.

Someone has always held my hand as we walk the steps up to each stranger's house. Sometimes the stranger yells at the person holding my hand, "Don't come back." Other times they smile at me and ask me my name: "Oh, he's a shy one."

Every person who answers their door reacts differently to the big person beside me talking about God and his Kingdom. I love going to these stranger's doors. It gives me a chance to meet new people.

We are members of a small congregation of some eighty members and five Elders. Before we sit down, Papa buys the latest literature and then Mama asks him if she could have a couple of quarters to donate to the hall. Mama gives them to me and tells me to put them in the contribution box that is discreetly placed at the back of the room.

Today, our two-hour meeting begins with a Bible talk by Elder Bryan Smith on the responsibilities of being the male head in a Christian family.

"The man as head of the household...." My mind drifts off as usual.

"What just happened couldn't have happened," I tell myself. I just imagined The Game with Papa took place. But Papa said it would happen again, and I'd be better at it as I get older. Well, I won't think about that now. I'll just not think about it at all. How can I do that? I know—I'll pretend it never happened. If it did, it happened to someone else. That's right. The Game never happened to me. I'll never think about it again.

While Brother Smith is delivering his sermon, specifically focusing on two biblical characters from the Old Testament, I slip into a daydream, fantasizing about living amongst them—Lot's wife, who disobeyed her husband, looked back at Sodom, and was turned into a pillar of salt, and Jonah, who lived for three days inside a whale. Although I'm not even five years old, I question how this is possible. I wonder what it must have felt like. It sounds all so terribly frightening and very exciting at the same time.

Chapter Three

I came out of...an institution namely the Roman Catholic Church and was not satisfied spiritually nor had I any knowledge of the Bible as I had never been instructed in it and did not even have a copy of it as it was ill advised according to the church to have one and as it was strictly forbidden for many years as Catholics to have one...(I) was sorely disappointed through the years of my childhood while growing up in the atmosphere of World War Two, it is no wonder that my feelings were very bitter towards the hypocrisy around me and no solid foundation of faith to build on.

Daniel D'Haene, *Praise the Lord I Am Saved*, p. 6

I was always interested in my parents' homeland. As a little boy, I'd ask my mother endless questions, never stopping until I had all the information I hungered for. What was her childhood like? Were my grandparents loving? Did they discipline her? Was she happy? Why did she marry my father? What was his family like? What was it like to be Catholic? Why couldn't my parents read the Bible in Belgium? Why change religions? I had to know. I needed to know the origins of my family, but I didn't question Father. Then, I didn't know why.

Geographically, my parents' homeland is cradled within the borders of France, Holland, and Germany. Historically, Flemish soil has been the battleground between opposing faiths, serving as host for conflicting philosophical belief systems. Steeped in Catholicism for a thousand years, Belgium's stubborn religiosity proved a formidable driving force responsible for nurturing her growth. After a tug of war between her neighbors, Belgium gained her independence in 1830.

My parents were weaned on its predominantly Roman Catholic faith, its saints and legends.

Sister Ursula lay silent, struggling no more. The Belgian nun had fought the conqueror's flesh-penetrating attack, trying to deflect his hunger to possess and control. Attila's brute strength stilled her protests, but could not extinguish her commitment to her vows. Good meets evil. Darkness engulfs her. Suffering precedes reward. Once exalted, great sorrow is transformed into that which is perceived as holy. Oh sweet, beautiful, silent, perfect, dead Saint Ursula.

Mother is not a well-educated woman, having quit school at the age of twelve to take care of her invalid mother. She was born on April 28, 1935, and my father on September 10, 1933, in the province of West Vlanderen, Belgium. A bicycle ride's distance separated their birthplaces, Ingelmunster and Emelgem, now known as Izegem.

West Vlanderen (Flanders) is famous for *In Flanders Fields* by Canadian John McCrae, written in honor of the fallen soldiers of World War I. The Flanders American Cemetery and Memorial lies on the edge of the town of Waregem, fifteen miles from Izegem.

West Vlanderen is a picturesque province where quaint villages dot a countryside of rolling hills and brilliant blue fields of flax. Everybody knows everyone and everyone else's business. Neighbors chatter over fences and no secret is kept for long. My paternal and maternal grandparents were born into this setting just prior to World War I.

"Mama, how did you meet Papa?"

"When I was twenty, I went wit' some friends to a local pub. A young male singer—your Papa—was singing at his Aunt Sasha's small cafe in Ingelmunster, in de home country, Belgium. I heard about him and went wit' Willy to see de performance."

"Who is Willy, Mama?"

"Willy was a neighbor who was in love wit' me. Well, some members in the band failed to show up, so de whole evening turned out to be very easygoing. Occasionally your *vader* would dance in between sets. He noticed me when I was dancing wit' Willy. Your Papa was good-looking and he had a good singing voice. Later when he finished a set of songs, he came down and asked me to dance. We danced de rest of de evening toget'er."

"What about Willy?"

"He understood we were dere toget'er as friends. We still sat at a table toget'er. I could tell your Papa was interested in me, especially when he showed me pictures of his family. When we said good night, I only let him kiss my cheek. I knew he was impressed."

My mother became captivated by this young man with the velvet voice. She spent the next week daydreaming that this might be the man with whom she could share her life. The young pair agreed to meet again the next Sunday at their local theater. They dated exclusively from that moment on. My father had found a special young woman. Mother was pleased she had found someone who wanted a serious relationship. In a short period of time, my father proposed marriage.

Chapter Four

Belgian(s) are not the easiest men to debate with.... They become very dogmatic and vigorous in the assertion of their own opinions, arguing from the first principle, and insisting on the paramount authority of philosophical axioms in complete indifference to the hard facts of the workaday world. As parting advice, it is well not to get into any warm discussion with Belgians, but to listen to the expression of their views, and to confine one's remarks to safe generalities.

Belgian Life In Town & County (Demetrius C. Foulger, 1904)

A couple of months after my parents' engagement, my father had asked my mother: "Some people may talk about me in a slanderous way. Would you listen to them?"

"No, since you warned me ahead of time."

Mother felt her fiancé's honesty assured her that she could trust him and did not ask him to elaborate. Besides, he had respected her wishes to abstain from sex until their wedding night.

They were joined in holy matrimony on May 19, 1956. Mother was twenty-one years old, Father, twenty-three. The wedding reception was held at the cafe where they had met. As the groom welcomed the kisses of female well-wishers in the receiving line, his young bride was forbidden, by her new husband, from accepting any such exchanges. The groom also made it clear that no man, neither friend nor brother, would be allowed to dance with his wife. My father's insistence on complete control over my mother began on that first day of their marriage.

While traveling on their honeymoon, the groom insisted on visiting his first cousin Raphael and his wife, Rachel. After the evening's festivities concluded, Rachel took my mother aside and confided that Daniel had been making sexual advances toward her during the course of the evening. Mother was shocked and humiliated but Rachel excused the behavior.

"It must have been the beer."

After the wedding, they lived with Mother's parents. Lack of privacy and finances proved a difficult situation for the newlyweds. Within days, the groom was frequently finding reasons to argue with his bride. Every time she refused to quarrel, he prodded her until she retaliated. Although he prohibited his wife from taking part in any activities outside the home, he joined a radical Catholic Youth Club. Having heard of the flirtatious nature of some of its members, his new bride drew the line, insisting, "Quit the Youth Club or don't come back."

She won this battle but the disagreements continued. The "man of the house" always had to have the last word. Worn from the bickering, tired of her husband's flirtations and fits of rage, she became despondent. She wanted to run from her troubles, but where was there to go?

Mother's older sister, Simonne, had moved to Canada three years earlier with her husband Achiel. Her sister had found happiness. Perhaps the new continent would provide her husband with a new perspective and revitalize their relationship. Mother believed a better life could be found there so she begged her husband to make the move. He agreed.

A young woman who had never slept a night away from home decided to leave her beloved parents, family, and friends and place her future in the hands of fate.

While saying her good-byes, Mother's father whispered: "Since marrying Daniel, you've changed so much. I hope you'll be all right."

With tears in her eyes, she hugged him, saying, "I know, I hope so too." No sooner had the taxi pulled away from her parents' house, than Mother wanted to jump out and run back home. But she stayed, sitting beside her husband. Her last sight of her family was her father chasing the taxi, waving good-bye.

Chapter Four

My parents boarded an ocean liner destined for Halifax, Nova Scotia, in the dead of winter, 1957. The voyage across the North Atlantic was cursed with January's blistering cold winds and a weeklong bout of seasickness. Father was so emaciated, he had to be carried off the ocean liner on a stretcher and taken to a hospital where he remained for three days. Mother, meanwhile, stayed in a boarding house with Hungarian refugees. No one spoke Flemish and she was only allowed a ten-minute visit with her husband per day.

Weak from their weight loss and tired from the seemingly endless train ride from Halifax to Toronto, the reunion with Simonne and Achiel was marred from the beginning. They were met by Achiel, who drove them to the house they would all share in Mt. Salem, a village in a tobacco region of Southwestern Ontario.

The happy reunion of the two sisters proved to be short-lived. For as the immigrants settled in, so did the arguments, which became increasingly violent. Mother had chosen this path. Now she had to learn how to live with her decision.

Although Mother had hoped to leave her problems behind, the new language and environment only served to magnify the bitter conflicts with Father and her own sense of isolation.

Within months of their arrival, she became pregnant. An earlier pregnancy in Belgium had ended in a miscarriage, and she feared losing yet another baby. Late one night, in the midst of one of his blind rages, Father hurled a toilet tank lid at her. The heavy porcelain object struck the bedroom wall, barely missing her, and awakened Simonne and Achiel in the adjoining room.

"What happened?" Achiel yelled.

"Sorry, I knocked somet'ing on de floor," exclaimed Mother, accepting responsibility.

Ashamed, Mother decided to keep her husband's abusive behavior a secret by encouraging him to get a place of their own. She surrendered to all his additional demands to keep the peace and to protect her unborn child.

Southwestern Ontario contained a thriving tobacco industry in the late 1950s. It was here my parents obtained employment. Affordable housing was found nearby. Mother worked during the full nine months of her pregnancy. A healthy six-pound baby boy named Ronny Danny Archie was born on October 28, 1957.

Shortly after my older brother's birth, my father found a Jehovah's Witness pamphlet that sparked his curiosity into this unknown religion. He read its description highlighting just a few of the religious tenets of the Witness faith. Then, he immediately called the telephone number listed on the back of the tract. Within a few days, a Flemish couple began a series of regular visits. They started a Bible study, a formal discussion of the church's belief, with him.

Father had disagreed with the Roman Catholic teachings of his youth for quite some time, so Mother was, although not pleased, not surprised at this interest in his new-found faith. Father became engrossed in the Witnesses' doctrine, which contradicted the Catholic dogma he'd known since his youth, embracing its different concepts wholeheartedly.

My father had also found another outlet for his obsessive-compulsive behavior—witnessing or preaching to nonbelievers. This is a mandatory task new converts must undertake. Father became overly zealous in his efforts to convert family members and acquaintances. My mother vehemently opposed his attempts to convert her. Carrying his efforts to the extreme, he burned the crucifix which adorned their wall, ripped a cross pendant from Mother's neck, and tore the rosary from her hands.

[A] fiery zeal would eat me up each time I walked into the house and saw all those images of so-called saints which were so generously distributed in the rooms of my home. And especially that crucifix right in the middle of it all, was a constant thorn in my eye for quite some time now. I mentioned to my wife one day that one of these days that crucifix together with all that other junk would have to go, to which my wife replied: "You are not going to throw God outside". That to me was the last straw and I rather forcefully removed it from the wall and threw it outside on the sidewalk where it shatter (sic) in pieces. In a fit of anger this was done as I had not learned to be tactful at that time. That very act started many a heated argument and produced a lot of tears on my wife's part as to her as a very devout Catholic, the very thing I threw out was God. As I look back

> at it now, I realize that it was not a very nice thing for me to
> do but that happened to be my state of mind at the time.
> **Daniel D'Haene,** *Praise the Lord I Am Saved,* **p. 2**

Father felt he had to control even Mother's private, personal beliefs. He needed to be certain he knew exactly what his wife was thinking at all times. He would not let up in his harassment until his goal of converting her was successful.

> **In time through my constant pushing and prodding (and
> pushing I did) my wife joined in the 'study'.**
> **Daniel D'Haene,** *Praise the Lord I Am Saved,* **p. 3**

His persistence was soon rewarded. During a visit to her sister, Mother confided she was beginning to have doubts regarding the Catholic teachings. When Simonne mocked Mother because of her confusion, Mother wept. As they drove home that evening, she told her husband they would no longer be arguing about religion. "My eyes have been opened to De Trut'."

Initially, Father was skeptical. Doubting the sincerity of her conversion, he invited a group of Witnesses to their home to test her. By the end of the evening, they were convinced the unbeliever had been successfully converted. During a convention assembly of area members, my parents were baptized into the Witness faith.

> **The subject of baptism came up and on November
> 21/1959 I was baptized by immersion as one of Jehovah's
> Witnesses at an assembly in London, Ontario. I can still hear
> the witnesses say to me, "Now you are an ordained Minister
> of Jehovah." Oh, yes! I was as they called it part of the 'New
> World Society' a Minister, just think of that! Now I was
> really going to show people out there what the truth was
> whether they like it or not.**
> **Daniel D'Haene,** *Praise the Lord I Am Saved,* **p. 4**

They met many Witnesses who shared both their devotion and their language. Many Flemish-speaking immigrants had also converted to the Witness faith. The camaraderie of this newfound family, coupled with the strict morals and values of her new beliefs, convinced Mother she had made the right decision in moving to Canada. She was confident that her husband would adopt the God-fearing principles of their religion: faithfulness, self-discipline, and the sanctity of marriage vows.

Initially it appeared there would be some relief. At the very least, my parents were momentarily united by their shared belief and the birth of their firstborn son.

Father's Catholic faith discouraged reading of the Bible in the 1950s, so he replaced it with a religion that required in-depth Bible study, challenged him intellectually, and fed his obsession for control.

> **My thirst for Bible knowledge was great back in 1957, and I came from Belgium very determined to get to know all about the Bible.**
>
> **I had obtained a Catholic New Testament while in the Army in 1954 and after carefully reading it's (sic) [message] found that the teachings of the Roman Catholic Church did not agree with this book that I held in my possession and was given to me by a Catholic Chaplain, so an inner conflict was waging inside of me as to whether I should reject the teaching of the church or this New Testament?**
>
> **When in Canada, I still did not have a complete Bible but was given one by a Mexican Mennonite.... I read and read that Bible so much that my wife said to me: "Daniel, you and your crazy Bible: Next thing you know you will be crazy!"... I read the Bible whenever I could.... No wonder my dear wife often wondered if indeed I had flipped my lid."**
>
> **Daniel D'Haene, *Praise the Lord I Am Saved* p. 2**

Meanwhile, in her new religion, Mother had found something to compensate for her feelings of isolation and hopelessness—a spiritual family of brothers and sisters who spoke her mother tongue.

Both adopted the new religion as absolute truth. Two years later, February 7, 1961, I made my entrance into this Christian family. Whereas, my brother made an uneventful arrival, my birth was prolonged, painful, and memorable. My sister, Marina, soon followed.

As Jehovah's Witnesses, there would be no nursery rhymes or tales of princes rescuing princesses, no holidays or birthdays to celebrate.

Father would play games with me. Mother would tell me about The Truth. I knew Papa and Mama would never lie to me.

"Don't ask questions, Donald; just do it 'cause I say so," Papa says.

Only associating with members of our faith, I hear discussions of The Truth: God's love for us, sin, preaching, strong and weak Christians, men praying, women secondary, children born in sin. These concepts cradle me to sleep. Lullabies are a waste of time—the world is coming to an end. No Santa Claus or Easter Bunny to look forward to.

"God loves you, Donald," Mama says.

During a visit to Belgium, my great-aunt showed me pictures of Mother when she was a little girl. This was a very moving moment for me as if I was connecting with my mother's inner child. Her face possessed the haunting look of a Renaissance Madonna. I was struck by the symbolism. Mother was chosen by my father for her virtuousness, her strong faith, and her innocence of the world. It's no wonder her family had believed she would become a nun.

Later that day, I stood within the church where my parents were married. Though so much pain ensued in the decades that followed, two people were joined here and I am a product of that union.

It took years to get to this point, but I could only think, *God, I am glad they did.*

Chapter Five

"Ten minutes and we're in Aylmer, Maurice. Whoopee!"

I mock what I find troublesome. Proceeding south on Highway 73, my eyes transfixed on the leaden sky in the distance, I am flooded with long-lost memories: hour-long bus rides, motion sickness as I attempt to catch up on a school assignment, the screeching sound of the bus's brakes as we stop for each new passenger, getting into the back seat of the car and listening to my father arguing with Mother to and from religious services at the hall.

"Maurice, with my father moving us practically every year, Mother was preoccupied with packing and unpacking, preparation and organization, cleaning...constant cleaning of the house we moved out of and the filthy ones we moved into. My father drove the truck and carried the heavy items with my older brother. We younger kids had the best time, riding on the back of the pick-up truck holding down mattresses, singing Ray Stevens's songs till our voices cracked. We considered these moves adventures to new worlds, new people, new experiences."

"God, you moved a lot!"

"Yes, and we learned never to get too attached to any person or place, for the next move was never planned. It was always spur of the moment, as if we were on the run—terribly exciting to us children. The only constants in our lives were our mother's love, our father's control, and our joint attendance at the Kingdom Hall."

My memories are interrupted by an unfamiliar sight.

My God, would you look at that?" A sign boasting a smiling chicken oddly greets visitors to Aylmer with the words: "Just Say No."

"How ironic, eh, Maurice?"

* * * * * * * * *

I am five now. I know because Mama just taught me how to spell my name on my brand new pink piggy bank. She says at five, it is time I learn. Ronny and Marina have piggy banks too, but Mama has to write my sister's name on hers.

Mama rubs her big tummy and says I am going to have a new baby to look after in a couple of months.

"Put your hand here, Donald."

"Wow."

"If it is a boy, I am going to name him Erik after my *broeder* in Belgium. If it is a girl, Erica. And when I t'ink de baby is going to show up I have to go to de hospital for a couple of days. A sister from de hall is going to babysit the t'ree of you. Lina will cook and clean and look after you when your *vader* is at work."

I will miss Mama terribly, but I look forward to talking to old lady Lina. She will have so many new stories to tell me.

I spent a lot of time talking to my mother and listening to her stories. She'd confide in me feelings and experiences she wouldn't reveal to another living soul. I remember our conversations fed my desire to understand why she had made her choices: leaving her mother, her family, and her country. The more I told her, "I will never leave you," the more she would confide in me.

"You will never leave me, will you, Donald? You will always look after your Mama, no matter what?"

"Of course, I will, Mama."

"I should never have left my parents. Every day I regret it. As soon as I waved good-bye for de last time, I wanted to turn back. Run back to my *vader* and *moeder*. But it was too late."

"I don't know why you did, but I will never leave you. 'Cause I will be sad like you."

I owe Mama happiness. She's missed out on so much in life.

Mother's stories feed my curiosity and paint a bleak portrait of her life with my father.

"My marriage to your *vader* looked normal for de first part. Oderwise he was a fanatic. I had not'ing to say in what we did. If I gave opinions, he would hit me. Right from de start I was scared of him. He told me right after we married dat I could say not'ing and it would be his way only. At first, I fought back a little but he would beat me. So I quieted down and let him be de boss."

Having witnessed my father's behavior first hand, I know my mother is telling me the truth.

I see Mama cringe when Papa shouts at her. Mama and Papa are shouting at each other. Papa is slapping my Mama. Mama is crying, holding her face and looking sadly into my eyes.

I hate you, I hate you, I hate you, Papa! How can I help you, Mama? I do not know what to do! I want to help Mama!

People outside our home validated Mother's stories of Father's early aggression. One of the Witness immigrants that Mother befriended in the late 1950s had known Father in Belgium before he had met Mother. After refusing his request to dance, she accepted the offer of another suitor, and my father slapped her across the face.

But I don't need any such accounts to believe my mother.

And he shouts at her a lot.

Papa won't let Mama wear makeup on her face. When we go to the hall, Mama tries to sneak a little bit of lipstick by Papa. If he catches it, he makes her cry. She has to go back in the house.

"It is just a little bit of de lipstick?"

"Get woman! Take that filth off your face. Who do you want to look pretty for at the hall? You look just like a harlot!"

Papa won't let her into the car unless her lips are spotless. When Mama returns, she bows her head as she opens the door to the car. Mama looks so unhappy. Ronny, Marina, and I cower in the back seat. We don't want to make things worse for Mama.

I wonder why Papa doesn't want Mama to look pretty.

I watch him interact with my older brother. He demands his eldest son's respect, but every time Papa promises that if Ronny confesses to a misdeed, he will be spared the rod, he beats him.

I vow I will never place myself in the position of either my brother or Mother.

If I do what Papa says and be a good boy, I won't ever get hit like Mama and Ronny. I don't want Papa yelling at me.

I learn I must never trust my father to keep his word. I will do anything so he'll always think of me as a good boy.

The more I listen to Mother's stories, the more I resolve to never be married like my parents.

"He did de t'inking for me. I had not'ing to say in de matter. I could never go away wit'out him for any reason. My place was in de kitchen and in de bed. For dese reasons, I did not have a life outside of de home and eventually got so used to it, dat I did not want to go out."

Marriage is something that involves a man shouting, hitting, and making a woman cry.

"I will never get married, ever!" I tell everyone.

"How can you know that? You're only five!"

"I *know*."

Mother's acceptance of her situation and her isolation from her peers served to protect her from most of the world outside and its concerns. However, some events were so extraordinary, so far-reaching in their cause and effect that they broke through the cocoon my father had built for her.

These events were a matter of public record.

They were imprinted into the conscious memory of all affected.

In 1966, we lived in New Sarum, halfway between Aylmer and St. Thomas, and attended meetings at the St. Thomas Kingdom Hall of Jehovah's Witnesses.

Early in the year, a young woman from Aylmer was reported missing. Witnesses from both congregations helped in the search for her.

Mama is watching the television and suddenly turns to me.

"Look, Donald. Georgia Jackson is missing."

I recognize Georgia's picture from visiting the Aylmer Kingdom Hall and the Jackson home. Mama's eyes are all watery. Something bad has happened.

"Poor Sister Jackson," Mama cries. "What could have happened to Georgia?"

My father joined the search party and early the following morning, he invited those in his group over for coffee. A spiritual "sister" was missing—it was natural that everyone would get involved.

In general, Witnesses have a strong sense of old-fashioned values. If a Witness needs help, members from the local congregation or, if need be, from miles around will respond immediately.

Georgia Jackson was a twenty-year-old member of the Aylmer congregation when she was abducted and murdered in 1966. Murder outside the community was expected, given the conditions of the world. Murder inside the community was unthinkable. Only someone who lived an ungodly life could possibly have done this to one of our own.

To the greater community, the murder of a Jehovah's Witness was also newsworthy, not only for its shock value, but because Witnesses were considered a curiosity—a religious organization with unique and controversial doctrines. But there were other factors that set this case apart from the norm.

During the inquest later that year, the Aylmer Police were much criticized for not declaring Georgia a missing person. Police Chief Harold Henderson was accused of "laxity and impoliteness" (*The London Free Press*, Sept. 20, 1966) at the beginning of the case.

Henderson freely admitted: "In this case we put the information over Telex and checked the town. We didn't take part in any outside search."

Sgt. Reg Armstrong added: "The first full-scale search by Aylmer police was carried out February 27 (nine days after Georgia went missing) after the dead girl's coat was found beside a tree off County Road 32.... I feel there is nothing more that could have been done at this time." The coroner's jury disagreed:

Police under fire at inquest in Georgia Jackson Slaying

ST. THOMAS — The coals of criticism against the Aylmer police department's handling of the rape-slaying Georgia Jackson case were fanned into open flame yesterday during a coroner's inquest here....

After deliberating almost two hours, the jury returned with their verdict:

"We find Georgia Jackson came to her death between 6:10 p.m. February 18 and March 16 on Lot 20, Conc. 8, of Malahide Township. Death was caused by asphyxia due to suffocation in a brutal murder and rape by person or persons unknown.

"We recommend in cases of missing persons in a small community police should start an immediate investigation and search where family and friends are duly concerned.

"If this course of action had been followed by the police, it may or may not have solved this case, but, on the other hand, such actions may save a life in the future.

"We also recommend that this investigation continue. We would urge all citizens having any information to come forward immediately."
The London Free Press, Tuesday, Sept. 20, 1966.

Laxity.
Impoliteness.
Delayed investigation.
Big words that mean so much.

I only knew my mother was in pain. And in times of crisis, Mother always spoke of her faith as the solution.

"A very bad person murdered Sister Jackson, Donald. De police don't know who it is, but God will punish him." Mama assures me. "Georgia is asleep and at peace until God resurrects her."

A beautiful young girl is now asleep. A bad man did this to her and God will wake her up. It sounds so strange but I believe Mama. Our God will make everything better soon.

I couldn't comprehend murder, death, or resurrection at five years of age. I had no real concept of what God was, but I understood him to be very powerful, very loving, and the opposite of evil.

Mama says I'm getting to be a big boy.

"You can walk across de street and get de mail, but you must remember to look bot' ways for cars coming before you cross de road."

"Don't worry, I will, Mama."

I walk down to the end of our gravel lane that faces Highway 3. It is a busy road today. I look back and forth, back and forth. I am tired of looking, so I walk across.

Screech!

I wake up on an outdoor bed with white sheets. Mama is crying. Two men in white uniforms are standing over me. So are Mama and several strangers. I hear lots of voices but I can't talk. I hear myself talking but everyone around me can't.

"I should never have let him get de mail. It is my fault," Mama tells the men in white.

"I did everything I could not to hit your son, Missus. Is he going to be all right?"

"The child was not hit. He's in a state of shock but he should be fine. We'll take him to the hospital overnight for observation."

Wow. All this attention just because I could not get the mail.

Now I am in the hospital. More people in white coats talk to me.

"Your father called. He's going to come and see you later tonight."

It's suppertime. A woman in a white dress with a white cap brings me a tray of food.

"Eat every bit of it because you need your strength."

The food is strange. I think I see squished potatoes but it looks more like pudding. The peas are hot. I'm used to Mama's cold peas with mayonnaise on them. And the bread is too tough to eat.

"Yuck."

Mama's cooking is a lot better than this, but I am glad to be in a strange place just the same. I feel like I am on a holiday.

When Papa arrives, he seems in a weird mood.

"Where's Mama?" I ask.

"She's too upset to come, so I told her to stay home. What did you tell the doctor and nurses?" asks Papa without looking in my direction.

I wonder why Papa never looks me in the eye. He always looks over my head, especially if he is upset with me.

"I said that I was tired of waiting for the cars to go by."

"And that's all?"

I nod my head up and down.

"Good."

"Oh, and…."

"And what?"

Now his eyeballs seem to be clear back behind his eyelids!

"That their food is yucky."

Another white-capped lady tells me it's time to sleep. She has a cross around her neck. She looks mean.

"Now you stay in bed and don't be making any noise."

This is the first time I am supposed to sleep away from home. I am bored, I want to go home, and I can't sleep because of the strange smell in this place.

In the morning, Papa picks me up to take me home before he goes to work.

I am so happy to see my Mama. But in the afternoon, Mama is in a lot of pain. She is calling her Witness friend to come pick her up to take her to the hospital.

"Donald and Marina, I am going to have to leave you to go have de new baby."

"I will miss you this much," I promise her stretching my arms wide above my head while I stand on the end of my toes.

"I miss you!" mimics my little sister.

Lina is an elderly woman with sun-colored skin. I pull on Mama's dress.

"Mama, she has been in the sun too long," I whisper.

"It's not from being out in de sun, Donald. Sister Lina is an Indian Witness. God created all colors of people."

I don't care if she is tanned. I'm more interested in her wooden leg. I have never seen anyone with a wooden leg before. She walks almost the same as those of us who don't have a wooden leg, but she does lean to one side a bit.

Chapter Five

Lina sleeps with me in Mama's bed because it's downstairs. "Can't do no stairs," she says. Papa sleeps with Ronny in my brother's bed. Playing The Game all night, no doubt. Marina sleeps in her own little bed. I think this is great until the morning.

I went to sleep with a pillow under my head, and I wake up with no pillow and Lina smiling at me with two pillows under her head. I know Lina stole my pillow, but Mama said to be nice to her or else I'll get it. I know Lina did a bad thing stealing my pillow so that my neck is sore when I wake up. But I don't say anything because I want to know her stories.

Especially the one about how she got that wooden leg.

Chapter Six

"Maurice, my father kept us isolated from the rest of the world. We never developed normal relationships. He would not allow us to bring friends home from school. He decided who would visit our world."

"Of course. He knew what he was doing."

"I did not have contact with the outside world until I went to school. Anyone who wasn't a Jehovah's Witness was 'bad association.' We'd watch television and my parents would tell us, 'those people are worldly and non-Christian.' We were normal and they were not. I didn't understand this concept, but my parents knew best. My father would only take us to visit a few families he knew well and that he considered safe for us to associate with. We never went to movies or sporting events and we never traveled. I guess we kids thought moving was traveling. Other than that, we only went to congregation meetings and some of the social functions they provided."

* * * * * * * * *

Within the year, 1966, we moved again, this time bringing with us our baby brother, Erik, to Mount Brydges. Before I went to my first day of school, my mother took me to the washroom, informing me: "Your private parts are just for you to touch. Don't let anyone at school touch you dere!"

"Okay, Mama."

This was the only time my mother talked to me about my private parts. I never made the connection between this instruction and my father's touching. I never saw it as a contradiction. I thought strangers were "bad touch" because my mother said so. But my father touching me was "good touch" because he said it was so. My father was bad to be mean to my mother, but I never thought his touching me was bad.

A tall man is giving me The Look. The Look Papa gives me. He wants to play The Game, I can tell. I'm waiting for him to grab my hand and take me somewhere. He doesn't. He just keeps giving me The Look. I am happy he gives me The Look because that means he likes me. Papa says all Papas play this game with their children. Mamas aren't supposed to know because they'd get jealous. They'd stop us from playing it. The Game is the only time Papa talks to me or pays me any attention. I will never tell.

I don't want to go to school. I don't want to leave my Mama but Papa takes me. The teacher is nice and tells me she'll look after me.

I don't realize I am different from other children until I go to school. Students and teachers ask me why I dress the way I do, talk the way I talk, and walk the way I walk. They wonder why they don't ever get to see my parents. I shrug my shoulders. I don't know why.

Who am I? Only one Donald knows about The Game with Papa. I fear Papa. Another Donald goes to school. I like learning. A third Donald is taken to Jehovah's Kingdom Hall. I love God.

Other kids discuss what they have for show and tell. I always know I could top them. I have no friends to discuss my show-and-tell secrets with.

I hate school because it is different. I am different. I have to be forced to play with other children. I love reading and talking with grown-ups because I know I can learn so much from them, but other than the teacher there are no grown-ups with stories here. And sometimes even she is not nice to me.

During naptime, I watch the classroom clock, religiously counting the hours until I can walk home. I never nap at home. Why do I have to pretend to sleep here? I whisper something to the girl beside me.

Swoosh!

My cheek smarts from the teacher's hand hitting my face from behind my chair. I hate her. I don't cry. I don't talk anymore during naptime because I don't want the teacher surprising me and touching me from behind again.

I can't wait to go home. Home is where I don't have to pretend to sleep in the afternoon. Home is where I don't get slapped from behind. Home is where I am loved and accepted.

Mama hugs and talks to me.
Papa plays The Game with me.
Home is normal to me.

Our houses are always surrounded by nature. Each house in the country is situated near a creek so fishing is a regular part of my childhood. Usually I sit and watch the interaction of wildlife. The turtles, frogs and fish, butterflies and insects, the flower and plant life keep me busy for hours. While Papa waits for a fish to bite his hook, Ronny makes bows and arrows out of tree branches so we can pretend to be wild hunters. Other times, Erik watches as I try to find turtles with the pretty patterns on their shell. I ask Papa if I can take them home as pets and sometimes, he even lets me.

Papa won't buy us any new toys but we never complain. He tells guests, "My kids will never be spoiled." We are thankful when Witness friends give us second-hand toys. I pretend I have an allowance, look at the toys in the Eaton's catalogues, and add up an imaginary list of items I can afford.

Mama feels bad that we don't have toys to play with so she makes us life-size dolls. We pretend one of us is pregnant and that person has a multiple birth—eight four-foot babies. We laugh ourselves silly. On the rare times we have Witness kids visiting, we drag out the babies and entertain them with our outrageous performance. They have fun too.

Even our clothes have already been worn by someone else. Ronny wears them, then me, and Erik grows into some of them. We laugh when we discover we wore the same shirt for our annual school pictures. At school, we are obviously dressed differently, because we don't wear anything close to the styles of the time. None of us ever wears blue jeans in public school. That would be an all-too-modern luxury.

The other students predictably make fun of us.

I look forward to the only time I visit the city outside of school or worship: a car ride with Papa when he shops for groceries. I love watching people and buildings. McDonald's becomes the fantasy restaurant I see on television commercials. I love watching the big yellow sign as it slips by the side window in my father's car. Of course, I don't dare ask Papa to stop and buy a burger and fries. He considers that a waste of money.

In the summer, on one of many such car rides, Papa stops on the side of the road. The routine is always familiar. He unzips his pants, reaches for a girlie magazine from under the seat, and I have to take care of business. The more it happens, the more daring he gets. On this one particular stop not too far from where we live, our landlord's oldest son pulls up alongside my Papa's car and asks if something is wrong. Papa strategically places a newspaper over his thing and I, the good son, smile appropriately. Nothing looks suspicious. Papa tells the man we are just stopping for a break. He believes Papa. Such split-second timing always prevents Mama or anyone else from ever catching us.

We don't usually have playmates outside of the family to interact with, but our landlord lives just down the road from us. His younger son, Corey, often comes to our house to play. One day Papa asks Corey if he wants to go fishing with us.

The boy sits between Papa and me in the front seat of the car.

Oh, Oh! Papa is giving Corey The Look. I know what that means.

Papa drives Corey and me to the creek where we always fish. All of a sudden, Papa is talking about The Game, so I know I am right. I'm mad at him for involving my friend. I feel protective of Corey.

Somehow I know he is innocent and I am not.

"Corey won't want to play The Game, Papa."

"Never mind. Get out of the car and walk down to the creek."

Corey is crying already and I know Papa should stop.

"You're upsetting Corey."

"Get!"

By the time I came back, Papa's deed was done. Corey doesn't look the same.

Corey and I go to school together. He is seven, a year older than me but we get along pretty well. At least he never makes fun of me. Sometimes I wonder why he doesn't when all the other boys do.

Chapter Six

I felt a tremendous guilt over what happened to my friend. At the time, instinctively, I thought it would change him and that it wasn't okay.

I was already different, so it was too late for me.

I don't know how I came to understand that it was wrong and that I had been changed as a result of The Game when I had never talked about it with anyone.

Perhaps witnessing my father's deception, his lies and selfish behavior, and the fact I had to play The Game upon his command had a cumulative effect on me. It wasn't one thing. It was all of the above that left me with an uneasy feeling about introducing outsiders to The Game, which to me seemed indecent and normal at the same time.

Chapter Seven

I know each of my siblings had a difficult life. Sheer brutal force introduced my older brother to The Game.

Papa tells Mama he is going to take Ronny out for a car ride.

"We're going to the garbage dump. Ronny will enjoy it."

"Yes, I want to go."

Papa drives the car off the main dirt road.

"I want to show you something."

"What?"

Papa unzips his pants and pulls out his thing.

"What are you doing?"

"We're going to play a game—"

"Oh no, we're not! I don't want to play this game!"

"You have to!"

Ronny starts crying.

"Stop crying. Give me your hand. Now go up and down!"

Ronny cries uncontrollably. Ronny leaves himself. He floats out of the car.

Papa is worried Ronny will tell.

"Don't you dare tell your Mama about this. I gave you life and I can take it away."

Afterwards, Ronny lays his head against the car window looking outside. He sees a large bird circling above. He straightens up.

Wham!

A hawk crashes through the front windshield.

Ronny remembers a horrific incident. I remember an innocent game. Yet, each incident was so unsettling that we both left ourselves in order to carry out Father's instructions.

When faced with overwhelming trauma, a child may resort to "going away" within his or her own mind. By this dissociation process, traumatic experiences, thoughts, feelings and perceptions can be separated psychologically, allowing the victim to function as if the trauma had never occurred. The child's personality is in part developed in response to the conflict.

Father discovered a recipe from his experience with my older brother.

Introduce the child to The Game at an earlier age so there is no resistance.

Add the pretence of importance and secrecy.

The child will want to play.

Ronny was six, and just old enough on the first occasion to be aware that something was wrong with even a suggestion of sexual contact between father and son. He fought back while I, introduced to The Game at four and before the age of understanding, did not. Ronny never considered his sexual abuse an act of love or a game as I did. He was coerced into being a "player" in an act of abuse in which he did not want to participate. The difference in our initiation to the same game no doubt deeply affected our personalities from that time forward. I became shy, Ronny outgoing.

Ronny and I were complete opposites, inside and out. Cain and Abel. Ronny loved sports, fast cars, The Beatles. I was interested in the arts, old black and white movies, Doris Day. Ronny was the doer; I was the thinker. My brother was the typical extrovert—his values were derived from his external environment. Whereas I internalized my problems, Ronny vented his difficulties outwardly. He became the predictable troublemaker, defying church and law, and turned hostile in relationships, both within and outside of our family. Ronny had his own demons to struggle with. He, too, had to overcome the fact that Daniel D'Haene was his father and mentor.

While Papa and Mama are working in the tobacco field, Ronny is left to babysit Marina and me. Sometimes we pick big worms in the field and take them home and put them in jars. Mama calls them tobacco worms. Some die but Ronny had one that made a cocoon for itself. We love looking at these big worms. They are beautiful and scary at the same time.

My brother keeps to himself for the most part but often spends the afternoon leaving the house in disarray. Ronny tears down the curtains, rips the Witness literature, scattering the pieces all over the house, places bath towels in the toilet, and sprays shaving cream everywhere. When our parents arrive home, Ronny shows them the damage.

"Donald and Marina did this while I was upstairs."

"Donald! Marina!" calls Mama. "Why did you do dis?"

"We never did a thing," I say.

"Ronny," adds Marina, pointing at him.

"Why are you lying?" asks Ronny.

"We are not!"

"Daniel! No!" cries Mama, as Papa looks for scissors. He grabs Marina's beautiful long hair and cuts it off. Next, Papa whisks me into the washroom and dunks my head into the toilet. Then Papa makes us kneel in the corner on the hard linoleum floor. One of us has to kneel on the air vent which hurts but leaves pretty marks on each knee that disappear after an hour or so.

"There! You'll never do that again."

For two years this chain of events was repeated. Papa and Mama always believed Ronny. Marina and I always pleaded innocence. We were always punished. Ronny would think of creative ways of destroying things. Papa would create new ways of punishing us.

Two of Mama's Witness friends, Ann and Hilda, didn't believe Ronny. Right in front of me, they would proclaim my innocence and my brother's guilt. They would tell Mama, "It has to be Ronny." Mama never listened to them.

Ann and her husband, Frank, and Hilda and her husband, Fred, always maintained an interest in my mother and us children. When they didn't see us at the hall, they would call Mama and make sure everything was all right. Because of the continuing problems with Marina and me, Fred, an Elder, was asked to speak to me.

"Donald, you can tell me. Why are you doing these bad things?" asks Elder DiAngelo.

Brother DiAngelo is always nice to me so I am not afraid to talk to him.

"I am not doing anything bad. Ronny is."

"Don't you agree that ripping up Bible literature is a bad thing?"

"Yes, but I didn't do it!"

"Why are you lying, Donald? Do you know how God feels about liars? If you confess to your sin and ask for forgiveness, it will be granted."

I stand in front of this big man, wide-eyed, speechless. I don't know what to say. I decide I will never be honest with other people. Why should I be? Elders don't believe me. My parents don't believe me. Why tell the truth when it is not believed? I don't want to talk to people who don't listen to me anymore. I won't tell my secrets to anyone. Not even to Mama or Ann or Hilda who do believe me. Papa always says, "Your Mama will punish you if you tell her about The Game." Now I know that is true.

"Do you want to do it?"

"I don't know."

"Sure you do. You like it, don't you? It feels good. I promise."

"Okay. Papa, do you do this with Mama?"

"Yes, all the time!"

"But why can't I tell her we do it too?"

"She won't BELIEVE you! She'll hit you. She'll beat you up. She's such a jealous person. She wouldn't want us to have fun. Do you want us to stop having fun?"

"Oh, no, Papa!"

Movie reels. Black and white. Monotone voices. These are my recollections of these events. I don't remember any pain or anger associated with them. I am merely testifying to their occurrence.

Chapter Eight

My memories are split evenly: light, sunny, happy images of Mother contrasted with dark, cloudy, and secret images of Father. I placed my mother in the role of a holy saint. Mother just couldn't be bad or make mistakes. My father was the opposite: evil, wicked, someone who never did anything good for anyone but himself. Yet both were equally strong—as if I had more than one childhood. One Donald lived in peace, the Other Donald, in chaos. Events, which would lead to the end of my innocence, were increasing in number and significance.

Papa does all the shopping and handling of business matters. Mama's place is in the kitchen and in the home in general. She never goes anywhere alone. Papa never takes her to the movies, shopping for clothes, or even to the dentist. Although Papa uses his dental plan on a regular basis, he won't take Mama or any of us. Over time, Mother's beautiful teeth have decayed. Papa doesn't want Mama to look good.

Papa takes Mama to congregation meetings now about once a month, to the bank to co-sign loans, and to the doctor when she was ill beyond a reasonable doubt.

Mom says there is a growth on her neck.

"The doctor says it is a tumor and he has to operate."

"Is Lina with the wooden leg going to look after me and steal my pillow again?"

"No, Ronny is old enough dat when your Papa is at work, he can take care of you and your sister and *broeder*."

I don't understand that big word Mama has, but I will miss her when she's at the hospital just the same. Papa says everything will be all right. I know what that means.

I wonder which one of us he will sleep with this time.

Other than infrequent attendance at the Kingdom Hall, we have two big yearly family outings. There is no hint as to when in any given year Papa will decide: "Let's go to Niagara Falls." We jump up and down, excited at seeing the Falls again. Of course, we never do anything but see the Falls. No museums, restaurants, not even Ripley's Believe It or Not. And depending on Papa's mood, we never know what to expect on the way, when we arrive, or on our return. Which one of us will he belittle? Will he argue with Mama? Will he be hostile toward Ronny?

We are happy to go just the same.

I am crunched in the back seat of the car beside Ronny, Marina, and Erik. I count the homes, trees, hydro poles, horses, and cows as they pass by my back seat window.

Squeal!

Papa slams on the brakes because he hit a pothole and his hubcap fell off.

"Ronny, get out and pick up the hub cap."

When Papa brakes, the rest of us hear a noise under his seat. Something moved.

"What's that?" asks Erik as he checks the source of the noise.

"Oh, it's nothing. Leave it alone, Erik."

"What is it?" asks Mama.

"Just forget about it," insists Papa.

I know what I am supposed to say.

"Oh, Mama, it's just some school books. I thought I would do some home work on the way if I got bored."

"Dat's a good boy, Donald," Mama replies.

Papa nods and smirks at me in the rear view mirror. He thinks I'm a good boy too.

Ronny returns. "I didn't know those big steel nuts held the tire on to the car!"

"What, are you stupid?"

The other trip was an hour-long drive to visit Aunt Simonne and Uncle Achiel and their three children. Aunt and uncle always kissed us hello and were nice to us children. Aunt was a glamorous, Sophia

Loren-type hostess, and uncle a quiet, chain-smoking listener. Complete opposites and I loved them both.

Papa would use these visits as an opportunity to belittle Mama.

"If I had been at your wedding, Simonne, I'd be the first in line to kiss you."

My aunt smiles. She is used to these compliments. But uncle speaks up.

"Jeannette is beautiful. It's just that she doesn't look happy."

"What doesn't she have that she wouldn't be happy? Doesn't she have a roof over her head and food for herself and the kids?"

"Yes, she does," sighs uncle.

Then Papa directs his attention to his children. Especially me.

"There's something wrong with Donald," Papa says out loud. "Come here, Donald."

I happen to be playing with my cousin. We're both wearing dresses.

"Yes, Papa."

"You're like a little girl, aren't you?"

Embarrassed, I run downstairs crying.

"Why did you have to do dat?" says Mama. "Leave Donald alone."

"I don't see anything wrong with Donald," adds Aunt Simonne. "He's just a little boy."

"It's just not right," Papa insists, as I listen from the bottom of the stairs.

"So he likes to wear dresses, so what?" insists Uncle Achiel.

Since it is uncle's home we are visiting, I am safe. I don't understand why everyone is talking about me, but maybe Papa is right. I am a boy but I feel like I am a girl in a boy's body. I don't like playing with either boys or girls though. Papa always says I am odd, freakish, and different. I know I am.

Papa caresses my skin.

"You are like a woman," he tells me. "You have a girl's body and you are beautiful. You look like the girls in these naked photos."

Yuck! How disgusting! You are attracted to this. I hate you.

"You have skin just like a woman. What do you like about these girls? Mom and Marina have bodies like this too."

Yuck, yuck, yuck. I hate you, I hate you, I hate you!

I don't want to be anything like you. Everything you are, everything you desire disgusts me. But I'll never tell you. I'm afraid of you. You're big and I'm small. You own me.

I can never say how I feel. Nobody will listen to me. I mean nothing. God says you are the boss. You know what's best. I know nothing. You tell me I am weak. I am stupid. I believe you.

God created you.

God is good.

You must be too.

Chapter Nine

"I'm telling you, Maurice, I lived in two separate worlds. Other Donald experienced the bad stuff, but Thinking Donald had a blast."

"How's that possible?"

"You've met her. That wonderful, fun-loving mother of mine."

* * * * * * * * *

I know I learned from Mother to escape unpleasant experiences. She made life with our father bearable. Because of Father's shifts at the factory, we could be lucky enough not to see him for up to five days in a row. So we were able to pretend he didn't exist for days at a time. We were living like we were dirt poor but rich because we had a mother who loved life, laughter, and most of all, us.

"Donald, never be ashamed of your moeder or de fact you have no money or nice clothes. T'ink of de starving people in de world. Many people have less dan you. My own moeder has not walked since she was in her twenties, but we never heard her complain. She is a proud woman. She taught me to never give up no matter what life brings you. Try to put negative t'oughts out of your mind. I do. Remember, God loves you, your broeders and sister love you, and I love you, so you are rich," says Mama. *"Look to God and he will always help you t'rough anyt'ing".*

"I will, Mama."

Mother escapes her immediate world not only through her faith, but also through soap operas, old movies, and TV sitcoms. I, too, take refuge in the world of TV, the world of make-believe. My favorite is

The Edge of Night. I prefer its suspense and mystery over the romance of soaps such as *The Doctors* and *Somerset*. After the soaps, we watch *I Love Lucy*, *Bewitched*, and *I Dream of Jeannie*. I envy Samantha's and Jeannie's power to cast spells and change their lives. I have ongoing fantasies of zapping this or that person or blinking myself to any place but here. Sometimes I daydream of a master like Jeannie's taking me away, but I don't know where or why. I can't watch *Bewitched* if my father is home. He says it is the work of the devil, that witches are real but evil and not like the good witches portrayed on television. We can't watch fantasy shows if he is around. I cannot believe that Samantha, the good witch, could be bad. If she is from the devil and my father who has God isn't, I would choose Samantha's witchcraft over my father's God any day.

I am happy because I have my friends in the land of make-believe. One such friend changes my life. *Funny Girl* is the movie version of the Broadway musical about Fanny Brice, vaudeville comedienne, starring Barbra Streisand. This creature is like nothing I have ever seen before: awkwardly beautiful, talented, unique, funny. She is my first role model. I identify with this character. I know I am talented. I know I am something. It is just that nobody else recognizes it yet. I know some day I'll make it.

I love watching TV so much, I hate it when anything interrupts my favorite programs.

Bang, bang, bang! Papa is stomping his feet again. Which one of us has to bring his milk and sleeping pill this time? We all dread going.

"Donald! Bring me some milk."

"I guess, Marina, it's my turn."

Today, I'm the chosen one. Sometimes he calls us by name. Other times he just tells Mama to send one of us up with whatever the latest request is. Sometimes he'd be in bed. Other times in the bathtub.

It always meant: "Donald D'Haene, come on down! It's your turn to play The Game!"

The smell is overwhelming—I feel dirty every time we are done and I will take a bath as soon as I can.

Luckily, I get to take a bath every day.

Papa is the only one who spoils my fun. When he is present, our environment is insanity, chaos, fear. But when he's not home, it's like we are on a holiday, each in control of his or her own space. We get to choose what shows we watch on TV. We aren't told: "Shut up," "You're stupid," "Do this," "Do that," "Don't do anything!" And best of all, we never have to play The Game.

Ronny, Marina, Erik, and I celebrate our freedom by roaming the countryside, discovering new trails, creating new ways of having fun. Sure we fight too, but who doesn't?

I remember our father made us laugh. Once.

My sister and I are watching a sitcom, and the actress in the series portrays someone rehearsing a commercial for an audition. My father is watching it too. About a half hour later, our father opens the door to the living room, steps in and pretends to be the woman doing the commercial. It is hilarious. My sister and I look at each other in disbelief.

He had never intentionally made us laugh before nor has he since.

Chapter Ten

[I] lost my zeal and became dead spiritually. I became a sinner in every way but in secret.

I dared not admit it for fear of [being] disfellowshipped which would mean losing the only friends I had.

Daniel D'Haene, *Praise the Lord I Am Saved*, p. 10

There were many people who visited my childhood, our little world, but I never attached myself to any one person because I knew we would be moving again soon.

I've just turned ten years old today. Even though we don't celebrate birthdays, Papa says he's got something special for me just the same.

"David and his wife Fran want me to do some work on their house. If you come with me, I'll get you something you'll like."

I don't like leaving Mama but it sounds exciting. I can't wait to get my gift. Maybe instead of passing McDonald's, Papa will stop and buy me a burger and fries. The kids always look like they're having so much fun. And, David and Fran are new people. Big people with great new stories to tell.

All little kids want to do is talk about games and dolls. Yuck. I hate playing little people's games.

Fran is very nice to me and gives me some cookies she just baked.

"You're a very mature young man for your age."

"Everyone tells me that. I don't get along with kids my own age. They're so immature."

David and Fran leave Papa and me alone while they go shopping.

"Papa, when do I get my gift?"

Papa unzips his pants and I know what I have to do.

"Come on, we have to be quick!"

I got tricked again.

It was nice meeting David and Fran just the same.

When I get home, Ronny, Marina, and I discuss The Game.

"Sometimes I don't want to play," I state matter-of-factly.

"I never want to play. It's disgusting," says Ronny angrily.

"What about you, Marina?" I ask.

"I don't know what to say."

My poor baby sister. Ronny and I feel sorry for her. I resolve to play The Game more often so that Marina doesn't have to anymore. Ronny resolves to be away from home as much as possible. He knows we will have to play The Game in his place, but he can't deal with that or anything having to do with Papa right now. When he's old enough, he will take us out of here.

"Wonder if he's tried it with Erik," suggests Ronny. "He'd better not."

"Right. Erik shouldn't have to play The Game. There's enough of us here to do that. Why bother Erik?" I say.

"Let's make sure Erik isn't touched. Watch him," Ronny tells us. Marina and I make a pact.

We don't understand why we fear Papa will damage our five-year-old brother by playing The Game but we make the pact just the same.

Papa takes Marina and Erik into the attic. Marina fears Papa will touch Erik.

"Don't play with Erik."

"You just never mind. Come here, Erik. I want to show you something."

Papa unzips his pants and asks Erik to play The Game. Marina is terrified. Erik is confused. He runs for the door.

"Marina, go get your brother. Bring him back."

Marina fears that Erik will tell Mama.

"Erik, come back!"

Ronny and I are downstairs watching television.

Erik is running down the stairs with Marina at his heels.

"What's wrong?" Ronny and I ask in unison.

Erik is acting funny.

Chapter Ten

"Papa wants me to play with his pee pee! I'm telling Mama," yells Erik, catching his breath.

"She's jealous."
"She'll hit you."
"Don't you dare tell."
"I gave you life and I can take it away."

"No!" we yell.

As strange as our life is, it is normal to us. What we fear is the unknown. Could things be any different?

Erik doesn't know that it is bad. He doesn't know it is a secret. We think that it is bad but we don't understand why. Erik marches right over to Mama in the kitchen and tells her about The Game. Ronny, Marina, and I look on in disbelief. We can't stop him. Erik is the tattletale in the family. We are terrified *and* relieved at the same time.

Papa is standing quietly at the bottom of the stairs. He looks at us like we have failed *him* in not keeping Erik from revealing "our little secret."

Mama turns white, and there are tears in her eyes.

"Is dis true?"

The look in our eyes answers her question. And since only the whites of Papa's eyes are visible, he doesn't need to.

Mama runs upstairs to her bedroom crying. Papa picks up his car keys and heads for the front door. On his way out, he stops and talks to Marina.

"Your mother will be all right. Nothing will change. Everything will be the same as always."

The screen door slams behind him.

We go to Mama. We explain what has been going on all these years. Mama believes Erik. She believes us. Everything might be the same but Mama isn't.

"I am completely shocked…. Dis is beyond belief—like someone is tearing up my heart. I t'ink I will lose my mind. I was never even suspicious somet'ing like dat was going on. I wondered why you all could not stand your *vader*. I t'ought it was just because he was weird."

Mama is suffering. I don't really understand why. We comfort her. Papa and I just play The Game. I am not in pain. I am perfectly healthy. Maybe she is jealous like Papa said she would be. But Papa said she would hit us and she hasn't. Papa must be lying.

Well, for some reason The Game is wrong. Wrong enough to make Mama cry.

The abuse is disclosed for the first time. Papa didn't count on a mere five-year-old breaking the code of silence.

No one comforts us. We comfort each other. Will our way of life continue to be part of an ordinary existence?

The contradictions continue.

Mama cries and cries. We think she is having a nervous breakdown.

When Papa returns home, Mama confronts him, yelling.

"You are disgusting, dirty, and no good. How could you do dis to your children? Dese disgusting t'ings? Why? How could you do dis to me? Dis cannot go on! Dis must stop!" she rages.

Papa looks like a cornered animal looking for a quick escape.

"I...I promise I'll stop. I'll...I'll go for therapy."

"You are sick. Doing it wit' me and de children at de same time. Do not come near me! Do not touch me again!"

Papa goes for a drive.

Papa says he is sick and will go see a psychiatrist. He doesn't mean it.

Mama still sleeps in his bed. We still visit his bed. His ownership of her is unconditional, of us, absolute.

Things won't be different.

And so, the year I turned ten years old, Erik outed our little secret. The disclosure left our mother feeling humiliated. Did her husband prefer sex with his children to relations with her? Why make that humiliation public knowledge? On some level Mother was thinking of herself, but for once in her life, why not?

This was not a woman who ordinarily lived for herself. She fulfilled the duties of wife, mother, and Christian. Her choice to move to Canada with my father had isolated her in every conceivable way. She was totally dependent upon her husband.

Once again Mom wanted to run away from her problems, but she couldn't run to anyone in Canada for help. By this time, she rarely saw her sister who worked full time while raising her own children. She saw her Witness friends infrequently because of her husband's poor attendance at the hall. Although her closest friends, Ann and Hilda, protested Father's treatment of her and us children, they never heard her complain about her relationship with my father. She wasn't about to shock them with her secret when she had never shared her personal thoughts before. She also never had any money, didn't know how to write or sign a check, and she didn't know how to drive an automobile. Father had refused to teach her so she couldn't go anywhere by herself.

Mother asked Father to move us all to Belgium. He agreed. Passports were updated, relatives in Belgium supportive, Witnesses informed. Then one day, I found Mother crying as she read a letter from her mother suggesting she should make the best of her life in Canada.

Mother said, "It is as if my *moeder* slapped me on de face." When Mother showed the letter to Father, the move was called off.

No one in Mother's world had ever separated or divorced. Even if she had considered leaving Father, where would she have sought shelter? Mother had never used a telephone book or read a newspaper. In 1971, how much community support was available anyway?

She wouldn't have known about such support. Father always kept her where he wanted her—isolated at home, controlling every aspect of her life. She wasn't allowed any decision-making or even the opportunity to think for herself. My father owned my mother as much as he did us.

A stronger, more independent woman might have left her husband, taking her children with her. Such a woman would have found a way. Such a woman, my father would never have married.

Think *for* herself? Never. Think *of* herself? For a moment, why not indeed?

Although Mother never hit us when we threatened to talk about our abuse outside of the home, she did tell us to keep silent. She was ashamed for her children, her faith, and herself. What would people think of her Witness husband who had sexually abused his kids? How could she go on preaching in the community? Wouldn't she be shaming her God if the secret slipped out? Mother was also keenly aware that her children were already having a difficult time at school for being different. Wouldn't the gossip in a small town make life more unbearable?

Sometimes we would tell Mama—"We are going to tell our secret!" and she would tell us not to. "We would have to run away. Where would we all go?" Mama felt our disclosure brought us all closer together. It did. It became us against him.

"I feel so ashamed. Do not tell anyone. I am scared. What would happen to us if it came out what your *vader* did? When I grew up, my *vader* would never have touched me dat way. How wrong it is."

Ronny informed me the earliest disclosure of the abuse outside my immediate family occurred in 1972. He told a doctor that we had been molested by our father.

"You're probably going to turn into a homosexual," the doctor told him. "Just be careful you don't turn into a molester too. It happens quite frequently."

"I don't believe you! I don't want to ever see you again!"

Ronny didn't want to believe him but he was scared. This was a doctor. He was supposed to know the truth.

The doctor sent him home to his abuser and did nothing further. I can only imagine the deep and personal anguish this ignorance caused my brother. In that moment, Ronny became homophobic. Was he going to turn into his father? Was he going to molest children? Or was he going to become a homosexual? Living in dread, he pursued as many girls as possible. As soon as a girl liked him, he'd discard her. She needed to be replaced with several others who would serve to combat his fears.

Fearing that a metamorphosis would take place, Ronny made a pact with God: "If I ever have the desire to molest children, I will kill myself."

So typical of all my family's experiences up to this point: fish the size of pike, apparently invisible, drowning in a small fish bowl.

Chapter Eleven

"Your Papa's *moeder*, your *grootmoeder*, is coming to Canada dis summer."

"What's her name?" I ask.

"Germaine, but you have to call her Meme."

"I can't wait to meet her."

Meme will be able to tell me all about Belgium. What it's like now. What my Papa was like when he was a child. We'll even be able to take her to Niagara Falls. Maybe because it's his mother, Papa will finally take us inside a museum, a McDonald's restaurant and if we're really lucky, Ripley's Believe It or Not.

As soon as Meme walks in the door, she hugs all of us. But she doesn't let go. It is strange getting hugged and kissed like this by a stranger but that must mean she loves us, I tell myself. After all, Mama hugs and kisses like that too.

"Mama, Meme is very pretty for her age, isn't she?"

"Yes, she is Donald," Mama answers, laughing, then to Meme she says, "Germaine."

"*Moeder*!"

Even though they speak Flemish to each other, I understand that Meme wants Mama to call her *Moeder*, not Germaine. She likes to talk all the time, and she patiently waits for Mama to translate everything she says to me and everything I ask to her.

"Ask her to tell me everything about Belgium, my grandfather, and Papa."

"Boys will be boys," my grandmother tells me. "Your Papa was always getting into trouble."

Germaine Noppe grew up in a large, lower-middle-class family. Her mother died soon after she gave birth to a son. Germaine, who was only in her teens, assumed the motherly role over her siblings and remained the mother figure throughout their lives. Germaine became the central character in her family. A sense of family grew very important to her. This role did not change with her marriage to Michiel D'Haene.

Michiel was a hardworking, physically striking man. Germaine would bear him three sons and one daughter. Their firstborn, a daughter, died in childhood. Papa kept a photo of his beautiful sister, but never talked about the circumstances surrounding her death. Meme's eyes watered as she talked about losing her baby girl. The second-born, my father, was named Daniel Noel Michiel D'Haene. Two more sons were to follow—Valere and Etienne.

Germaine was a proud woman. She wanted her sons to carry the D'Haene name with heads held high. They did.

When my grandmother goes for a walk with Marina, Mama tells me what she knows about my Papa's upbringing.

"Papa must have been upset when his sister died!"

"Yes, but he never talks about dat."

Mama says Meme and Papa were a lot alike.

Germaine had a hard time with her iron-willed son. Their strong personalities conflicted because Father challenged his mother's authority at every turn. He resented being controlled by a woman even if that woman was his mother.

After carefully scrutinizing both the teachings of the church and what it said in the scriptures, I left the church. This was not going over very smoothly as my mother in fact as a very devout Catholic blamed my turning away from the church on No. 1) "that bad book" 2) "the army has done it to you". With the latter to some degree I had to agree as the things that I saw in the army really were an eye opener to me in many respects as I did not at all agree with the far from Christian behaviour by professing Christians.

But with the former as to it being a bad book: I took issue with that statement as I said to my mother, "Now Mother, listen if this is a bad book then what is there left over to

believe in. For this New Testament has been approved by the Pope and the bishops of the Netherlands and Belgium". She replied, "It's a BAD BOOK and I am going to burn it." I had to put the little Testament in a box with a padlock on it from that moment on.
   Daniel D'Haene, *Praise the Lord I Am Saved*, p. 2

Daniel watched his father passively take a back seat to his mother's domineering personality. He vowed that when he married, he would be head of his household. He would actively seek a bride who would "love, honor, and obey" *him*. What Father sought in a woman was his idea of the perfect wife: obedient, dutiful, faithful, and above all, unquestioning. She had to be a woman he could dominate.

Daniel saw his father as weak and couldn't understand how a man could be so passive. Daniel became one of the boys, a man's man. He believed men who displayed emotions were weak.

Mama doesn't know much else about Papa and says it might not be a good idea to ask Meme too many questions since it would upset Papa. Papa remains a mystery, so I ask Mama to tell me all she knows about her own family.

My mother's parents, Remi Bataille and Maria Priem, also came from lower-middle-class backgrounds. Their firstborn was named Simonne, followed by my mother, Jeannette, a third daughter Blanche and finally, a son, Erik. Three daughters and a son.

When Maria was in her twenties, a mishandled operation performed on her legs left her permanently disabled. Everyone's role in the house would be changed forever. Her daughters would have to do the chores at home while Remi worked at a local factory. Yet, Jeannette had a happy childhood. Remi and Maria were loving parents and their children found security in a household run with their parents' strong, firm hands.

Mama told me the 1930s were simpler times. Young people would take a few francs and go to the cinema to watch the latest movie at the Sunday matinee. Children invented games to play. Toys were scarce. Children managed with what they had. My parents walked to their schools. Everything was within walking or biking distance. Neither Father's nor Mother's families owned automobiles. Cars were for the rich. The poor also could not afford the luxury of a telephone. My mother never picked up a phone until she was in her teens working as a cleaner at a nearby farmhouse. Her boss asked her to answer the phone, and she didn't know what to do. She was literally afraid of it.

Neighbors were extended family. Children and women could walk alone and not worry about their safety.

World War II shattered this placid and peaceful existence. Belgium's neighbors, Germany and France, were at war. Jeannette's father was a socialist, and he often hid soldiers in his cellar. Once a German officer kicked the front door down, walked in and told Remi to make coffee for him. Jeannette and the rest of the family hid in the basement. Knowing he placed the entire family at risk by hiding Allied soldiers, Remi persisted just the same.

Exploding grenades were not uncommon in the neighborhood.

During one such incident, while the children were playing in the street, fighting suddenly erupted. Maria yelled to Jeannette, "Jump in the ditch." Instead, she ran, narrowly escaping injury as a grenade blew up meters behind her.

Due to rationing, Remi and Maria had to work hard to make ends meet. Maria would spend tedious hours rolling cigarettes to sell on the black market. Jeannette made the cigarette boxes. After her father would fill the lining of his coat with packages, she often would accompany him in the middle of the night to sell their wares. A neighbor tipped off the police about the Bataille family selling cigarettes. As soon as Remi got wind of it, he stuffed Jeannette's mattress with dozens of little boxes. He told his daughter to lie in bed and pretend she was deathly ill. When the police arrived, they searched the house but didn't check her mattress.

Jeannette, the actress, was born.

Living through a war just served to strengthen the bonds in the family. There was no place for selfish thinking. Survival of family became paramount.

My mother was timid and shy. She didn't always fit in with the school crowd and was often ridiculed for being "too quiet" and "too good." She rarely fought back, feeling it was better to turn the other cheek than to retaliate. Her best friend would often have to jump to her defense.

Jeannette felt she must pray to God for help in accepting circumstances she could not change. Her mother had instilled in her a deep sense of faith in God. Yet she, like my father, was not allowed to read the Bible.

The Bible was a mysterious book, both respected and feared. A traveling insurance salesman once bragged to Jeannette that he had read the Bible, but his priest scolded him and told him to lock it up and never read it again.

"Parishioners would only get confused," the priest told him. "Look what happened to the Protestants!"

But Jeannette, also like my father, was intrigued by a holy book she wasn't supposed to read. Perhaps this explains why my parents were later attracted to a faith that encouraged the opposite.

While Jeannette found solace in her faith, her sister, Simonne daydreamed that a better life lay in store for her elsewhere.

Watching a plane fly overhead, she shouted, "Someday, I'm going to be in one of those planes. I'm going to live far, far away."

"Not me," Jeannette responded. Jeannette would never leave home even for an overnight stay. If a relative invited her to, she would choose the security that her parents' home provided over the unknown. She looked forward to marriage when a husband would take care of her.

"Good girls do just what Mama says, even when Mama's not around," Maria would teach her daughters. Their mother was the disciplinarian and only on rare occasions did Remi punish his daughters.

Maria kept little chocolates on top of the china cabinet. Once, little Simonne climbed up a chair, onto the cabinet, and reached for the candies. The whole upper glass unit fell, breaking the antique dishes. Simonne was so scared she ran away. Maria had to promise she wouldn't hurt her before she would come back. Simonne was Maria's favorite. Maria kept her word.

Once Jeannette heard a joke at school about fathers. Later she was playing outside with some neighbors, looked around to see if her parents were listening and when she was sure they were alone, she told the joke. Suddenly, the back door opened and out comes Remi, giving Jeannette a swift kick on the backside.

Parents were not to be ridiculed.

I never understood how my grandfather could kick my mother. I hated someone hurting her in any shape or form. I never want to get hit.

"How could grandpa kick his own daughter?"

"I deserved it, Donald. I knew he loved me and dat was de important t'ing. My *vader* was not a violent man. He had to be pushed. I was just extra careful after dat."

The only other time Remi hit Jeannette happened at the kitchen table. Jeannette used a curse word and was smacked hard on the head from behind. The shock made her want to laugh but when she saw her mother's face, she knew that if she made one false move she would get the beating of her life.

She knew not to cross her mother. One day a neighbor's child lied to his mother saying that Jeannette and Simonne had pushed him into the ditch. When Maria found out, she didn't ask whether it was true or not. Her children had embarrassed her in front of her neighbor so her children would be punished. Jeannette would occasionally remind her mother of this incident throughout her life. Maria would always respond, "I thought I was right, and there is nothing I can do about it now." She never did apologize.

These isolated incidents of discipline were translated into a lifetime of obedience. Jeannette would never cause her parents, her neighbors, her teachers, or her employers any trouble.

Jeannette was a good child.

Jeannette fell in love for the first time when she was sixteen years old. She would kiss her boyfriend, but he always wanted to do more.

"When can we do it?"

"Never!"

Eventually she broke up with him because of his insistence on having sex before marriage. He did not want to wait. She was heartbroken. She felt so alone, dead inside.

To support the family, Jeannette obtained two jobs outside the home. During the day she worked on the assembly line at the shoe factory. After work, she cleaned the home of a farmer's wife, Godlieve, who was a friend of her mother. Jeannette had a reputation as a hardworking young woman.

She also had a number of young suitors. One of the farmer's helpers took a special interest in her.

Lecien was older than Jeannette and raised in a middle-class family. On their first date, they went to see a movie. Jeannette liked Lecien but when she told him they could only be friends, he was crushed. Lecien cried the day Jeannette married. He would never marry.

Mama could not see herself dating Lecien. He stood a foot shorter than her. Mama would tell me this story throughout my childh ood. I always told her she would have been happier with this short man. So would we. I didn't understand how my mother could have been so naïve.

Why didn't she see through our father's g ood looks? Why did she base a relationship on physical appearance? And why did she choose a life of unhappiness? By telling me her stories, my mother unwittingly influenced my views on love and marriage, further strengthening my resolution never to marry. Perhaps that was her intention.

One day while her mother was visiting neighbors, teenage Jeannette was alone when their landlord came over to visit.

"I've been waiting a long time for this. I think you're beautiful. I love your body."

"What are you talking about? Stay away from me. T'ink of your wife and your baby."

The more Jeannette resisted the more the man was visibly aroused.

"I could take you out to the coal shed. No one would know. No one would believe you."

"I'll scream. I'll hurt you if you come near me."

"You can't hurt me."

Jeannette grabbed the lid hook from the stove and brandished her weapon in front of his face.

"I'll tell everyone what you do to me. I swear I will."

Jeannette didn't stop talking. Her cool head, meeting threats with threat, and standing firm shocked the man, but a noise from outside stopped the potential rape.

I believed her. I never connected Mother's story to anything I was experiencing. Once, while playing The Game when his mother was outside in the garden, I even dared to ask my father if anyone had done "it" with him? He told me a male neighbor introduced him to The Game when he was a child. I believed him.

Of course, I was interested in these stories. I loved hearing adults talk. They knew so much more than children.

Mother's stories involved love, force and violence. Father's one and only tale involved a game. My father and mother are both the second eldest in their respective families of four children. I am their second child in a family of four children.

"You are my favorite," Father told me. "You play The Game so well!"

"You are most like me," Mother told me. "You are my special son."

My mother told me about her childhood, her courtship, and her relationship with my father. Because I listened.

I was the child who asked too many questions. The child who sat at the kitchen table with the adults while other children played. The child my parents discussed their sexual relationships with.

The good son, the good child, the different one.

A child who knew too much.

Chapter Twelve

"You have got a bad cold," Mama tells me. I cough and I cough. We go to the hall and I cough some more. "Maybe Donald should see de doctor, Daniel."

"He doesn't need no medication or no doctor," states Papa.

I know. A doctor is for when Mama has a baby, an operation on her neck, or her gall bladder is removed. Sickness is something you have to learn to live with until you get better.

Papa never takes us to the doctor except when we are there to wait in the big room with sick people for Mama to come out of the doctor's smaller room. It's always fun to look at picture books and watch the other people cough, blow their noses, or tell their children to behave. Even though I do not want Mama to be sick, it is a time when things are different.

Things are also different at school. My grade four teacher, Ms. Shaw asks me to draw a picture on the chalkboard. After recess, she returns to class and says I must have traced the picture. "You can't draw that well."

Just because Ms. Shaw can draw beautifully doesn't mean she has to call me a liar. I don't know how to trace on the blackboard. Why can't she believe I did this on my own? I don't insist it is my own. I think she is jealous. I keep quiet just the same.

Another teacher says we have to find a book at the school library, then report on the story in class. It can be fiction or non-fiction. I go to the library and study the wall-to-wall books. *Margaret Atwood, Canadian author, fiction*. I don't like fiction. I just like true stories. I finally find a non-fiction book, *The Steven Truscott Story*. I am fascinated with this young boy's tragic life. At the age of 14, Steven was wrongfully convicted of murdering a twelve-year-old girl. He was sentenced to die by hanging. The sentence was later changed to life in prison, and he was released 10 years later.

"I think Steven is innocent," I declare to Mrs. White in front of the whole class. "What do you think, Mrs. White?"

"I think he's guilty."

"I know he's innocent and I'm not changing my mind!"

Even though I rarely speak up in class, no one can get me to say something or do anything I don't believe in. My mother is the one responsible for instilling in me a commitment in belief, for Father never speaks of God to me. I never for a moment, consider swearing, smoking, drinking, or taking drugs. These are not options for a child who "knows" God could kill him in the future and his father can kill him in the present.

Because I am one of Jehovah's Witnesses, I have to stand out in the hallway when the national anthem is played over the classroom speaker, sit down while everyone else stands up if the anthem is played in the auditorium, and never participate in any Christmas, Easter, Valentine, Halloween, or birthday festivities. For a Witness, these are matters of life-and-death importance. Standing up for what I believe to be right and putting up with ridicule for being different is a typical, if somewhat difficult, part of my everyday school life.

So was an attraction to drama in my own little world.

I finally found it: Charlotte's Web, *the book on which my favorite cartoon movie is based. How I identified with both Charlotte, the mature, mother-like spider, and Wilbur, the innocent, lovable pig. Wilbur couldn't understand why it was necessary for sweet Charlotte to kill and feed off a fly that flew into and got caught in her web.*

"Mama, why do innocent living things have to die so that others may live?"

It had been six years since Georgia Jackson's death. Gossip and innuendo stoked the flames of mistrust and unanswered questions surrounding the case. Had the police handled the Jackson homicide differently because the victim had been a member of the Jehovah's Witness faith? Who killed Georgia and why? For the past six years, the Jackson case was kept open both by the Ontario Provincial Police and the Witnesses' Watchtower Society.

Chapter Twelve

Then in 1972, seemingly out of nowhere, David Bodemer, a Jehovah's Witness, confessed to and was subsequently convicted of the crime.

I'm eleven now. Mother tells me who Bodemer is. And do I remember him sitting in the hall in Aylmer when he visited with his wife and children?

"I always heard weird t'ings about dat man."

I guess the more weird the outside world appeared, the more normal we perceived ourselves to be.

The trial's sensational aspects were reported daily in the press. The St. Thomas courtroom was packed with local Witnesses and other members of the community.

Witnesses consider this Aylmer homicide, a Witness slaying a fellow member, to be the first in their religion's 100-year history. This is remarkable given the fact that Witnesses' membership had grown to number in the millions in more than two hundred countries.

After the Bodemer trial ended with his conviction, The Watchtower Society's file remained open. Speculation haunted the case from the beginning and did not end with Bodemer's incarceration. Certain members of the Witnesses' organization believed there had been a deliberate, calculated cover-up and that more than one person was involved in the murder. Meanwhile, the police were equally satisfied with Bodemer's conviction as they were with their initial investigation.

An unresolved mystery, suspicions, gossip—a scandal. No wonder that within months of the trial's conclusion, Elder Adam Sandor was assigned to the Aylmer congregation to spearhead recovery and healing amongst its troubled members. A congregation traumatized both by the sheer brutality of the crime and the reality that a fellow Witness had committed the act.

Adam Sandor became interested in the secrets locked away behind the walls of the Aylmer Hall. Why had it taken six years for Bodemer to confess? Had something other than his professed feelings of guilt motivated his disclosure? Were others, in fact, involved in a cover-up? Sandor believed that his mission was divinely inspired and the Jackson case became his obsession. He befriended Max Leder, an Overseer Elder responsible for several Kingdom Halls in his designated area. Leder played a major role in obtaining a confession from Bodemer and in the subsequent trial. Sandor and Leder were inseparable as the two worked closely together in their quest for "the truth."

Fate, in the form of Father's constantly relocating our family, brought me once again to this little town of Aylmer. I was raised on the secrets and tales of the notorious Jackson murder case. The characters involved were people who visited my world and the never-ending story held my interest.

Yes, Sandor and Leder visited our world, asked questions, and gossiped to discover more gossip. Had we seen anything unusual? Would Ronny and I spy for them? All the while coffee and cookies were being served.

I spent my early childhood more often as an observer than a participant in these events. Because I was a quiet child, I listened rather than spoke.

Sometimes adults would say, "Perhaps we shouldn't speak in front of the children." Then others would respond, "They're only children. How could they possibly understand anyway? They're busy playing."

I never played. Not children's games, anyway.

Eavesdropping on adult conversations was one way I could gather information. Therefore, as a child, I lived in a grown-up world, learning games that adults in my world played—creating a web of secrets and lies.

No wonder I only looked for non-fiction books to read. I didn't need to read fiction to discover drama.

Chapter Thirteen

"Secrets, lies, games, and God thrown in as seasoning. You must have been a pretty mixed up kid!"

"Actually, I didn't think so, Maurice. Situations that seem unbelievable now were normal back then."

* * * * * * * * * *

The older I grew, the more stubborn and outspoken I became at home in contrast to the shy behavior I displayed to the real world.

Mama is the disciplinarian, but she only punishes us if we do something really bad. More often than not, she lets us get away with too much. "I'm spanking you because I love you," she says.

She is also afraid if she doesn't and Papa finds out, his anger will inspire an even worse licking. That's because, when Papa hits us, we are scared to death since he can't control his temper. He weighs over 200 pounds and stands six feet tall. We younger kids are small. We do whatever Papa says for the most part anyway.

"Donald," Papa yells, "Are you drinking coffee again? I told you before, you'll never drink coffee under my roof!"

I say nothing, but my eyes telegraph a message of hate.

"Dere is not'ing wrong with a cup of coffee now and den!" Mama counters in my defense.

Swoosh!

Papa throws the cup of hot coffee in my face. After the hundreds my mother poured for me in secret, this is worth it.

"I hate you!" I mumble under my breath. Nothing will stop me from drinking coffee.

"After dis, I will hide de coffee in de pantry for you and you can gulp it down," Mama whispers.

Defiance—us against him. Papa is unfair in many ways outside of The Game. Gradually I perfected the role of Good Son in order to avoid confrontation. It is in my best interests to let Papa think I always obey his "commandments".

Even after Erik's disclosure, The Game continues, often daily. We play in the barn, in the car, in washrooms, in the shed, in the fields, and in our bedrooms. Anywhere and everywhere. Mama never catches us. One Donald despises Papa with a passion, while the Other Donald participates in The Game.

I lie in the tall grass watching the clouds pass by. There are bodies around me, but I am alone. I exist in a world separate from anyone. What is reality? What is fantasy? I know I will escape and never turn back. No matter how bad it is out there, God, it must be better than here. At least it will be my choice. For now, I will do my time and wait patiently.

"I want him out of our life. Let's kill him. It's our only way out, Mama."

"Now, Donald, you do not want to go to jail, do you? It's not wort' ruining your life to kill your *vader*."

I think this is twisted logic. I'm only 12. Would jail be that much worse than living with Papa? I only have two choices: continue playing The Game or kill Papa so I don't have to play any more. Life would look better if Papa was out of the picture. Nevertheless, Mama must be right. I don't want to go to jail. God says, "Thou shall not murder." And besides, it is only a game after all.

Only a game?

While Other Donald plays The Game with Papa, I am ashamed of my body. No one sees me nude except my father. Why is it okay for my father to see me nude and no one else? I won't allow my brothers, my sister, or my mother to see me naked. In gym class at school, I go to great pains to protect my modesty. I avoid urinals for the same reason. But with my father, I become completely opposite. I am never self-conscious about my body with him.

Papa makes it clear to Marina and me that he will be the first to have intercourse with her, the first to initiate her to sex, the first to be her lover. He says I can have her after he is finished. Marina and I live thinking this could happen any time soon. I am afraid my sister will want him to do it and she will get pregnant. We have no choice but to accept the inevitability that one day he will fulfill his wishes.

I tell him I am never going to have sex with Marina. I tell him I would hate that. I hate touching my sister sexually.

"Come on and play with each other!"
It's wrong! It feels wrong. I know it's wrong. Why is it okay for Papa to play The Game with me? I don't know anything about sex. Nobody discusses sex with me. It or any part of our body is not named.

A few times, he makes us touch one another. I hate myself for touching my sister there. Somehow I feel so dirty doing that. It is so gross, even not knowing it is wrong. But why do I remember wanting to have a body like Marina's—a girl's body?

Father praises the female body, never a male's, as an ideal. Papa treats me as if I am his daughter although he sneers at my girlishness. Eventually I think it will be more advantageous if I have the female anatomy.

"Hide your thing between your legs. You'll look more like Marina," he says as I stroke him. "If you put pins in your hair, you can curl it. You'll look like a girl."

I must feel unworthy of his complete attention unless I have the female body parts and looks he desires. And if I have those things, I can offer myself so that he won't do it with my sister. My mind cannot handle him doing what he does to Mother, to Marina.

Before going to bed, I say my prayers:

"...and take care of my sister. And God, please change me into a girl."

Since my prayers are never answered, I make an announcement to my family at supper.

"When I get older and have enough money, I am going to have a sex change operation."

"Could you pass the salt, Donald?"

Silence.

My announcement is not acknowledged. There is no point in bringing it up again.

Chapter Fourteen

"Originally Satan's name was Lucifer," preaches Mama. "He was de beautiful angel of light who fell t'rough overweening pride and jealousy into darkness."

Papa moved us so much because he was running. Running from people who might have suspected him. Brainwashed and obedient, his family was his most reliable ally. He trusted that his secrets were safe with us.

We knew from experience that telling our secret didn't change anything. So why bother telling? The chain of events became more predictable.

We tell Mama, "It happened again."
She condemns Papa.
He promises to change.
Nothing changes.

There are, however, cracks in what had become my father's predictable arrangement, for Ronny is unaware that the abuse has continued. The last time Ronny was attacked by Father took place two years earlier. He was 13.

Papa takes Ronny on a hunting trip. But Papa and Ronny aren't there to hunt. Papa stops on a country dirt road.
Papa whips out his thing.
"Okay, come on already."
"NO!"
"You do as I say, boy!"

Ronny is six feet tall now. No one, including his father, is going to make my brother do something he doesn't want to do. He not only rejects Father, he threatens him.

"Don't you ever touch me or any of us kids again. If I find out you've touched Donald, Marina, or Erik, you're a dead man."

Nothing more is said.

Papa never approaches Ronny again.

We tell our brother The Game has continued. Ronny is furious. He also feels guilty.

Ronny became the only one of us able to achieve some semblance of independence. He made sure he was rarely home. He wanted to believe Papa had stopped playing The Game with us and so he did. He naïvely thought there was a chance we could be one big happy family. The truth shocked him. Meanwhile, we assumed that The Game continued with him too. There was no reason to discuss it. Why would we want to?

Ronny knows he has to do something. He promised he would. But now, as a baptized Christian, he can't physically hurt his father. Instead, he reaches out and cries for help. He decides to confide in the Elders of the Aylmer Hall of Jehovah's Witnesses.

Mama says, "Don't tell."

Papa says nothing, as though this disclosure is inevitable. God knows he plays The Game. Now God's Elders will know too. Papa's silence is a brilliant and calculated turn.

Me, I am ecstatic. No more secrets and lies.

And Ronny? As the oldest son, the pressure on him is unbearable. He fears physical retribution from his father, not only for himself, but for us, too. But now he also has to deal with another unknown factor—how will the Elders react to the news?

He breaks down, confiding in the men of God, that our father has played with us sexually for years. Their reaction: a mix of detachment, curiosity, and confirmation.

Within the Witness society, spiritually weak males are suspect. Where there is no sign of progress, there is genuine concern. During his fourteen years as a Witness, my father's involvement with Jehovah's Witnesses had been sporadic at best. The Elders "knew" there was something wrong with him. Now they have the "evidence" on him.

They assume because my father is guilty of perverse behavior, and both he and Bodemer have had a connection to the Aylmer Congregation, he might have something to do with Georgia Jackson's death, or at the very least he is withholding pertinent information about the case.

With the murder and rape of one of the sisters in our congregation, everybody became a target of a veritable witchhunt and accusations of every sort was (sic) hurled at everybody. I was the subject of question and doubts like everybody else and everybody was becoming a spy on each other. The congregation had one of it's (sic) worst moments of backbiting and gossiping that just about ripped everybody wide open. When the one who did it was found and brought to trial a sigh of relief came over everybody. "Finally," we thought, "everything will settle down." Not so!!! Every mistake of the past by individuals was raked up and I was also exposed as to my behaviour pattern which brought about my disfellowshipping. I was relieved at first as the load was off my mind but then it really hit me.
Daniel D'Haene, Praise the Lord I Am Saved, p. 10

Papa is called into a meeting with three Elders. Mama is angry with Ronny for breaking the silence. Her private humiliation is about to go outside her inner circle. The four of us are told we must testify before the Elders. Ronny is fifteen, I'm twelve, Marina is ten, and Erik is seven.

Papa confesses to the accusations. How could he not? Why would his four children lie? Why would Mother? Following his silence upon Erik's disclosure two years earlier, his quiet admission of guilt now is really not that surprising. Perhaps his silence serves a purpose. Wouldn't a self-defensive posture or an antagonistic approach add to an already explosive situation?

My naiveté and innocence are thrown into the public arena for the first time. I feel like a witness for the prosecution. I'm excited that our secret is finally coming out. "My life will change for the better," I tell myself. "God's Elders will hug me and tell me God loves me just like Jesus did to his disciples."

We four children are called to the hall to tell the Elders about Papa's abuse of us. I am nervous but not frightened. After Ronny leaves the room at the end of the hall, I am called in.

I walk into a tiny room with five chairs. I sit before three men of God. I completely believe that these men are God's chosen Elders. I know Mama believes in them. Even Papa believes in them. I cannot, and will not lie to God's helpers.

"You realize how important it is to tell the truth, don't you, Donald? It's God's will that you do," one Elder tells me.

"Yes!" I promise.

"Describe the sexual acts with your father. What did your father do? What did you do exactly? How often? How many years?"

As odd as I feel, I am enjoying this attention. Thinking Donald describes The Game perfectly. I've repeated this monologue before. Explaining Erik's disclosure to Mama was a rehearsal for this revelation now. After all, she asked the same kinds of questions, but when we told her, she cried. I am on a stage again, but this time God is listening. I know what I say has significance. Why, I do not know, but I know just the same.

No one asks me how I feel or how I felt. No one touches me. The questions are cold, blunt, and matter of fact. I haven't the nerve to ask questions. As always, Thinking Donald has no tears.

"Thank you. We'll call you back later." I am dismissed.

An Elder steps out of the small room.

"Next, Marina."

The assembly line of D'Haene children continues into the back room. I sit on a chair in the main hall. To say I have no comprehension of what is happening to me is an understatement.

"Papa is bad and he is going to be punished," Mama tells me.

I'm involved in something very bad. I feel like I'm in a television courtroom drama and the show is long and boring. I can't turn the channel! Erik is sitting next to me waiting his turn. I kick the legs of the chair in front of me...waiting and waiting.

Finally, Mama is called in to answer questions.

"I did not tell anyone because I was embarrassed for de kids, for me, even for Daniel. What would you Elders t'ink of us? I kept everyt'ing to myself for so long, I didn't know what to do or how to feel. I know dat Daniel influenced me to keep everyt'ing quiet."

"It was very wrong of you not to report this situation to us, Sister D'Haene."

"I truly feel horrible and guilty and pray God will forgive me. I am ashamed. Yes, at first I was shocked and angry at Ronny for telling and den I knew it was de best t'ing to do. But still I was ashamed and did not want many to know about de situation."

Within days, another meeting is called. Once again, I find myself in the little room with the big men. This time, Mama and my brothers and sister are with me. One of the men starts talking.

"Your father will be disfellowshipped and your mother publicly reproved for conduct unbecoming a Christian....When your father comes to meetings, he will sit at the back of the hall. You will sit with him and your mother. Remember, you must still honor your father as head of the household."

I am dizzy. "Mother publicly reproved...sit at the back of the hall ...honor your Father." I can't hear the rest of what this Elder is mumbling.

I am happy. I understand Papa's excommunication will mean he is no longer a Jehovah's Witness. That makes sense. God's people do not play The Game with their children. They also don't ask their children to lie about it to their Mama.

I am confused. How shall we "honor" our father? He never talks to us unless we play The Game. Does God expect my siblings and me to honor our father in some things but not in others?

I am sad. Mama's being punished because of my testimony. Why? I don't understand! Mama's hurting and Papa has something to do with it. I have something to do with my mother's pain.

How can I feel sad yet happy at the same time? The big secret is out, but a dark cloud continues to hover over us. I am afraid of these men, but God must have told them to do this.

As we drive home, Mama talks first.

"It is God's will. I made a mistake. I should have told de Elders."

Again Papa is silent.

We're driving to the big four-bedroom house on top of the hill with the barn, silo, and chicken coop. Nothing's changed. People know and we're still living with Papa as one family. Will the abuse continue? I believe it will. I know it will.

On Sunday, we go to the congregation meeting and the public announcement is made.

"Daniel D'Haene is disfellowshipped for conduct unbecoming a Christian. Jeannette D'Haene is publicly reproved. Now, let us stand and sing song number...."

We're at the center of a sick kind of circus. Yet no one looks at us. I don't understand why. I feel nothing. What am I supposed to feel?

Witnesses use Biblical scripture to back their beliefs, believing that every word is directly inspired by God. Even though interpretation is relative, they are sincere in their views. While much of the Bible they consider symbolic, other verses are taken literally. Therefore, they follow the examples of the first century Christians as reported by the Apostle Paul—if a member sins and is then removed from the congregation for not repenting, all must ostracize the erring member to help him repent and return to the flock. If a member were to associate with the excommunicated member, he himself would risk being ostracized. There are variations on this theme; in the late '70s, the Witnesses' Watchtower Society counseled members to have limited contact with an erring member and even then, only regarding necessary family matters.

Publicly reproving those who do not show repentance for committing acts contrary to church doctrine is a common practice. Once disfellowshipped, an ex-member may continue to attend meetings. However, the congregation is not allowed to acknowledge his presence. An ex-member may be reinstated after six months.

But were the Elders aware that an adult who engages in a sexual act with a child is committing a criminal offense? There was no talk of contacting the police, reporting our disclosure to the Children's Aid Society, or offers of escape.

How could a twelve-year-old boy know this event would be the beginning of a long series of disclosures, public announcements, hearings, and media attention? I didn't. The only emotion I remember during that period was sadness over my mother being punished. She was being punished for knowing about the abuse and not reporting it for two years.

Would it have been such a sin to stand up, say, "This is a load of crap!" and walk out of that meeting? Such a blasphemous move would have labeled one a devil's disciple. We four children believed in this system of discipline, even if we didn't understand it. How could we know better? The Elders dealt with our problems internally because their perspective was focused on not being a part of the ungodly world.

Jehovah's Witnesses believed in separating church and state. They had a desire to remain detached from the outside world. In general, though, if someone broke the law of the land, the Elders encouraged the individual to initiate the unwieldy process of settling accounts with the appropriate law agencies. Even David Bodemer was encouraged to confess his guilt to the police. It appears there was a double standard in our case. Why had the Elders not encouraged Daniel D'Haene to go as well? Was incest not also a serious crime?

No doubt the fact that Ronny's disclosure followed on the heels of the Jackson murder conviction worked against us. One of the Elders handling our father's case, Elder Surin, was married to a relative of the murdered victim. Four physically healthy children came before him to testify. We were not seen as Daniel's victims. We were witnesses and participants in a series of sinful acts. More importantly, we were alive—what did we have to complain about? Such was the depth of ignorance of sexual abuse within the Witness society in 1973.

Yet Elder Surin wasn't completely naïve. He told me, "I warned my wife to keep our children away from your father."

Did the adult players in this fiasco act out of self-interest? I was a child. What did I know? I wished someone would take us away from my father, but I did not understand the legalities of the situation. Outside the looking glass that was my childhood, one could ask why Mother had not taken action to remove us. Were we asking more of the Elders than of her? Perhaps. But Judgment Day seemed far off. Was it so wrong to look to the shepherds of the flock to be our immediate saviors? The Elders were well educated. Mother was not. Who had more responsibility to act upon the knowledge given them?

I know that I associated disclosure with hurtful consequences, unfair punishment. These experiences only encouraged my separation from reality. I was a body without a voice, programmed to be silent, to feel nothing. There was no acknowledgement of my worth. In fact, my public image was negative by association. I was my father's child. I had hardly begun my life and already the strikes were building against me. Worst of all, a condescending attitude from certain ministers— God's chosen Elders—fed the feeling that a negative energy was coming to us in an indirect way from God. One traveling overseer told me that from the moment he heard of our being sexually abused, he vowed never to touch another glass or cup in the Aylmer hall—because, "it was tainted by your father's touch."

He was truly horrified by our experience. He always expressed genuine caring for my family—and chose a symbolic act that would signify his personal protest to the abuse, yet he never made an overt gesture of help. He never said, "Get out! Call the police or I will!" His revelation was like an abused victim of a Catholic priest receiving a get-well card from the Pope. Too little—too late.

My family had been conditioned to view the world as separate. "We are in the world but not of the world" was an oft-quoted teaching. Hence, problems within the Witness organization were handled internally, within a small congregation, by each local body of Elders. I did not understand the Elder's judgment, but I certainly never questioned their decisions.

After Father was disfellowshipped in 1973, members of our faith did not associate with him or visit us when he was home. At least their children didn't have to play The Game with him.

I did take comfort in the fact that we would no longer have to listen to Papa self-righteously preach to visitors.

And once, just once I heard from my father's lips: "We have to stop." Even at twelve years of age, Thinking Donald found that laughable. "We" have to stop?

The implication was that we had been consensual sexual partners. His excommunication had him sufficiently worried that he decided to lie low for a while, but Other Donald knew he would be back.

Chapter Fifteen

Our youth is comparable to that lived by army brats. I've attended seven schools by the time I reach grade nine. This constant relocation prevents bonding with any students and definitely affects our education.

We get labeled early on. The popular television comedy, *Green Acres*, featured an oddball character named Mr. Haney. Because he sells an odd assortment of junk and lives in a community where animals are as unusual as their owners, kids constantly tease us over the similarity of our names.

"There go the Haney Goats."

But we fulfill other stereotypes for our peers as well. My older brother excels at sports, but more often is noticed for his lanky body, height, and backward manners. "Tex," they call him. I am characterized as the nerdy, feminine, somewhat intellectual one. My sister is centered out for her weight. And Erik, well, he is labeled "trouble" with a capital "T."

Oddly enough, Erik is the only one of us who vocalizes how he feels in the present moment, and he is judged most harshly for it. After Erik fails yet another grade, his principal requests a meeting with our father to discuss his "problem child." It is mutually agreed the youngest D'Haene will join a special education class.

Is there something wrong with my baby brother? No more than is wrong with the rest of us, but Erik hasn't had years of being conditioned to play by the rules as we have. No doubt our constant moving and increasingly warped environment contributes to Erik's difficulties. How could it not? Although he plays The Game infrequently, he experiences and displays numerous manifestations of a hellish upbringing. It is easier for everyone to focus on his external behavioral problems rather than the source of his dysfunction.

We too focus on the external rather than the internal, for labels cover a multitude of sins.

My brothers and sister rebel. They fight with other children at school, talk back to teachers, don't complete assignments, or skip classes entirely. Each new report card contributes to their history of erratic behavior. Some years they manage excellent grades which no doubt leads teachers to believe my siblings are individually responsible for their problems with learning and discipline.

Marina brings home her report card.

"Marina's excess weight makes it difficult for her to participate in physical education. She also finds it difficult to make friends with other students...."

My gut aches. Why don't you see my sister as a person instead of as an object? I hate you, Mr. Smith. Poor Marina. I wish she hadn't seen this.

I, on the other hand, receive one and only one detention. "Acting out" is unusual behavior for me so it gets noticed, and my father makes a noisy commotion about it.

I wonder what it would be like to be "bad" for a day and decide to stay late for an extracurricular activity, a series of games in the school gymnasium. Donald committing a deliberate act of defiance is unheard of. It is the first time I attempt such willful behavior. Or at least, an act of behavior that I know will be discovered.

I am not physically punished on this occasion, but Papa makes me write out, "I shall not..." one hundred times.

"You call this a punishment," I laugh to myself. It must have something to do with his playing The Game with me. Nevertheless, I resolve not to be bad in this way again. It seems a waste of everyone's time including my own.

I am no angel. I am just extra careful. One time I get caught, but only by a process of elimination and investigation. We eat the same lunch for school, every day, five days a week, forty-odd weeks a year: brown sugar sandwiches.

"Brown sugar again!" I complain.

Chapter Fifteen

"Your Mama has no money to buy anyt'ing else, so be happy you have somet'ing to eat!"

I don't blame Mama but I'm sick of these sandwiches. The other kids' lunches look so good. They wouldn't notice if I take a couple of their items, would they? After several complaints to the teacher, and the discovery of sugar sandwiches in the garbage bin, my jig is up.

"Donald, if we ever catch you stealing other students' food again, you'll get the strap. You hear me?" commands the principal.

"I promise, I won't."

I am humiliated by the teacher who announces to the class that I stole the food. Of course, I won't steal again, although the others' lunches still look mighty good. I just don't want to get hit. It might be worth it though, if I just had to write out, "I will not steal," one hundred times like I did for Papa.

My crimes are of a secret nature. I never act out in school again as my siblings do, but there are signs something is definitely wrong. My introversion is visible. Everyone around me tells me how different I am. I don't understand why, but I believe them. Nobody talks to me, they talk at me. My school life is becoming increasingly insane. I talk to no one and avoid speaking in school at all costs. I stare down at my books when I am in class.

I overhear students talk about going skating last weekend. How can Other Donald tell them what he did on the weekend?

I listen to students complaining about their parents' restrictions, homework and the like. I envy them. I tell a student that I wish my father were dead. A look of horror and disbelief shades his countenance.

Only one student gets close enough to me to ask what it is that I'm hiding.

"Come on. You can trust me."

Those are the magic words that betray his intent. How often I have heard that promise before. I can't trust him with my secret. It would be nice to think he cares what happens to me, but I doubt it. I think he's interested in knowing my secret because it's a challenge to get it out of me. He is the only person who approaches a semblance of friendship with me. He sees through my appearance and recognizes wit and intelligence, but just asking me to trust is not enough.

I'm called to visit the guidance counselor who also happens to be my math teacher. He's a very nice man.

"Is there anything you'd like to talk about, Donald?"

I shake my head. Does he really think I would talk to him about my other self, my secret life? Feeling Donald doesn't exist when I am at school. Why would I speak about The Game? The Game might not be normal, but neither am I.

Since nothing changed before, would life become any different if I talked now?

I am programmed. Brainwashed into this life of deception, denial, and self-hatred. My school world responds to my low self-esteem by targeting me as easy prey. They are right. I am outwardly what they think me to be.

Chapter Sixteen

"You'd think with the Elders and your mother knowing about the abuse, things would have been different."

"You know what, Maurice? Life became even more absurd!"

* * * * * * * * * *

Since Ronny's disclosure, the family dynamics have changed. The secret is no longer a secret. The Game is now labeled EVIL, SIN, and WICKED. The Elders don't want us to be involved in sin. Mama doesn't want us to play The Game. Papa wants us to continue playing.

Now little insignificant Donald is a player with choices. Or do I only think I am in control? Play The Game and you get called into a meeting in a small room with three Elders. "You realize how important it is to tell the truth, don't you?" Play The Game and disappoint Mama. "How could you do dis to de children? To me?" Play The Game and make Papa happy. "We don't have to tell Mama, do we?" Or play The Game and get something out of it. "You do me and I'll do you. I'll get you that toy you want."

Perhaps the only way to improve my circumstances is to continue playing The Game.

One day, when I get home from school, Ronny announces to Mama and me that he has a serious matter to discuss. As we sit at the kitchen table, he informs us with great hesitation, that he's having a problem with self-abuse and has gone to the Elders for help.

Ronny is sixteen and I am almost thirteen. I think this is ridiculous. I've been doing it for a couple of years now. Initially, I thought it was senseless to pleasure myself. That's what The Game was for, wasn't it?

Yet my father encouraged me to do it. And when I started I almost went out of my mind with guilt because I thought: "Oh, my God. Another practice that makes me like Papa."

I never told my father I played with myself, and I'm certainly not going to the Elders to tell them. They might disfellowship or reprove me. I feel sorry for Ronny. Why does he feel he has to tell Mama and me about something so personal? I will never be that open.

Let the games continue....

I'm playing with myself while taking a bath. There is a large window behind me. Suddenly, I sense someone is watching me. I swing around. I look up. I see Papa's smiling face. Instantly I freak out, aware that this will mean betrayal and blackmail! I am scared to death, yet I do not panic. In fact, I notice the curtains have been deliberately separated in order to get the best possible view from outside.

Quickly closing the curtains, I dry off, and get dressed. I go upstairs to my bedroom. I glance at the calendar on the wall: January 16, 1974. I will never forget this day, for I know my father will use what just transpired against me. Everyone will hate me if they know I play with myself. I will be compared to Papa. I hate him.

I await Papa's next move. It comes.

While in the barn, attending to my chores, Papa approaches me and says, "If you don't do it with me, I'll tell your mother and the Elders you masturbate, and you'll be disfellowshipped too."

I have to think quickly. I didn't say no to Papa, but I didn't say yes either. I have never said no to The Game. I just try to avoid it and Papa as much as possible. This time is different.

Immediately, I march straight to the house and announce to my family: "Remember what Ronny told you about his problem? Well, I tried it but it's not for me. I thought it might be a problem, but I've got it under control."

I walk outside, smiling. I've won this battle. It is important for me, at the very least, to think I am in control. I don't know why.

Of course, Papa did not act upon his threat. He didn't tell Mama and he rarely went to the hall, let alone talked to the Elders. But that didn't mean he gave up the challenge to get me to play The Game. He knew there were only two ways to get what he wanted.

Papa gives me The Look followed by the obligatory nod. Obeying the signal, I enter the washroom first. Papa enters and locks the door behind him.

"Today, we're going to play a new game. Bend over the bathtub with your legs spread wide."

I do as I am commanded.

"What are you going to do?"

Suddenly, I feel a sharp pain as Papa enters me.

"Ouch! That hurts."

"Be quiet!"

The pain is continuous and I can't move because of my vulnerable position. I hope this ends soon. This is no game. I will never get tricked this way again.

"I'm not playing this Game again."

I don't say another word. Neither does Papa.

I am sore for days.

This version of Papa's Game is never discussed or repeated again. Papa is smart enough to know that The Game can only be played if the players are willing. Otherwise, I might find someone to tell our little secret to, just as Erik and Ronny had done.

Brutal force was one avenue to victory, but as it had not proven successful with his physically strongest, oldest son, it was even riskier behavior with the child Papa declares, "plays The Game the best." Papa makes a sport out of developing new ways to entice me.

Mama and I are watching *I Love Lucy*. I get up to get a glass of water and when I walk in the kitchen, Papa opens the newspaper on the table to an advertisement for adult movies. "Do you want to go to an all-night drive-in porn festival?" he whispers.

I'm in the middle of puberty. My hormones are raging. Of course, I want to see a porn movie. I've never seen one before. I know what I have to do to go, but this time I figure it is worth it. The Game is my only bartering tool.

"Yes, I'll go."

Since I was underage, yet looked like a girl, Papa asks me to wear sunglasses.

"You can pass as my girlfriend. Wife, we're going to drive to London, and I'm taking Donald to a movie. It's a comedy."

Now I have to work my end of the bargain.

"Mama, I want to go. I've only been to the movies once in my whole life and that was to see *The Bible*. Way back in 1966. Please let me go."

"Okay," Mama says, but with a suspicious look in her eye.

Papa's car nears the gate.

"You know what to do."

I flash a smile at the drive-in ticket counter, and they let us in without questioning. I am pretending to look forward to playing The Game just so I can see a couple of movies. I enjoy the excitement of being bad, tricking the attendants, acting with Papa, and I'm seeing a drive-in motion picture for the first time.

The movie begins. What a stupid movie! I am used to watching great movies with Mama, but this story line is boring me to death.

"We're going home after this movie, right Papa?"

"Of course we will. Now, pull it out."

I've made such a mistake.

I hate this. My hand is getting tired, and I want to go home but I'm trapped. I can't even tell the truth to Mama because I'm responsible for our being here.

Suddenly, an actress appears on the screen who plays a secretary on a law show I've seen many times. Don't tell me she's going to take her clothes off? Oh my God, she's taking off her bra. I can't believe this woman would take off her clothes in a dumb movie and have sex with that ugly guy! Yuck.

I can't watch that law show ever again, and I can't tell Mama it's because I don't respect that actress any more.

Papa used my curiosity about pornography as the enticing factor. I can see how I felt responsible—I chose which movies we watched that day. I could have said, "No, I'd rather see a comedy." There was something disgusting about this. I felt strange for days. I guessed that Mama silently suspected Papa of playing with us every time he took us for a car ride. She knew Papa never did anything for unselfish reasons. Why else would he give her children the time of day? Why did Mother "allow" Father to take us on car rides? She had no say, no influence over my father whatsoever. My father cleverly made it appear that we needed Mother's "permission." Father did whatever he wanted, when he wanted. He never asked for her opinion in his life. But the older we grew, the more he seemed to realize forcing us lacked the challenge of getting us to approach him. And the older I got, the better I became at lying. The more I lied like my father, the more I could get away with. He got away with everything. Why couldn't I?

Certainly The Game continued but Mother did not know about it. A year went by before one of us confessed to our "sin." Of course, our game-playing and success at each new level made us feel like we were co-conspirators with Father.

Mother couldn't stop The Game from happening. Father kept a shotgun in the pantry in the kitchen. On several occasions, he blew our favorite pets to smithereens. We all knew enough not to get Papa angry.

Mother's main concern and fear was that we would want to play The Game. She did not tell me, "You cannot do it." She said, "You should not do it."

I think she was right.

Chapter Seventeen

I had no friend in the world. After being quite bitter for a year or so I approached the elder for reinstatement but despite my breaking down in tears was turned down flat. That hit me like a ton bricks as it threw me as I saw into the cold and right in Satan's lap. I turned very bitter and lashed out at everybody at home and at work.

I must at this time add that before and after my disfellowshipping I had a lot of nervous breakdowns and my nerves were very bad. I took four nerve pills a day to keep calm. I had as a witness many sleepless nights and truly believe that I was under demon control. Occasionally, still felt a need for spiritual food and due to my witness indoctrination sought it by attending sporadically at the kingdom Hall. But fell off again, I had no communication with my wife and children for that's what disfellowshipping from Jehovah's Witnesses means, no spiritual communication at all and you are strictly forbidden to visit the witness at their homes. I became a very belligerent man at work and had started to use vile language and got intoxicated, too. But did that make me happy? No, not in the least. How long was I to continue on like that?

Daniel D'Haene, Praise the Lord I Am Saved, pp. 10, 11

While Mother had reason to be suspicious, the Elders on the other hand, were clueless. They felt their job was done. The congregation was protected after all.

Daniel continued to attend meetings and sit at the back of the hall. The Elders understood that action to mean he was, at the very least, showing respect for their decision, but it would require more than tears to get him reinstated into the congregation.

The truth remained that getting "found out" was not enough to put an end to The Game. Father took a short break but not a permanent one. He soon resumed The Game.

On two different occasions, in the second and third year of his disfellowshipping, Ronny and I informed the Elders of the ongoing abuse. The reaction was predictable.

"I guess he wasn't sincere when he applied for reinstatement."

"I want to take my family out of there!" Ronny says.

"You can't do that. You have to respect your father as head of the household. But you must take over the spiritual leadership."

And so he did. Ronny focused his energy on getting us to as many meetings as possible. He made a point of studying the literature with us weekly, whether we wanted to or not. Though he never expressed it to us, he harbored a fear: we secretly wanted to play The Game. He believed a spiritual life would replace that desire.

Meanwhile, I spent more time playing The Game than I ever did talking about it. A year or two would go by, and I'd state, "Yup, it happened again." Between incidents, I'd never even think about it.

I was too busy exploring our property. We were surrounded by forests and creeks. We had chickens, ducks, and rabbits to look after as well as our cats, dog, cow, pony, and goats. These were my friends and besides the occasional peck, scratch, bite or kick, the animal kingdom did not hurt me.

Other than frequently barking orders, Father continued ignoring us younger children. Yet he sparred frequently with Ronny. They were constantly at odds because of Ronny's ever-increasing freedom and Father's ever-decreasing control.

They were a study in contrasts. Ronny was becoming more involved in the Witness faith, while Father's interest waned. Ronny was becoming more confident, Father less so. He did everything to sabotage Ronny's friendships and deflate an already fragile ego. He appeared jealous of Ronny's charisma, personality, youthful looks, and attractive appearance. Ronny was in many ways a young version of the "Daniel" Father used to be. Father resented him.

Any attempts, whether internal or external, to affect the control Father had over his family were to be nipped in the bud. This was never more evident than in the summer of 1976.

My father's first cousin and his wife are arriving from Belgium for a month-long summer visit. Of course, my parents have no intention of showing them anything but a grand time. We are trained to pretend everything is all right for company. We are excellent actors. It is necessary in order to keep our secret.

But the mirror's reflection continued to crack. Why pretend? What do we owe Father?

When grandmother and grandfather visited in '75 for a second time, all they witnessed and participated in was fighting and arguments, yet those disagreements were partly based on their own dysfunctional relationship with their son and each other. They never had a problem with us nor did we with them. We were their adorable, lovable, perfect grandchildren, or so they told us.

Both grandparents were loving to us but to experience Grandpa's hugs, holding our hands as we walked, conversing and playing with us was like experiencing something out of a dream. He never wanted to play The Game. His touch was warm and safe and true. We stopped and asked each other, "How could Grandpa be so wonderful and Papa be completely opposite?" And although unspoken, we knew Papa's parents were asking themselves the same thing.

Grandpa and Grandma couldn't help but observe that we had no respect for their son and that Mother was unhappy as well. They also noticed that Father had stopped preaching to them about the Witness faith. We never for a moment considered telling them the real reason why. Perhaps we should have, for when they returned to Belgium, Grandmother told her nephew and his wife we were living a wonderful life in a large, beautiful house in Canada. The need to keep up appearances seemed to be a family trait.

Mother told Father: "It will not work out. Your cousins will figure out somet'ing is wrong." He was going to stop them from coming, but Mom told him his relatives "will become more suspicious if you change your mind now."

Father's cousins have no idea what they are getting themselves into. Imagine their reaction as they are driven up to a run-down, two-story house with unevenly painted pink-and-green siding and a five acre plot of land that looks like Dorothy's dream come to life: Kansas after the tornado.

Within two days, they simply ask what no one previously dared: "What in the hell is going on here? Why don't you talk to your father? Why are you so unhappy, Jeannette?" This time we don't hide our resentment, hatred, or disgust. Horrified at discovering our poverty, Mother's repression, and our abuse, they condemn Daniel: "You don't have to live like this. You must not live like this."

It's the first time I hear that I don't have to live with abuse. Instead of, "You shouldn't be playing The Game," they say, "This should not be happening to you." I have a choice? At fifteen years of age, do I?

Encouraging as their words may be, our visitors from the homeland offer no immediate support or plans for escape. Still, prior to this experience, I was convinced I was destined for a life as Father's sexual partner.

Am I afraid of Papa? I participate in The Game willingly. I believe I can say no, and that I am in control of the outcome. Can I say "No"? Am I in control? Is it only a game?

I never realized how much I loathe my father until this year. I've never hated him for having sex with me. I think I'm guilty, as much as he is. I hate everything else about him though. He owns me. He is indifferent toward me. He torments my mother and brothers and sister. We are worth less than furniture to him.

Does he assume because I'm party to The Game, that I like him? That I'll grow into manhood and everything will be okay? He doesn't know us. How can he? He never asks how we feel about anything.

But somehow, after experiencing my grandfather's love last year and my cousins' reactions this year, things are different. Unconditional love is what they give me. They tell me I am worthy of love, of something more than I am experiencing. Love without ulterior motives. I don't understand what that means. All I know is that when I'm with Grandpa or my cousins, I feel better about myself.

My cousins don't say The Game is evil. They don't say it is a sin. They say it shouldn't be happening to us, period. Mama's and the

Elders' reasons aren't enough to get me to say "No" to The Game. But my cousins' reasons make sense to me.

I decide to turn Papa down for the first time in eleven years. That's easier said than done. Avoiding The Game is far different than saying, "No." I'm determined that Marina and Erik will never be alone with him again. In the past I offered myself up sexually in order that Father wouldn't totally corrupt my siblings. Like Mother and Ronny, I too fear they'll want to play The Game. I thought it was okay with me but not with them. Now I don't think it is okay with me either.

I call for a family meeting. We make a pact amongst ourselves never to be alone with him again. It is the only way to ensure our individual safety. Marina opens up about her experiences with Papa. She says she smashed her hands with Papa's hammer so she wouldn't have to play The Game.

"If my hands are messy with scabs, Papa says we can't play. It hurts him."

Marina's disclosure makes me more determined than ever to put an end to Papa's Game.

Papa's true character comes to life when we say "No." He connives and twists things around to get one of us alone.

Papa orders Marina to feed the rabbits, which is normally my job. I know something is up because she hasn't returned to the house. I go to the barn to look for her, and sure enough, I intercept an assault in the hayloft. Papa is unzipping his pants in front of my sister. I shout to Marina to run, and then yell for Mama. Papa isn't afraid of any of us, but he doesn't want an audience either. Marina and I are sure Papa is going to rape her soon. It will take constant vigilance to avoid his snare from now on.

Papa has become violent—much like a jealous lover. Papa isn't upset because he can't have sex with us. Rather, he knows he's losing power and control over his family. We never witness an ounce of sorrow, responsibility, or self-hatred in Father, just anger over the fact that people he introduced us to encouraged our independence.

He is jealous of my relationship with them, yet remains convinced I want to continue The Game as much as he does. He tells me I perform better than my sister and brothers. He thinks I love him the most. What a fool. He lost all of us a long time ago. He never thought we'd grow up and want to leave him.

Within weeks of his cousins' departure, Papa started inviting a fellow employee and his wife to our house to visit. It was obvious Papa hoped to engage this woman in an affair. Even her husband announced in front of Mama that his wife was a "slut." This woman flirted with Papa, Ronny, and me at the same time. What must Mama have felt? Her husband flaunting "another woman" in front of her eyes. He bought hippy clothes, jewelry, and came home drunk for the first time in their twenty-year marriage. Yet she refused to believe Papa was having an affair.

"He would never do dat to me."

"What, you think he'd play with his kids and not with a woman?" was my blunt response.

Ronny and I decide to prove her wrong. We drive Mama to the couple's house when both Papa and the woman's husband are supposed to be at work. Sure enough, Papa's truck is hidden behind the house on the back lawn. Confronted with the evidence, Mama weeps uncontrollably. Strangely, Ronny and I draw no comfort from the knowledge that our suspicions are confirmed. Still the evidence isn't enough to convince Mother to leave him. "But he might change," she cries.

Ronny talks to Elder Jack about our ongoing difficulties with Father.

"Now that we believe our father is having an affair, we want our mother to divorce him."

"You know, your mother has no grounds for divorce if she had sexual intercourse with Daniel after she knew about the affair."

"We're leaving anyway."

The Elder wants Mother to leave with her Christian principles intact. He coyly passes on information she could use in a divorce proceeding.

"Is there anything that man hasn't done? Sexual abuse, bestiality, and now he's having an affair with a—"

"What did you say?" Ronny is in shock. "That's disgusting. We never knew about the bestiality!"

"That's definitely grounds for divorce. I probably shouldn't have told you. Make sure you tell your mother not to have relations with Daniel. I mean, if you choose to use this information and share it with her."

Chapter Seventeen

Jehovah's Witnesses follow strict rules governing divorce proceedings. My parents believed if intercourse happens between a married couple after a confession of fornication, an act that broke the marriage bond, forgiveness is granted. Therefore, because Father had sex with Mother after the disclosure of abuse, all previous acts are pardoned and religious grounds for divorce no longer exist. My father brainwashed her into believing this logic, an exaggeration of Witness dogma. We certainly never listed every single sexual experience with Papa for our mother. Did one copulation automatically give Father a clean slate?

Ronny tells me and we jointly tell Mama. The Elder confided in Ronny that Father had admitted to this sin in 1973 when my brother first reported our abuse. The Elders read off a list of acts that were condemned in the Bible, and Father admitted to acts of bestiality. Elder Jack is a young man in his early twenties. He isn't supposed to reveal confidences from within an Elders' meeting, but we are awfully glad he did. Ronny and I are sure God will forgive him. We are thankful for the disclosure. Finally, the trump card we need to convince Mama to leave her empty sham of a marriage is in our hands.

Mama is owned body, mind, and soul. The idea of leaving never enters her mind. But Mama stops sleeping with Papa. This revelation seems to send her over the edge.

In order to rid myself of the thought of Papa touching my animals, I distance myself from my pets. I block it out of mind, separating from my emotional self. Will I ever be able to enjoy my pets again?

Mama is the uncritical, submissive wife. That's why she was chosen. Papa didn't foresee us educating not only ourselves but Mother too. He programmed us to be with him "Till death do us part." Our only hope is to get away from his house. Our salvation depends on it. We must convince Mama to leave Papa. We couldn't live with ourselves if we left her here! Never.

We resent the fact that we have to convince her to leave. It's difficult to reconcile this knowledge with the concept that Mama loves us unconditionally. Her husband has sex with her babies. Is that not reason enough to leave? These feelings are sidelined for the moment. We are united in a mission: to free Mother from her jailer. Her liberation from captivity takes on more importance than our own.

The roles of parent/child are forever reversed. At fifteen, I am counselor, caretaker, therapist, and tower of strength to my mother. Finally, our pact is cemented—all or none of us.

We must escape.

Leave questions unanswered. Feel later.

Chapter Eighteen

I've just entered tenth grade but I never go. I can't leave my Mama, my brother, and my sister alone anymore. I will probably fail my year at school, though. I'll worry about that tomorrow.

Ronny is out and about with his Witness friends, tinkering on cars or with girlfriends. Marina and Erik play and fight as all kids do. Mama is still cooking or cleaning. Papa is still working or sleeping.

I spend a lot of time writing to our relatives in Belgium. I have a burning desire to someday visit my parents' birthplace. I asked our cousins before they left to give me as many addresses of our family as possible. I hand-draw thirty cards in color to send. When I finish, I decide to draw cards for every family at our Kingdom Hall. It's fun creating something that makes people smile. Almost makes me forget Papa is coming home soon. Almost.

When Mama finally agrees to leave him, it doesn't take Papa long to figure out Ronny and I are the ones behind it. But he also accuses the Elders of being responsible for his current dilemma. He swiftly moves into action.

Papa tries to sweet talk Mama into staying with him. So much so, she actually bends, and experiences a change of heart.

"I cannot leave him now. He is being nicer. Maybe he has changed."

"You are unbelievable!" I explode. "He makes me sick to my stomach. He'll show his true colors soon enough."

"I know you are right, Donald. But it is difficult to leave de marriage after so many years."

Father is suspicious Mother will separate from him and won't leave her alone until he finds out if, when, and on what grounds she is going to divorce him.

"You know of my molesting the children and of my bestiality. You have slept with me since knowing so you cannot divorce me on Christian grounds." How did Papa find out about our trump card?

I tell Mama: "Never answer him. You'll just give him ammunition against us." She resists for a time but he finally wears her down with his persistent nagging.

"Yes, I am going to divorce you."

Mama feels that he will stop badgering her if she answers him. And Papa, he feels vulnerable for a moment, knowing that at long last we are going to leave him and for good.

But only for a moment.

Then he goes nuts. His life is spinning out of control. His affair has cooled off. His children have rejected him. Now his wife, the one woman he knows to be faithful and true, the person that he mistreats but can always count on to be there to forgive him, is about to disappear. How can he prevent her from leaving?

There is only one way. He will become born-again and all of his sins will be washed away.

Papa works at the Ford factory in Talbotville where a small group of born-again Christians are well known for their preaching to other workers. Papa seeks solace in his co-workers' faith and quickly adopts its teachings.

I felt so miserable and expressed the desire to speak to a councillor (sic) and to open my heart. My foreman said he could not do it as he was not a religious man but said a supervisor might be willing to speak to me. Then in the afternoon something made me do some writing. I was so low that I wrote on a piece of cardboard that I apologized to everyone on the line for the way I behaved and asked their forgiveness. My foreman realized that I was very low spirited, arranged for the supervisor to talk to me. I went to his office and when asked what the problem was, really opened my heart to him. He said, "Daniel, just because you are no longer one of Jehovah's Witnesses is no reason for

**you to throw all your high moral principles out the door." I
said, "Yes, but I've sinned!"**

**[Being Born Again]...no longer do I need pills because
...look, no bad nerves!**

Daniel D'Haene, Praise the Lord I Am Saved, p. 11

Immediately, he witnesses to us, proclaiming his conversion and its
message, much the same way he had forced the Witness faith on his
wife, eighteen years earlier. For Mama it is a flashback. Once again
Papa hounds her to change her current beliefs. If it worked once, why
wouldn't it work again?

Now, from dawn to dusk, all we hear is how Father is a changed
man. To us, this amazing recovery began the moment he found out
Mama is going to divorce him!

He begins to exercise his Christian authority as head of the house.
He becomes physically abusive and targets Ronny.

"I am your father. You must listen to me."

"You're my father in blood only. You're a disgrace to the title."

Soon their anger and tempers lead to a terrible fistfight. We are
rooting for my older brother, scared for him and for us. If Papa wins,
he'll come after us next. We fear for our lives. Ronny and Papa are
rolling on the floor, with us three kids and Mama circling them.

"Oh Daniel, please stop!" Mama cries.

"Don't hurt my brother!" yells Marina.

"Go, Ronny! Go!" I shout, but unlike my roosters, only one of these
competitors is my friend. Ronny wins! But only the wrestling match.

"Don't you ever set foot in this house again!" says Papa as he
heaves himself up from the floor.

Ronny's face is redder than I've ever seen it but so is Papa's. Ronny
is worried about us. He did make that promise to protect us when he
was 13. And Papa does have that gun.

"I'll take care of Mama, Marina, and Erik. We'll be okay," I assure
him.

But I'm not so sure. I just said that so Ronny won't want to return
and fight Papa again. Mama and us kids wave good-bye as Ronny
drives off to stay with Witness friends down the road.

Ronny and I don't have to say anything. We both know we must
plan our family's escape, and soon.

We try to live by the code that Mama had learned as a newlywed—do as Papa says and you won't get hurt—but that isn't enough to please him. Papa controls us in every way but one.

"You are all going to Hell if you don't accept Christ as your savior. You must be born again in order to join me in heaven," Papa repeats over and over again. He hounds us day and night with his newfound insight into God's Word.

I think I'd rather get hit.

Papa is losing control. I find it strange that to get us to be born-again, his current brand of Christianity, he displays such unchristian behavior. He owns us in the flesh. Now he wants to own our spirit too. He burns our Witness books in bonfires, locks up the photo albums in his car trunk, and repeatedly calls Witnesses in the middle of the night and hangs up on them.

Papa follows us everywhere preaching with Bible in hand. Around and around the house we go. We sing our Witness songs to drown out his voice. The louder we sing, the louder he preaches. We are mentally exhausted.

He plays the good preacher-father and makes Marina, Erik, and I sit and listen to him read scripture on fornication and adultery. For this man to read to us from a book we respect makes us sick. Every time his back is turned, we make faces at him.

Tactics that might have worked on Mama eighteen years ago, won't work with me. I knew he was wrong then, and I know he is wrong now. I have never read of Christ acting like this when he preached. And if he did, I wouldn't listen to him either.

Chapter Nineteen

In the middle of the night, Mama wakes up with Papa staring down at her, breathing into her face. Before her eyes have a chance to focus, he grabs her hand and removes the ring Germaine had given her.

"If you're going to leave me, you don't need Mother's ring. This is mine."

Mama wishes he would take her wedding ring instead.

In the morning, Papa grabs Mama's purse and goes through it. He pockets her two dollars in small change and roars when he discovers she's kept the latest baby bonus check.

"Sign it, wife!"

"Don't do it. Mama, he can't make you," I shout.

"Oh yeah?"

Papa squeezes Mama's hand and attempts to force her to sign.

"He is hurting my hand, Donald. I have to."

That night, a Witness picks us up to take us to the Kingdom Hall. "At least we have peace of mind here," I whisper to Mama. "Remember, De Trut' will always set you free!"

When we arrive home, Papa says there's been a break-in while he was in town.

"The police will be here shortly. Someone stole the ice cream, killed the fish, and butchered your bunnies, Donald."

I run outside. All I see is a red and white landscape. My bunnies have been massacred!

"Oh Donald, I am sorry," Mama says.

I know someone who isn't sorry. When the officer arrives, Papa explains that he found the screen door busted open, the fish on the floor in a pool of water, and an ice cream box eaten.

"Is there anything else missing?" asks the officer.

"Yeah, my bunnies."

"I found all the rabbits killed in and outside of the barn," adds Papa.

"Why would a crook only eat an already half-eaten box of ice cream and nothing else?" I ask. "How did he know the ice cream was in the deep freezer in the pantry?"

"I think you should stay out of it and let us adults handle this," answers the police officer.

Who do they think shot the rabbits, Elmer Fudd? I know Papa shot my bunnies. Papa knows they won't work as a bartering tool anymore. I don't say another word. No one listens anyway.

I call Ronny at the neighbor's house and relay the past day's events. Ronny says he'll ask Elder Jack if he could recommend a good lawyer. When we obtain that information, we convince Mama to contact the lawyer from Tillsonburg. The attorney tells her she definitely has grounds for a divorce. He will represent her but he requires a $250 deposit. Although the lawyer is made aware we don't have the money, he never suggests we contact Legal Aid or welfare.

Why didn't our attorney contact the police or tell us to? We would have been out of our father's house sooner had he or anyone who had knowledge of the abuse just picked up the phone and placed an anonymous call to the Children's Aid Society: "I know of children who are being abused." Better yet, Father might have been the one taken away.

The only person Mama can ask for the retainer fee is Aunt Simonne. Ronny drives us to Innerkip to see our aunt and uncle. The fact we have to ask our relatives for the deposit emphasizes our role as a burden. Of course, uncle doesn't mind helping out.

When Ronny drops us off after midnight, Papa is waiting for us at the door.

"You were at Simonne's, weren't you? I got on my knees and I have spoken with Jesus. He told me where you were. I have seen the light."

"And when and where did this blessed miracle occur?" I inquire.

"11:30 P.M., right here in the kitchen," he replies, pointing to the floor.

"I don't believe you. At that time of night, it was pretty dark from where I stood!"

I think he is going to deck me. The nerve he has. Of all people, would Jesus send him a message?

I won't leave Mama alone for a second. I'm afraid Papa will rape her. I know he will.

Papa hounds Mother with the words: "You owe me my marital due. Even if I rape you, it isn't rape. You *Jehovahs* even believe that, and you know it."

Marina and I take turns watching her. Today I'm in the washroom with Mama. Papa busts the door down.

"I don't want any disgusting incest happening in my house!"

"YOU are telling US not to commit incest!"

"Don't you ever go in the washroom with your mother again!"

He whips off his belt and starts beating me. Mama tries to stop him. He grabs her arms leaving nail marks in his wake.

I cry hysterically. I stop. I leave myself. I go to another part of the room. I watch this man, Daniel D'Haene, beating Donald. I will never feel again. I must not.

Papa, noticing my change in mood, becomes outraged all the more by my calmness. I smile. Feeling Donald has departed. Thinking Donald takes over. He must.

Mama reaches for the phone, but Papa won't let her call anyone. He grabs her and forces her to sit down at the kitchen table.

Then he does an about-face, crawling on his knees crying, begging for forgiveness.

Ronny and I must take my mother, brother, and sister out of here before they become like me, unconnected to my reality, my feelings, my existence. They don't recognize the real Daniel D'Haene for what he really is. Am I the only one who sees the eyes of the Devil?

As soon as Papa leaves for work the next day, I tell Mama to telephone our lawyer and tell him what happened.

"Go to emergency at the hospital and move out as soon as possible," he instructs. "Have the children write down in their own words a statement about their experience. I'll need them as evidence."

On October 27, 1976, a fifteen-year-old wrote his statement.

DONALD D'HAENE'S STATEMENT FOR JEANNETTE BATAILLE'S DIVORCE FROM DANIEL D'HAENE DATED OCTOBER 27, 1976

My first sexual assault was in 1965 when I was four years old.... He came to me, most of all the children because I guess I was easiest and would not tell, he WAS sure of that.... He never touched me really until I was six years old because I was small but he made me do it with [to] him every time. After I was six, he started with me.

What really became sick for me was when he touched Marina.... He used to put his thing on Marina's part and just push a little and then say, "When you are older I can put my thing right in your part," I heard him say it. He used to make Marina & me just watch each other take turns on him. I asked him many times does he do it often with Mom—sex I mean, because I knew what it was since I was four. He told us and showed us with dirty books— pornography—what he does and what people do.

I began to hate sex because I thought, if everybody does this I would never do it with children myself and sex between man and woman to me was very dirty and disgusting.

All our friends who came by, I used to ask father if they do it and he would say yes. I became really disgusted with sex and even now it's the same way.

The only reason Mom found out was because Dad started playing with Erik and Erik after a couple of times told Mom what he did and she was shocked.... He told Mama he would change and then I guess she was sucked in. I don't know about Marina and Erik and Ron, but I sure wasn't. When I found out what he did WAS sick, wicked, etc. I hated his guts more than Mom would ever...

When Mom found out [about an incident with Marina], she went outside and told him he was crazy and a sick man and do you know what he had the nerve to tell Mom: that he was glad that Marina had told her. My foot he was, because he came to me about a week after.

Then he knew that there was no way we would let him touch us, so he had to find another outlet for his sexual desires so he went to a friendly loose women who was married and wanted to have sex with her and loved her but because he was an older man she refused him—(he actually told us all this, admitting he loved her and wanted her).

After all this, then about nine weeks he has been driving us crazy with his so-called religion. But we had to go through it before!!

It takes a beating to inspire an "okay" to move out. I call Ronny at his new home. He comes to our house to drive Mom and me to the hospital.

A doctor physically examines us.

"Mrs. D'Haene, you can charge Daniel with assault. Unfortunately, you, on the other hand, Donald, won't be able to because you're underage. You know, you should get some medication for that acne on your back."

I cover myself, ashamed of how I look.

Is it any wonder why I didn't tell him about The Game? No doubt, I might have opened up to someone as a child about the abuse, had anyone made the effort to get to know me beyond the Physical Donald I displayed for them.

I don't remember a time when I considered telling someone about my secret while I was living with my father. Any friends that I had were Witness adults who befriended my parents first, and therefore, could not be trusted. The fact that my father had told me all men play The Game with their children sabotaged my ability to trust adult males. My father's brainwashing techniques were masterful. Why would I tell when I thought it was normal to keep secrets, and that other children were as good as I was at remaining silent?

No one in my father's house articulated feelings. We'd argue about everyday matters—chores and punishments. Who would listen to how we felt, anyway?

Ronny just called to say he's on his way. Fortunately, our father is holding down two jobs and we know his schedule. There is no time to plan a move, no time to stop and think. We pack Ronny's car with large garbage bags filled with the bare essentials—clothes, schoolbooks, a sewing machine, a few plants, and some cutlery. I want to take all the cutlery but Mama says: "We have to leave him somet'ing. He has to eat." I can't believe Mama is concerned about Papa right to this bitter end.

"What if he comes after us?"

"You're right, Mama. I'll go back in and get the gun."

Ronny runs in and out in a flash. He locks the gun in the trunk. We drive off in a daze. A forty-five minute move. I can't believe Mama is finally leaving her husband, my father in name only, my molester. I had long wanted to stop calling him Papa. In fact, when we found out about his abusing our animals, we nicknamed him "Cow," after our beloved Bessie.

This is it. I'm finally rid of him—I think—I hope—I shout: "I'll never see 'Cow' again!"

Yes, I am outspoken with my family. Thinking Donald always speaks his mind when Papa is not present. I can't believe Papa won't ever be present again. He certainly won't miss me. He's never known of Thinking Donald's existence. I only existed for him when he needed Other Donald to play The Game.

How fitting there is no good-bye. There has never been a hello. The experience is surreal. A movie reel spinning off its projector. I'll wake up tomorrow and I'll be living with him once again. How can fifteen awful years be left in the dust without even one last final hurrah?

I've always wanted to leave my father's house. I'm never going back.

Chapter Twenty

"People wonder why women don't take their children and just up and leave their abusive husbands. Isn't the real question though, is it possible to ever really leave an abuser behind? Back then we thought so. God, we were naïve!"

"Donald, twenty-five years ago, you were a child. How could you possibly understand your experience?"

"Yeah, if I only I knew then what I know now."

* * * * * * * * * *

"We're free!!! We'll never have to call him P-A-P-A again!" I shout.

I'm sitting at our friends' kitchen table with what photos we have left of our family.

"I don't think we should call him 'Cow' anymore either, Mama," I continue. "That's an insult to Bessie."

"I agree. And to t'ink, he seemed so sad de day de truck came to pick her up! Now I know why," jokes Mama.

"He'll be your ex-husband soon, so let's call him Mr. X."

I cut Mr. X out of every single picture we have of him.

"I think that's a great idea," agrees Ronny.

"Look, I've cut Mr. X out of here and replaced him with another picture of the five of us in the same space. What do you think?"

"Hey, cool, Donald."

"And Ronny, if I help you clean the hotel every morning, can you pay me a couple of bucks? I want to start replacing everything we have that reminds me of Mr. X. Our clothes, knick-knacks, you name it."

"Sure. Besides, I'll get done faster."

The truth? I want to forget The Game.

I can drink all the coffee I want. I don't have to hide in the cold pantry. I will never feel those whiskers rubbing against my cheek again. I never have to bring him his milk so I won't hear that bloody stomping again. I won't have to hear him preaching, singing, and yelling again. I'll never have to listen to his voice again. And I remind myself, I won't ever have to play The Game again.

I must be dreaming.

I'm 15, unhappy at school, poorer than a beggar, don't know what's going to happen to my family or where we will live, but I feel like the luckiest person alive. I know that yesterday I was owned, from head to toe. I lived in a prison. No matter what happens today or tomorrow, I am free. The shackles are gone. Sure I'm afraid of this man, but there is no way he'll get me back there. I'd rather be dead.

For the first time in a long time, I feel alive!

While my siblings and I embraced our independence, Mama had a difficult time with her newfound freedom. She felt like a failure, embarrassed that her marriage was, for all purposes, over. It was a scary place to be. She had never been free. She had lived under her parents' rules, then married a man whose rules she'd discover were stricter than The Ten Commandments. There is a false sense of security that comes with being accustomed to someone else's set of rules.

Our mother was a forty-one-year-old woman with no skills, only a basic grasp of English, no money, no car, and four children to feed and clothe. Ronny and I knew this. We took her out of her prison, and we promised her we would look after her. That promise dried her tears and calmed her fears.

Her new freedom allowed her to focus on her faith. Witnesses picked us up and took us to meetings three times a week. Those meetings kept us going, gave us a sense of purpose, and provided a great source of strength.

Many of the Witnesses supported our decision to leave and helped in any way they could. We appreciated what they did for us once we decided to escape the house on the hill. While Ronny stayed at Witness friends across the road, another family provided immediate assistance by inviting the four of us to move into their house on Sunday afternoon, October 31, 1976.

All five of us were living just one mile away from Daniel.

In the days that followed, other members of the congregation gave us used clothing, furniture and money to pay bills until we could get on our feet. But for the moment, daily survival had become our focus—buying food and being forever vigilant, knowing that the newly christened Mr. X could retaliate at any moment. Living such a short distance from him, we feared for our safety, so much so, that at times we questioned whether we'd live through the night. The euphoria of our freedom proved to be short-lived.

The self-proclaimed "Christian" stalks us as we get off the school bus.

I am babysitting the children of the family providing us shelter. Suddenly, I hear a voice screaming. I look out the large veranda door and see Erik running up the lane. Right behind him is Mr. X reaching out to grab him. I open the door, pull Erik inside, and slam the door shut, locking it just in time.

"I love you. Erik is my son. He should be with his father," yells Mr. X.

I gather the young children and tell Erik to follow me into the washroom, the one room that has a lock. Even if Mr. X breaks in, he'll have to break into this room as well.

I tell everyone to be quiet as can be, but my heart doesn't quit pounding. I'm scared for the children, but take comfort in the fact that I saved Erik, that I can handle a crisis, and that I can do the right thing. I should not be surprised. I've shown grace under pressure before. Thinking Donald is progressing at an accelerated rate. I am an old child at fifteen. I have been my father's second wife, my mother's surrogate therapist, and now I am my younger siblings' keeper.

I had no time to be a child and now have no time to be a teenager.

An hour goes bye. Everything is still. I open the bathroom door, walk through the living room and peek out the front window down the lane. Mr. X's car is gone. But he would be back.

In December, an elderly Witness couple rent us their second home in Belmont.

The day following our move, Mr. X makes an appearance. Before we get off our school bus, we notice he is waiting for us, reading his Bible. We know he wants to find out where we live. We're afraid but this isn't the time to play games. There is no time to explain the situation to the bus driver. Mr. X watches us as we get off the bus and we make a run for home.

He is more fanatical in his new faith than he ever was as a Jehovah's Witness. The fact that he never stops making attempts at communication affects all of our actions. It is as if he is everywhere we are, lurking about waiting for the right moment to pounce on us.

Every time I walk downtown to the post office or the variety store, I am afraid he will confront me.

In hindsight, it makes complete sense that Daniel would convert to another Christian denomination when he lost control of his family. As intelligent as he was, he chose a faith that fed his need for dominance, whose teachings erased his record of abuse for his own purposes.

When we left, with literally the clothes on our backs, he called the police to report that a sewing machine was stolen. That was the one household item my mother took. How ridiculous! We left all the furniture and he complained about a darn sewing machine! Wasn't that the only thing he ever gave Mother in twenty years of marriage? That tells the story as much as anything. Mr. X was a selfish, childish, fanatic. He had the audacity to call the police about a sewing machine when he could have been arrested for molesting us. The policeman told us he laughed off the complaint. We never even thought of mentioning the abuse. Why was Daniel so certain no one would contact the police?

As we struggled to make ends meet, Daniel was for the first time in two decades free of the financial responsibility of a wife and four children. He had two jobs and was making reasonably good money. We, on the other hand, were living on Ronny's income of $150 a month and the generosity of the Witnesses.

Since Daniel could devote all his energies to his new-found faith, he moved up their social ladder quickly. Because we were identified as Witnesses and our molester as an ex-Witness, people in the community with a bias would side with his story. Since we did not publicly disclose the abuse, our silence served his purpose. In his writings, he'd refer to the sexual abuse as "my past sins as a Jehovah's Witness," and that he was "disfellowshipped for drunkenness and drug abuse." We even received letters from strangers condemning us for not acknowledging our "father."

Letters from a few of Daniel's relatives in Belgium to my mother betrayed an underlying judgment of her Witness faith. Daniel wrote to my mother's mother: "Jeannette has left me because of her religious beliefs." Within weeks, Mama received a letter from her mother asking, "How could you do this, Jeannette?" Of course, once they understood what really happened, Mama's family supported her.

The combination of these experiences took its toll on us. We were made to feel guilty for doing the right thing and praised for pretending nothing happened.

Is it any wonder Mr. X became self-righteous and verbal in his quest for revenge? Because Mother left him and kept the abuse a secret, he was able to paint his wife and children in the color of his choice. Non-Witnesses blamed us for the split. Even to our brothers and sisters in the faith, we felt obligated to explain over and over again.

"He is a bad, bad man."

"Daniel is evil and selfish."

"We hate him."

Families didn't break up in Witnessville, not unless they had a darn good reason. Most didn't know about the abuse, and neither we nor the Elders revealed our secret. Many Witnesses, as well as our neighbors and relatives, believed we left because Daniel had abandoned the Jehovah's Witness faith. People misdirected their own prejudiced feelings about the Witnesses on to us. It was a horrible time. An emotional roller coaster that never seemed to stop.

Now that Mr. X knows where we live in Belmont, he arrives at our doorstep every day, ringing the doorbell, yelling, "Let me in. I love you. I am your father." Other times, he rings the bell repeatedly, then vanishes. Once he even dropped a dead rabbit on our doorstep.

"Like we're going to eat it," says Ronny.

"I know. 'Thanks for din-din, Pa,'" I joke. "Give me a break!"

We're not sure if it is meant as a joke or if we're supposed to take this seriously. I wonder if it's a personal message to me: a dead rabbit to remind me we no longer play The Game.

"You don't think it's an omen, do you?" asks Ronny.

"It's a sign of something, all right. He's nuts!"

I really wanted to say, "A sign of my disobedience in freeing myself from The Game." But there is no need to upset Ronny with my thoughts. He doesn't realize the role rabbits played in The Game.

Sometimes Mr. X doesn't leave quietly.

The front window is smashed open. He's ringing the doorbell again. We are shaking in fear.

"Oh, my God!" cries Mama. "Ronny is not home. What are we going to do?"

"Call the police immediately!" I demand. "Dial 9-1-1."

While Mama is on the telephone, I watch the front door. The lady on the phone tells Mama to keep talking.

"He broke de window! He can come right in!"

"He's not doing anything yet," I call from the living room window.

Amazingly, Mr. X disappears.

"He has left. T'anks for talking to me."

"Call us back if there's any trouble, ma'am."

We're convinced Jehovah God is protecting our house today, but we have to keep on the watch. We continue to live in fear, never knowing when Mr. X will return.

I don't feel safe. I won't let anyone near me and I trust no one. I check my room every time I go in to see if someone is hiding under the bed or in the closet. I don't walk out at night alone because Mr. X could be following me. I am scared to death he will kidnap me and keep me as his sexual slave forever.

I am even more afraid that he could take Marina, Erik or Mom. I am fanatically over-protective. I am scared that Mom might go back to him.

The doorbell rings.

"It's probably Mr. X again," I guess. "Thank God, Ronny's home now."

More ringing. Ronny goes to the door.

"You're right. He's crying and babbling on again."

The screen door is locked.

"Go away!"

Mr. X doesn't quit yapping. Ronny grabs the shotgun and shells he took from him. He sits on the bottom step in front of the door and loads one shell. Ronny walks to the screen door, unlocks it, and returns to the step.

"Come in." states Ronny, inviting Mr. X to enter, his gun pointed at the unwanted visitor's head.

We're hysterical. Jumping up and down. Afraid for Ronny.

"Mr. X is not wort' going to jail for, Ronny!" cries Mama.

We keep silent hoping he will leave so that Ronny won't have to go to jail.

Mr. X knows what will happen if he opens the door.

"How can you do this to me, my son? I am your father."

More crying. More babbling. It stops. We run to the living room window and close the curtains. We peek out, watching to make sure he drives off. But as he walks to the end of the sidewalk, he falls and lies on the front lawn. We wonder what we should do—call the police?

After ten minutes, Mama says, "We can't just leave him dere. Someone should go out and check on him."

"You have got to be kidding!" I exclaim dumbfounded.

Ten more minutes we wait. He's still lying there.

"What if he had a heart attack or somet'ing?" Mama exclaims. "I cannot afford to pay for de funeral!"

We are laughing and scared at the same time. Suddenly, I notice Mr. X's hand is moving. First it shakes and then it swishes in a brushing motion against the ice.

"He's faking it!" I yell. "If he really had a heart attack, he wouldn't be able to move his hand in such a controlled fashion. What a faker! He's just testing us to see if we care!"

We laugh uncontrollably now.

"I'm calling the police!" says Ronny.

After Ronny gets off the phone, he informs us, "They're sending an ambulance and a cruiser out!" Within 10 minutes they arrive. The attendants help Daniel up to his feet. Ronny goes out and talks to the police officer, who reproves my brother for not helping his own "father." When Ronny matter-of-factly tells the officer what Daniel had done to us, he's more than understanding.

Another outsider finds out we were sexually abused and does nothing.

Molesters are pathologically selfish. They don't weigh the consequences of their behavior. I'm sure it was a shock to our father that none of his kids cared about him. Although he never considered our individual feelings to be important, he was keenly aware of their existence. He used our emotions, our insecurities, our exposed psyches to develop new ways to control our minds. When he lost the ability to physically dominate us, religion became his weapon of revenge, a powerful tool to manipulate public perception of the family break up.

Although we managed to leave our abuser, one form of earthly hell was replaced by another. In the 1970s, many people believed that once a child's abuser was removed, the trauma for the victim ended. We certainly didn't realize that our experiences would have ongoing, long-term repercussions. Being free from this controlling dictator, the worst was behind us, or so we thought.

Chapter Twenty-One

Before we get to our next stop, I need a diversion. Too many painful memories lie there. Maurice and I spend some time browsing at a garage sale. I learned long ago to turn off unpleasant thoughts or experiences, so mixing shopping with a psychological excursion is not out of character.

Finally reaching the school, we walk from the parking lot to the north side of the building, stopping to look through the auditorium windows. I recall rarely spending time here. In fact, I probably ate in the cafeteria only once or twice in four years, and I made sure I had excuses to miss every single school assembly. Maurice wonders if I notice any changes after twenty years. I think I'm the one who has made the most changes.

Stressing the positive, I tell him: "East Elgin was proud of its own colors, purple and gold. To show I had school spirit, I wore bright, ugly, oversized yellow slippers Mom made me, with purple socks, yellow pants, and a purple t-shirt. Ugh, what a sight!"

"So even then, you liked to get attention, eh?"

"Indirectly, I guess I liked the recognition, but I didn't realize it then."

* * * * * * * * * *

Don't they say, "The eyes are the windows of the soul?" My years in high school remain the darkest period of my life. My 1976 high school photo does not hide the sadness, loneliness, and terror of my private hell.

I rarely go to school and beg Ronny to let me quit and look for employment.

"I hate school and I've missed so many days, please let me quit! The kids make fun of me. You don't know—it's hell."

"Donald, you have to get a diploma. Look at me. I don't even have a grade ten because I quit at 16. I can't get a good-paying job. You'll hate me now but you'll thank me later."

I *do* hate Ronny for not letting me quit school. Three more years just to get a diploma. I don't know if I want to live that long.

The abuse has ended, but I have become a freak.

I feel ugly, unloved, and unwanted.

I am.

Nobody at school talks to me. They talk at me. Some students think I'm a child from the local Mennonite community. Those children are frequent victims of harassment.

I walk between classes as quickly as possible trying not to be noticed. I stare at the floor, never looking up. There is not a part of me from head to toe that is not picked on.

Two popular girls call me over.

"If my dog had a face like yours, I'd shave its ass and make it walk backwards."

Why deliberately torture me? These girls are in Christian families as I am.

I never fight back, verbally or physically. I don't know how to defend or protect myself. I have no friends and no self-esteem.

I am a freak, a fake, a "polyester" Witness! I am ashamed of my very person. The outside world judges the external package: bad clothes, unfashionable hair, acne-covered skin, nerdy glasses, and an androgynous voice and face. My differences are on display for the world to see, especially when I stand in the hallway as the national anthem is played.

Even Ronny and Marina make fun of my appearance.

Who but Mother and God could love me?

I pray that God will kill me—snuff me out of existence. If it weren't for the fact that my mother, my younger brother and my sister need me, I'd opt out of this life. They keep me alive.

I slip further and further into a fantasy world. It's the only way to escape the present.

I daydream in class, a recurring fantasy: I am locked in prison. Men rape me but they only do to me what I want done. Even in my daydream, I need to feel in control, and a prison with bars seems like an attractive alternative to the real-life prison I inhabit. I also fantasize about becoming a hooker. I get attention, physical contact, and extra cash. It seems like an appealing career choice. After all, it can't be worse than my previous "Life With Papa." I can move out on my own and turn tricks for a living. At least then I'd feel as if I were in control and at the same time, get mistreated like I deserve. Now that would be normal.

On many days, the pain is unbearable.

I want to shoot all the people who make fun of me. The problem is, it would mean a considerable percentage of the students around me. No, I can't kill them. How can I pay them back? By not letting them see the real me. I will never exist to them.

Such daydreaming doesn't help me totally escape.

Ring, ring, ring...

Oh no! That dreaded fire alarm again. I hate going outside. It means being in a large crowd of people. Everyone will look at me. Make fun of me. Why me?

I start perspiring at the very thought.

The school starts evacuating. Another exercise in isolation begins. The students congregate on one side of the high school building. Although I walk out among them, no one talks to me or wants to be seen with me. I am probably the biggest freak at this school and everyone knows it. I know it.

As there are no mirrors for my reflection to disappear into, I try to find a piece of wall to hide against. I do. The students within a two-meter radius move away. Because there are no bunny clouds to provide me comfort, I close my eyes and pray that God kills me right here and now. When I open my eyes, the entire school body is in one massive group directly opposite me. I notice a couple of Witness children looking at me with pity in their eyes. They do not walk up to me.

My mind is spinning. I feel faint. I know that there is nothing lower than this moment. How do I go on? I cannot stand the pain of this existence, but I shed no tears. I cannot cry. I don't know how anymore. All emotions are shut off.

I must leave this place at once, so I do. I can't take the emotional pain of my existence any longer, so I won't. Now my separation is complete.

I am no longer here.

Thinking-self put the last nail in the coffin of Feeling-self once and for all. There is no time to mourn. I am now an iceberg. I do not talk. I have completely left myself. I am in another world. No one will get to me any more. No one will ever see the real me. The only weapon I have left is my mind.

This Donald is dead.

I am dead.

Chapter Twenty-Two

"Well, visiting my high school wasn't as bad as I thought it would be," I blather. Maurice is unconvinced. He's aware it's too painful to remember, and I just can't go there today. I can't speak of this pain even with him, so I talk about something else. "Aylmer. I can't get over that smiling chicken!"

"Yeah, well, speaking of chicken, I'm hungry." Seizing on the relief of laughter, Maurice suggests, "Why don't we stop and get a bite to eat? Any fast-food, bunny restaurants in Aylmer?"

"MAURICE!"

He considers this journey important. It was he who suggested it, but he also knows we both use humor to deflect pain. Timing is key.

"Sounds like a good idea, wise guy. There are a couple of restaurants on THE main street. We could park and walk around."

Pointing out the significance of several buildings, I tell him: "I cleaned at that hotel when I was twelve. When I was a kid, this street seemed to require a lot of walking. Now it's like a miniature version of a town, the inhabitants no longer towering."

I pass by an Elder from my childhood faith who doesn't recognize me. Startling as his whitened hair is to me, his basic features remain the same. In contrast, although I have matured physically, it is my spirit and disposition that clearly make me unrecognizable. I'm still 6' 2" and wear glasses, but my eyes now shine with love and happiness, my heart is light, and I smile freely and naturally. The Former Donald is invisible.

"Let's try this place—I haven't been here since '75."

Nothing has changed in the restaurant's decor in all these years but as we look over the menus, my perception has changed. The experience is much more enjoyable this time around. I realize I'm not really hungry. Instead, I'm fascinated by the feeling of anonymity and the surreal surroundings of this experience.

Our second stop in Aylmer is my old Kingdom Hall, a building modest in size and appearance. Two decades later, the rectangular building painted cream with brown trim, is identical except a Pentecostal God is worshipped there now. That fact does not ease my discomfort although I tell myself it should. How can such an insignificant building be the source of so much pain? I have no desire to leave the car and walk around. In fact, I tell Maurice to get me out of here as quickly as possible. I don't look back.

* * * * * * * * * *

I just turned seventeen. Just one more year of school and I can escape. I don't like going to the Kingdom Hall either. But sitting in a meeting or a classroom, a quiet, invisible, unassuming wallflower, gives me an interesting vantage point. Nothing is expected of me. No one considers what I might be thinking, observing, feeling. I have all the time in the world to take mental snapshots of others—how they respond to me and each other. Do they discount me because of my appearance, my demeanor, my silence?

Almost always, but is everything as it appears to be? Am I really lacking personality, passion, verbal, and social skills? Not only do I not trust these people, I have every reason not to open up and reveal my true self.

Does God really want me to attend meetings where I am not happy? Does that not contradict the image of a loving God? I can't understand that kind of God. I don't go for the people who don't understand me but rather for the message from the Bible. It helps me to escape my suicidal thoughts: no small feat. It's not that I don't want to live. It's just that I don't want to live under the present circumstances. I feel worthless and I see no future for myself.

How can I explain my survival? Religion plays a significant role, especially since my older brother left home.

As the eldest, Ronny felt overwhelmed by the sense of responsibility for us. Though we seemed to be forever at odds, I never once doubted he cared for us. Unfortunately, the only role model Ronny had was his father. Ronny displayed many of the same characteristics. He became bullying, forceful, domineering, and fanatical. He'd order us all around. He'd demand respect before he allowed time to earn it. He'd physically punish us if we'd disobey his wishes. He even went as far as threatening Mother when she pushed him too far. Of course, we hated this behavior while at the same time we considered it normal. What else did we know?

Ronny would force us to study biblical literature and attend meetings. We'd resist his attempts at total control to no avail. The caring part of his nature was overshadowed by displays of violent fits of rage and fanatical zeal. Even outsiders would comment, "You're just like your father." This would provoke even greater rage.

We left one bully to live with another, but it became obvious Ronny was not happy, a ticking bomb ready to explode. When he did, it took the form of a dramatic rebellion.

We weren't surprised when Ronny's difficulties led to a drug-induced, break-and-entry charge by the local police. He and his buddies wanted something to wash down their pills, so they broke into a beer store. Unfortunately, the drugs he took that night did not leave the desired effect. He carved into his friend's tabletop what he was feeling in words:

> *"Sometimes I wish I had a cock 10 miles long and 2 miles thick,*
> *'Cause not only could I say, 'Fuck the world,' I could do it!"*

Such actions prompted his being disfellowshipped by the congregation. His probation officer asked if I wanted to talk about our life with Daniel. I informed him that I had God and that talking to someone sure didn't help Ronny. Why would I talk to him? This man was a non-Witness who was helping my excommunicated brother. Why would I trust him or accept his help? I was so confused that I viewed a genuine gesture of concern with suspicion.

When Mama asked Ronny to leave because he had become unmanageable, I was relieved. In fact, I encouraged this decision. I resented his control over me. So much so that I thought I hated him. I wanted him gone but never dreamed it would happen so soon. I also did not really think these matters through. Who would replace Ronny as disciplinarian?

Although none of us were able to get along with him, Marina and Erik did have a difficult time when he departed. They missed him. Although he disciplined them, in good times he had been their playmate. With Ronny gone, the torch was passed to someone who wanted it least: now I assumed the responsibility of caring for my family. A teenager myself, I did not want my mother and siblings relying on me, but I couldn't abandon them. I never thought I would be staying with my family in a caretaker role. I had always planned on pursuing a life of my own—running away as soon as I graduated to a place, far, far away, much like Simonne had done. I wondered if Ronny's unplanned exit had changed my own destiny? I had to put my dreams on hold and I resented it. I did not want to be "man" of the house.

After Ronny left, he lost faith in God for a short while before he was introduced to the Baptist faith. Abandoned by us and by his religion, he discovered a new spiritual family. Daniel had professed to be a born-again Christian for quite some time by this point. Ronny felt it was important for his own peace of mind and spiritual growth that he verbally express forgiveness to his father. He re-established communication with Daniel.

When I found out, I was enraged and felt betrayed, realizing how the Elders and our relatives might view this situation: If Ronny went back to the father who had abused him, it couldn't have been all that bad.

How can one explain cutting off one's flesh and blood? Witnesses do not consider their religion a sect or a cult, but there are definitely cultish aspects to it. They put the group before the needs of the individual. Although living in the real world, they live completely apart socially, isolating themselves. I believe many of them are happy with this doctrine; I thought I was.

At the time Ronny was disfellowshipped and changed his religion, this was viewed as an apostate crime—the worst sin in their belief system. Having deserted the cause, Ronny was perceived as someone who had died, especially to his immediate family. Of course, this greatly influenced our decision not to see or speak with Ronny. How could we have known any better?

As horrible as it must have been for Ronny, his road of discovery was immediate—suddenly, he was responsible for no one but himself.

He was free: alone, but free—to experiment, first with drugs and sex, and then with religion on his journey of survival.

But would he find love and peace with a Baptist God? Would he find a God unlike the one he believed exists? Would any of us?

With Ronny gone, we are stuck living in a hellish routine with no money to pay bills. We have to move.

We had stayed at the Witnesses' home in Belmont for five months, but they needed to rent it out to a family who could pay what the property was worth. We really appreciated their help and understood their situation. Ronny had found us a small apartment in Aylmer that was rented out by the town's social service's office.

Our landlord says he didn't realize how destitute we were.

"You must apply for welfare immediately, Mrs. D'Haene. No one with children should have to worry about food and shelter. Canada is a great country."

"T'ank you. I do not understand de laws of dis land. I appreciate your helping us out."

"I think you might even qualify for Mother's Allowance. That will require some time because an application will have to be filed. I'll look into it for you. Meanwhile, the welfare check should help you pay for the rent and food."

Mama's divorce proceedings are moving at a snail's pace. Daniel writes constantly telling us how evil we were to abandon him and he refuses to support us financially. He sends two $1 checks and a box of smelly clothes, though. He writes that our religion forced us to leave and shut the door on him.

Elder Harold Mayson and his family move to Aylmer. Elder Mayson delivers interesting Bible talks. Even though I never leave my seat in the hall, he always comes over and says hello to me. He reminds me of TV's Mr. Rogers. I can tell he is analyzing me. I hope he is sincere and doesn't want to play The Game with me.

One day, he asks Mama and I if it would be all right if he conducts a Bible study with me.

"A fatherless boy needs a spiritual father."

Not wanting to create suspicion in God's Elder by saying no, I agree. I don't trust Elder Mayson for a long time, but eventually his sincerity and perseverance prevail. He wonders why someone didn't try to help me spiritually before. I wonder, why would they? But I appreciate this Elder's kindness. He says he loves me like a father would a son, and I'm sure he doesn't want to play The Game with me. I don't understand this, but I definitely don't want to play The Game either.

I want to feel loved but I can't. It's as if I carry my body around but I'm porous. Expressions of love come at me but disappear as they go through me. I can't explain this to Elder Mayson. He wouldn't understand and I might upset him so much he would stop visiting me. He says only God's love matters, so I study the Bible every day, hoping to feel what he feels for God. I want to feel this more than anything in the world.

I have always believed I am in The Truth, but now I care about God and believe He cares about me. I will come out of my shell but only for Him. If I do what He wants, I will be okay, says Elder Mayson. I will, so I can make God happy.

My new obsession with Mama's "Truth" does give me escape from my problems. I will never marry, so I must make a vow of celibacy. Anything else would be a sin. To help me on my path, faith strengthens my resolve to be head of the house, disciplinarian, and Mama's strong right arm. God wants me to take care of my family. I will put this duty above all else.

Of course, I don't have the physical build to intimidate as my father and brother have, but I quickly learn not to underestimate the power of spiritual armor.

The seeds are sown for another Donald to emerge: Christian Donald will appear fearless, aggressive, determined, and unstoppable.

With my new Christian armor fortifying me, I help Mama get through her divorce. She has no knowledge of legal matters, let alone the emotional or intellectual strength to fight her husband in court. Although I am taking a law class, the real court process proves to be more of an education. Introverted Donald never says a word in school, but I could give a lecture on our experience with law. I write the speech in my mind and leave it there.

Coincidentally, this same year, 1978, major new legislation affecting divorce and distribution of assets passes in Parliament. If my mother is granted her Decree Absolute, she will receive one half of the sale of the house on the hill minus costs of sale, Daniel's debts which Mother had co-signed for during the marriage, and lawyer fees. This leaves approximately $2,000. Since we are living on welfare, we think this is a lot of money.

At the courthouse, like an episode of TV's *Perry Mason* without the commercials, the process seems as if it is over before it begins. As the witness for Mama's case, I am briefed in a private room about the types of questions I will be asked. The lawyer doesn't know how many times I have told this story before—I am a professional witness, matter-of-factly answering questions using expressions I have just learned.

"Tell the Court what it was like living with your father."

I am certainly not going to call him Mr. X. Judge R. L. Bannister won't understand that, but he really seems to have a sincere and kind face. I'll give him a short version of my story.

"Papa would have us masturbate him. It was mutual masturbation. Sometimes he would have Marina and I perform together with him. Papa would show us pornography, sometimes photographs of nude or partially nude women. He performed fellatio on me and tried to make me do the same. I just couldn't. Once he raped my anus with his penis. I was sore for days. As hellish as that was, the real problem was that he owned us all, including my Mama. She never had a life outside the home. He owned her completely. We finally left because we found out about his performing bestiality. And the fact he started to beat Mama and me."

I instinctively realize it is important to emphasize other matters besides the sexual abuse. By objectively pointing out Daniel D'Haene's abuse of my mother, I personalize the case which I know will have more impact. Devoid of emotion, I look the judge squarely in the eye and select words I know will be effective. Intellectual Donald will make more of an impression than any display of tears. There is no emotion to be had anyway. Because I appear clear and focused, my words shoot out like bullets into the silence of the courtroom. A young man testifying about sex with his father is unheard of in 1978.

Daniel's lawyer specifically asked him not to appear in court. There are no objections or cross-examination to my testimony. I am the perfect witness of my own experience. I speak the truth with conviction and no histrionics.

After what seems like minutes, Mama is granted her divorce, *decree nisi*. My Mama is free at last and it is a joyous occasion. As far as I am concerned, the only reason I talked about The Game was to help Mama get her divorce. There was no other expectation or agenda. Mission accomplished, I can bury the past once and for all. Besides, a court heard I was abused. Who was there left to tell?

I was the perfect witness—maybe too perfect. No one in that courtroom listening to my testimony, watching my demeanor, observing my conviction, seemed to see me as a recent victim of a crime. My detachment and ability to display the ultimate survival model blinded everyone to the importance of my disclosure. Yes, I described horrible acts to my audience, but I appeared to be doing well now. Why would anyone force me to relive it in a criminal trial? I did not testify that Mother was aware of the abuse since 1971 and the Elders, since 1973. What did that have to do with getting Mom a well-deserved divorce? This was an uncontested divorce. There were no antagonistic forces present, and hence, there seemed no reason for Judge Bannister to question my testimony.

In the afternoon, I return to school. As usual, I never share the drama of the moment with anyone, but an outsider might notice a smile on my face. Mr. X is finally an ex-husband to my mother.

A couple of months after the hearing, my grade eleven teacher tells our class we should read the newspaper daily. I go out and order a subscription.

I start reading Ann Landers' advice column religiously. One day, I read a letter from a woman who was molested as a child. Miss Landers responds that incest is a crime and that her abuser should be reported to the police. This is a major shock to me. No one has ever told me I could have my father charged.

Immediately, I am propelled outside the inner sphere of my small universe. My "computer" registers this information in a big way. I can't handle the implications. Sexual abuse is a crime—such a foreign concept to me. There are people who knew what happened to me. Did they know it's a crime? If so, why didn't they tell me? What has been going on here?

Why didn't Judge Bannister ask why the authorities had not been contacted? The fact that I discover sexual abuse is a crime after testifying about it in a court of law makes me question our judicial system. Even after reading Ann Landers, I'm certainly not going to approach another lawyer about a possible case. Besides, I am devoted to God now.

I've put the past behind me and I will succeed.

Helping Mom with her divorce, assisting her in disciplining Erik and Marina, and handling our finances are empowering acts. Maybe I don't know how to talk outside the four walls of our home, but I certainly display a dynamic personality when it comes to my mother and siblings. I become assertive, domineering, demanding—seemingly overnight. I become the thing I dread the most but it seems inevitable: the third bully in our household. But I can't waste time worrying about such things now. I cannot change. Instead, I focus on the obvious.

"I'm working part-time now, Mom, and with your Mothers' Allowance being approved, our situation will improve dramatically. I don't want to stay on welfare. I think we should plan on moving to a nicer apartment, buy you all some new clothes, and try to better our life."

"Do not worry about me. De new styles are not for me."

"Mom, your clothes are so old, I think you still have some clothes from when you came to Canada on the boat!"

"Yes, I do. But de winter coat is still good."

"You're kidding. That coat is that old? That's it. I'm chucking it out! And I'm going to buy a size 16 coat this week. It's only spring now. Mom and Marina, whoever loses the most weight gets to wear the new coat."

"Yeah, but what if we can't?"

"Can't? You will! Be positive. And your clothes—"

"Oh no, not de dresses!"

"Oh yes, come on. Model your dresses for Marina and me."

As Mom displays her wardrobe, Marina and I take scissors and rip each dress to shreds while Mom's still wearing them. We have never laughed so hard in our lives. Mom sheepishly appears around the corner: "Dis one is good. Look at de nice lace on de trim." Each time Marina and I give each other a knowing look. We practically destroy her whole outdated collection. Mother enjoys the attention.

While I create diversions, Mr. X develops new ways of making his presence known.

As I read *The Aylmer Express*, I notice a church advertising a special speaker: Don D'Haene. Of course, I know this is Daniel, but this shocking misprint is all the more intrusive because the church is located right across from our apartment. He just won't leave Aylmer, its Witnesses, or us alone. It seems his targets are only those who know or could discover the abuse.

By this point, I am distanced enough to view this self-proclaimed minister as a stranger, a faceless figure that haunts my dreams and my environment, but never my intellectual frame of mind.

The week that Mom's Decree Absolute is granted, a card arrives in the mail:

> *Roses are Red*
> *Violets are Blue*
> *Boy Am I Glad*
> *To Be Rid of You*

I take the card and show our next-door neighbor who has earlier described Daniel as a fine example of Christianity.

"It's normal to be a little bitter when you get divorced," she insists.

I walk away shaking my head. I can't win. Why do I have to prove that my father isn't the Christian he proposes to be? The thought of confiding in her about The Game never even enters my mind.

Three months later, Mr. X marries a much younger born-again Christian woman in London. He puts their wedding photo and notice in Aylmer's newspaper.

"The happy couple are residing in London where they are engaged in The Help Jesus Ministry, dedicated to reaching Jehovah's Witnesses for Christ."

"Mom, you are going to go back to your maiden name, Bataille."

"I do not t'ink dat is a good idea."

"What do you mean, you don't know? You are not Mrs. D'Haene any more. Someone else is. You are Ms. Bataille. I wish I could change my name to Bataille, but it would cost too much money. But you, you can do it legally."

"You are right. In Belgium, every woman keeps de maiden name."

"Too bad they don't do that here."

I do everything in my power to distance my family from our past. Changing Mom's name is just the first step. Leading my family to look to God for help is the second. Personally excelling at school is my final means of escape. To get good grades, I will need to devote all my time and attention to my studies. I will be rewarded immediately with praise, and in the long term, with employment.

"Anything girls can do, I can do better," I write for my graduation yearbook listing. I'm strangely attracted to such challenges. When I find out boys don't take shorthand at my high school, I not only enroll in the class, I also receive the highest mark in the school. When I find out boys don't become secretaries, that becomes my first career choice. During my last two years, I average 86 and 87 percent. In three of my final year courses, I obtain the top mark in the school.

I never go to school assemblies, so I miss my shorthand teacher's retirement speech when she mentions I earned the highest mark in the school, and could I please stand up. A Witness acquaintance informs me of it afterwards. Of course, he has to add that he was surprised that every one of the students in the auditorium stood up and applauded for me.

But I don't care. I have the final day of school marked out in my calendar as a countdown to freedom. Emancipation from these narrow-minded, predictably cloned students in this conservative, bible-belt town. Because I have the highest grade standing in typing and shorthand, I receive the Lena Baillie Award and will be recommended for a job placement upon completing high school.

I am an overachiever because I have no personal life. I go to school, religious meetings, and escape in the fantasy world of television. Opting out of life would be easier, but I want to achieve something. I don't know where this desire originates. Someday I'll be somebody. Someday I'll show everyone.

But for now, I have accomplished something. My family has a focus. My plan seems to be working out. We have found a form of happiness and escape. We feel safe.

Finally, I'm free again.

Chapter Twenty-Three

Maurice drives slowly down Main Street.

"That's where the old Dominion store used to be. I applied for a grocery clerk's job in '79 and the manager told me: 'We only hire girls to be clerks. I want you to try out for a manager trainee position.' You should have seen the shocked look on his face when I shot back— 'Sorry, but I have no aspiration to be a manager. Thanks but no thanks.' How times have changed!"

I notice a man mowing his lawn. He waves at us in a natural way, so uncharacteristic of city life. I take a closer look.

"That's Dr. Billingsley. I haven't seen him since I visited his office way back in '81. Hasn't changed a bit, but he doesn't recognize me. I'm glad."

Within minutes, we're on Spruce Street, two blocks away. We stop at another home from my past. Here is my final connection to Aylmer. Fragments of memories dart around my mind, frustrating me, as if I have found only ten pieces of a thousand-piece puzzle.

"God, they haven't changed a thing. The yellow aluminum siding still looks good. Doesn't it look like a doll's house? You know, I don't ever remember seeing a single neighbor. I hated gardening, but I enjoyed hoeing weeds in the back yard! Oh, the fights we had."

"You going to be all right?"

"Yeah. After twenty years, I guess it goes with the territory. It's just so weird being here."

"We can leave if you want. Is being here helping to make your memories real?"

"No, I mean, yes—visuals are coming back non-stop...."

Fragmented memories. A large basement. Mom is threatening to take all the lawn chairs down the rickety staircase if I don't. Marina is sneaking chocolate cookies from the freezer. Erik brings a friend home who takes an egg out of the fridge and smashes it on the floor.

"Goodnight, Mama."

"Goodnight, Donald and Marina."

Erik always has to be the last one to say goodnight.

"Yes, I am remembering, Maurice. We were a twisted version of The Waltons, for God's sake. It's not pretty, but at least it's a picture."

* * * * * * * * * *

My mind was stimulated from birth by religion, adult conversations, drama, and intrigue, as if it couldn't take enough in. I felt bored by the social box my circumstances destined for me. As a teenager, the games became increasingly complex, the deceptions deadly. As I entered my twenties, I felt like I was being held hostage in a psychological and religious war.

Although my parents' beliefs were instilled in me, I did not become a zealous disciple until my late teens. In order to make that transition, I had to disassociate myself from my past. I had to lock away nearly two decades of memories which up until then had plagued me.

My mission to forget the past became all the more difficult because my family remained in the Aylmer area where most of the abuse had taken place. I was rewarded by the Witnesses for apparently transcending that horrific experience, though in the long term, it cost me dearly. My older brother, who had rebelled against our faith, and my younger brother and sister, who were rebelling against our mother, were considered the "bad seeds."

Even if I, "the good son," had wanted to defy the church at that time, I would not have done so. The Witnesses were my peers, my family, the only group of people I associated with. I did not want to choose a course of behavior that would ostracize me from them.

The "other selves" and fantasy environment I created as a child were necessary tools for functioning as a Witness, as a student, and as an employee. Thinking Donald could live comfortably with the labels "good son, good student, and good employee."

In 1981, I believed Witness doctrine to be absolute truth. Everything else took a back seat to my faith, especially any difficulties we were experiencing as a family. The Bible had all the answers for the problems that had befallen us my faith assured me, and if we had the right spiritual "heart condition" (a Witness expression meaning that good or bad desires may take root, depending on the spiritual condition of the heart), we would find them there. As such, my fellow Christians believed in placing negative experiences behind them through the practice of prayer and positive thinking. Putting it behind us seemed an easier course of action than actually dealing with the dysfunction in my family. We certainly had problems and I wanted them to disappear. And I did have bad memories, but they only showed up in the black and white movie reels that played in my head. New events would be added to that memory bank daily. The only way I could feel better was to make believe each new problem was non-existent. Each would be assigned a certain amount of space on a new reel.

I exorcised my memories better than my spiritual and immediate family could have dreamed possible. I wouldn't let anyone inside or outside my family discuss our history with me unless it was at my initiation or for humorous effect, which kept secrets safe and distant. One way I achieved this separation was by referring to our father by his first name, Daniel.

I stressed the positive and that's all I wanted to hear. This was a necessary, temporarily successful survival tactic.

I had been steadily employed as an office clerk for two years. I even had enough money to buy a car, which gave me independence. I was a surrogate father caring for my younger siblings. By all appearances, I was doing fine.

My plan had worked: "Forget the past. No, get rid of the past. Who is Daniel? Don't think of Ronny." For three years I found this path rewarding. Why not continue?

The non-feeling, perfectionist personality I adopted resulted in my becoming judgmental of my siblings' shortcomings. I wanted the members of my family to excel at everything they did. As there were four very different strong personalities living under one roof, this was more easily dreamed than achieved.

Mother is a middle-aged woman now, her sharp features marred by thinning eyebrows and eyelashes and years of neglected teeth.

She is blessed with wrinkle-free skin and rarely wears make-up. Most of the time, there is an air of sadness in her countenance. There are other times, when she is in her element and displays the flirtatious behavior that must have attracted young men when she was a teenager.

With a very limited budget, buying clothes is difficult. Her one affordable passion is costume jewelry. With a sharp eye for a bargain, at dollar stores and flea markets, she has amassed an earring collection numbering into the hundreds. When we want to get her a gift, we know costume jewelry will elicit a rare glimpse of schoolgirl glee.

Since she has never taught us how to cook or do laundry, she does much of the work around the house. When we point this fact out to her, she replies, "I love doing it. Dat's what I am supposed to do."

When a piece of her front tooth broke off, Mother super-glued the broken chip to the other half left in her mouth. She did an amazing job. It's been several months and no one besides us has noticed. Every time she bites into some food, we do wonder if she will lose the tooth. Nothing has happened yet.

No matter what tribulations we go through, we find reasons to look on the bright side of life. Mom always tells us we are special, and that God cares about us. I love her more than anything in the world. There's nothing I wouldn't do for her and she knows it.

Every street in town is a quiet one, but since our little house on Spruce Street is located on the outskirts, privacy is guaranteed. Our home is my sanctuary. I discovered it last December for only $375 a month rent. By my own design, there is no history here. Letters are hidden away. Clothes from our former life have been outgrown and discarded. Although our garments are conservative in style and second-hand in origin, they seem new to us. Without history, they are safe and warm.

I share the biggest bedroom with my younger brother. It is the only room that will accommodate our two single beds. A desk, filing cabinet, and a dresser complete our uncluttered room. Our drawings and acrylic paintings decorate the walls. I chose this house with white, panel-free walls, open spaces, and numerous windows because I crave the light. An ugly, brown shag carpet is the compromise I must make to have this large room.

Chapter Twenty-Three

Across the hall, Marina escapes behind her closed door, music blaring from her stereo. Downstairs, Erik lies in front of our television, as is his routine, watching a series of cartoons and sitcoms.

I'm usually upstairs in my bedroom. I sing along with the medley of songs on the turntable over and over again. I've just turned twenty yet I seem out of sync with my generation, favoring the music of the forties and fifties. I memorize every phrase, nuance, and hesitation in each singer's voice. Whenever we watch *Solid Gold* as a family, I'm always reviewing the vocals and the stage presence of the performers. Everyone in my family is a pretty good singer.

I am never alone and rarely experience silence. I long for peace and quiet. I don't like shouting and arguing. Yet I have chosen the role of referee in the daily fights between my siblings and Mother. If they argue continually, does that make them un-Christian?

Privacy is at a premium. The only time I achieve complete isolation is by cranking up the volume on my record player and singing my heart out. My favorite vocalists express what I cannot. Through the lyrics of their songs, the notes that are sung, I escape my world. I can only feel by making believe I am someone else. I don't understand why. I just do.

I care about Marina and Erik as though they are my own children. When they make mistakes, I feel accountable and set about correcting their problems. I live my life through taking care of them and their troubles. I will never abandon them. Besides, dealing with my family's never-ending problems helps me fill a void in my life. Why do I keep so busy that I have no time for myself? What am I afraid of? I've taken on a lot of extra responsibilities since graduating from high school two years ago. I have maintained steady employment since then, and although the pay is low, I am still thankful God is watching over us. I will make sure we survive financial hardship and will stop at nothing to achieve that goal.

Writing is the best way I communicate, if not feelings, then my innermost thoughts. Just yesterday, I sent a letter to my Witness friend in London. Roland is a unique character: intellectual, eccentric, musically inclined. The closest thing I've had to a true friend. He knows my family history, my innermost thoughts, and has encouraged me in my devotion to God and not giving up in my role as spiritual leader of my family. I've come a long way. So has my family.

I inform him the district overseer and his wife are going to be staying with us. It's such an honor to be able to help out our congregation in this way. More importantly, I remind him of Marina's baptism in London this weekend. It's a miracle that my sister has finally taken our faith seriously.

I hope Roland will be able to visit for a weekend soon. I always find our private conversations encouraging. I've taken his advice and started reading the Bible from beginning to end. I'm up to Psalms now. I keep a notebook of all the scriptures I find the most uplifting. I'm on my second one already. Keeping my mind on spiritual matters helps me to stay in a positive frame of mind. I must do my best for my family who needs me.

I can't wait to go to our next meeting, although I'm not sure which I long for more: sitting in the Kingdom Hall listening to biblical instruction or having a rest from the incessant arguments which have nothing to do with anything in particular.

"Don't tell me what to do!"
"Erik's bugging me."
"No, you're bugging me."
"You're the bigger bug."
"You're the biggest!"
"Donald, what am I going to do wit' dem?"
"I don't know, but P-L-E-A-S-E be quiet!"

During the semi-peaceful portion of our trip to the hall, I reflect on how old I feel and act. The reason I don't play with my siblings is that I have skipped my childhood. While I expect much from my family, I am no harder on them than I am on myself.

I have determined that my purpose in life is to ignore my problems and encourage my family to be the best they can be, despite all obstacles. Only interested in attracting flawless attention to our name, I am fanatical about appearances, especially my sister's and mother's weight.

I have been obsessed about my own weight since I was twelve, when someone said those two crushing words, "You're fat!" Because I am borderline anorexic, I either overeat or starve myself depending on the mood I'm in. Sometimes I weigh as little as 145 pounds. I still think

150

I'm overweight. When people comment I'm too thin, I take it as a compliment.

I am obsessed with my family's weight problem too, so much so that I pay my sister to lose a few pounds. Because Marina will have to wear a bathing suit at her public baptism, her weight loss couldn't be more timely. I want her to be thinner so people won't make fun of her. I expect worldly people to be cruel, but when members of my faith make fun of Marina, I find it even more disgusting. I don't understand how Christians can act this way.

With uncompromising zeal, I badger Marina and Mom to take care of their health and appearance, but it pays off. Mom's lost 100 pounds during the past two years. Not only does she look better than ever, she's feeling good about herself too. I've saved up enough money to send her to Belgium next month. It's the first time she'll travel back since leaving there twenty-four years ago. The trip to see her mother and family has given Mom extra motivation in her diet. Her goal, or more to the point, my goal for her, is to fit into the dress size she wore before she left her homeland. She's almost there. I just want everybody to look their best. They must.

I'm so tired of the conflicts during the drive to the hall, that it takes all my energy just to make an appearance. Mom and I have the ability to switch from full-volume referees to actors with perfect smiles. Marina and Erik hate our controlling nature. On the ride home, I know I'm going to hear what phonies we are, but I can't help myself. Everything I've experienced up to this point in my life has taught me to pretend and put on a good face.

The hall is abuzz with conversation today. Most of the time, I approach members I am comfortable with. I pick out people who are usually ignored. I never go up to anyone I consider stuck-up or popular. If they've ever made fun of my family, it takes all the control I can muster to even smile at them. I remind myself God wants me to, so I do. Personally, I know I want to forgive, but I never forget. I have perfected the skill of not letting my facial expressions give away what I'm really thinking. Mother, the actress, taught me well.

"Marina and Erik, the meeting is starting."

Marina's ill-fitting clothes seem to hug her body, as she stumbles to find a seat. My sister considers wearing a dress, high heels, and nylons torture, but suffers through the discomfort because she believes rebelling against society's norms is not worth the trouble. But outside of Witness functions, her tomboyish nature rebels against wearing anything she deems frilly. I offer to buy her clothes, but she refuses to wear the feminine styles I point out. Yet her choice in attire, her chubby cheeks, and stocky frame can't hide a natural beauty. Her shoulder-length, light brown hair attractively frames her face, overshadowed only by her awkwardness in the alien heels.

Today's Bible talk is on The Book of Job. I can relate to Job. I hate my body—my acne-covered face, gangly arms and torso, my prominent nose—I rarely look at it. The mirror lies to me. I never believe it. Like Job, I will not renounce my faith for anybody. I present Christian Donald to the world—a world in which I am constantly disconnected from my surroundings. Bible characters are more real to me than the people who surround me. I question reality as I know it, sometimes even my own existence. What is my purpose on this planet? I don't understand why I feel and think the way I do. I am detached from my body. It's as though I have two bodies, one of which I haven't discovered yet.

What am I? Am I human? I act out behavior my religion dictates as normal. I don't know how to feel, yet words come out of my mouth expressing a concept that implies that I do. I have no sensory connection to my limbs or skin. Something happened to make this so. Is it my fault? I want to cry, scream, shout—but about what? True, my life is a series of dramas—some of my own creation—yet why? I never share these thoughts with anyone outside my family because I am afraid they'll think I am crazy. I've talked about this with Marina, and even she questions my sanity.

A voice interrupts my thoughts.

"Stop playing wit' de pen."

Once again, Mom sounds off on deaf ears. Erik continues to argue with the child in the seat in front of us.

Erik is a restless teenager who hasn't yet outgrown his baby fat. He still fits into my hand-me-downs, which helps to save a dollar or two. His ever-present devilish, tooth-filled grin and troublemaking behavior hide a sensitivity he likes to pretend he doesn't have. Sometimes he makes it very difficult to be with him or even like him. His constant teasing of others, especially his sister, is met with the attention he seeks. More often than not, it's delivered negatively, in the form of a physical blow or a verbal scolding. Knowing his sister can physically overpower him, he creates new ways of mentally persecuting her. In one moment, a battle of wits and power erupts, and in the next, they're playing and joking with one another.

Every time Erik and Colin sit near each other, all hell breaks loose.
"Colin, give it to me," Erik demands.
"No, you threw it, so it's mine!"
"Donald, Colin won't give me back my pen."
"Erik, quit it. You're making a scene."
As Colin's mother gives the pen back to Erik, dirty looks dart our way.

Of course, I can see Colin is a troublemaker but he isn't my responsibility. In our hall, it's a toss-up which is the bigger brat. There's no question about it, Colin has the devil in him, but my brother, being five years older, always ends up the one blamed. For the most part, they're just acting up because they're bored.

"Thank you for that encouraging talk, Brother Sandor. Before closing, let us stand and sing Song No. 119, 'Keep Your Eyes on the Prize.'"

Driving home after the meeting, I just want to get out of my dress clothes and the control they demand. Although I am able to keep Erik and Marina apart at the hall, the gloves come off as soon as they settle into the back seat of my car.

"You're such a phony, Donald. Why don't you show them who you really are?"

"Marina, I don't understand why it's any of their business if we argue or not. They probably do the same thing. Anyway, you seemed to enjoy the meeting."

"Yes, I answered three times."

"What a little browner," chides Erik.

I'm so used to their dialogue that, for the most part, I am able to tune them out. While I remain silent, Mom talks about the information delivered at the meeting and who talked to her this week and who didn't. She is extremely introverted, and only lately have I begun to feel uncomfortable with just how much she relies on me for friendship and companionship.

Am I a phony? There might be truth in Marina's accusation.

I don't know what I am.

Marina is being baptized at a London Witness convention today. There is an unspoken feeling amongst local Witnesses that it is *just* a D'Haene getting baptized. Sometimes that feeling is voiced.

During intermission, I overhear one of the Witness girls gossiping with two of her friends.

"I think Marina is so weird. I don't feel comfortable around her."

"Neither do I."

"Me either."

They aren't even careful enough to make sure the older brother of the object of their scorn is out of earshot.

"Oh, hi, Donald. Great assembly, eh?"

I think Witnesses would like Marina if she lost weight and wore nicer clothes. I want my sister to find acceptance. I just want her to be happy. Still I'm so proud to see her progressing in The Truth despite such hostility.

It's quite a weekend for me too. I'm going to be answering some questions on the platform about struggling to survive as a Christian. As I am waiting to go on, a couple of Elders ask to read my written answers. They edit two sentences from my speech where I talk about trying to keep a positive frame of mind despite negativity from even within the congregation of spiritual brothers and sisters. I knew that would get their attention, but I think it's so strange that I'm being censored for speaking from the heart. They're cutting my best lines.

Nevertheless, afterwards, many people compliment me on my courage. I was just being truthful. I don't know what the big deal is. Mom is a divorced woman raising three children, and I, as the eldest son living at home, choose to support them and set the best example possible. We have problems just like everybody else, but we're okay. At least I am finding a measure of happiness in my role as a Christian leader. I believe this is the only way for my siblings to achieve happiness.

I enjoy the attention even if it is controversial.

Once again, Christian Donald performs in front of an audience of strangers, and once again, my performance upstages my past.

Mission accomplished.

Chapter Twenty-Four

Our human subconscious has no sense of time, so reliving an ancient trauma can be as fresh and raw as if it had happened yesterday. For people who have experienced such devastation in their lives, blocking out memories may be a necessary, and often repeated, survival tactic. All the material I've read and the countless survivors I've spoken to concur: blocking out memories is common. An equally common reaction is questioning our own memories.

During a traumatic experience, a person may dissociate the circumstances surrounding the incident from his ongoing memory, hence avoiding the resulting fear and pain. Unfortunately, this action also affects one's sense of personal history and identity.

I have used this survival method successfully, having blanked out events through a conscious decision to will them out of my emotional data bank. However, when someone is successful at disconnecting from his history, current behavior that is irrational or conditions that are disturbing, such as insomnia, phobias, nightmares, seem to descend from nowhere. Reality blurs with fiction. One begins to question one's own sanity.

In the severest cases, long-term childhood trauma may lead to a condition known as Multiple Personality Disorder, also referred to as Dissociative Identity Disorder. In such extreme cases, repeated dissociation may result in the creation of separate entities, or mental states, which take on identities of their own. My dissociation did not reach that extreme continuum of severity.

Unfortunately, survivors who are as successful at blocking out their demons as I was, are often labeled healthy and rewarded with encouragement for their "amazing recovery," while those who experience ongoing difficulties dealing with memories often find limited support. Our society rewards controlled, acceptable behavior and is less prepared to support victims who require ongoing assistance.

This is never more evident than in sectarian faiths. Those whose progress is limited are labeled spiritually weak. Those who can detach and act in ways that fulfill their faith's expectations will find support and rewards for their apparent success.

Reviewing the limited resources at my disposal, I ask Elder Adam Sandor and his wife Cora to study the Bible with Marina and Erik. Mom needs help in handling her younger children. The Sandors have successfully raised two children who have remained faithful to Witness teachings. They might be able to accomplish what I can't. My weekly Bible studies have been nothing but a disaster. Sandor has befriended me over the last couple of years, especially since I began to take the Witness faith seriously. I wouldn't say that we hit it off in a natural way. We get along, providing I say yes and no when I'm supposed to. Personally, I haven't entrusted this couple with my own problems and feelings, but maybe if religious instruction comes from someone else, it will have more impact on my brother and sister. Since Marina is now baptized, I want her to continue to do well.

I wonder why the Sandors volunteer their time with them. What is their motive? I will not jeopardize their ongoing help by voicing my distrust to Marina and Erik or to them.

Initially, Marina and Erik progress with the Sandors' help but soon their erratic behavior, at home and elsewhere, becomes the topic of conversation at the Kingdom Hall.

A Witness pen pal moves to Aylmer. A couple of weeks after his arrival, he invites me out for a drive. Not having much of a social life, I accept this offer with reservations.

"I want to go!" Erik yells.

"Erik, it's the first time my friend has asked me to go anywhere."

"I don't care. Take me."

"I can't. He's driving and I'm expecting him any minute."

Erik is screaming, crying, stomping hysterically. I am in shock. I know he can sulk and whine if he doesn't get his way, but nothing prepares me for this reaction. He acts possessed. It's so upsetting I cancel the trip. My pen pal does not understand.

Perhaps this was Erik's intention, but his reaction to my attempts at a social life scares me.

The Elders are upset with my brother's antics as well. Erik frequently discovers ways of disrupting their meetings. Upon reflection, they seem humorous.

My brother needs to be the center of attention and in his unique way, develops new avenues to succeed, taking great pleasure in teasing me. I can hold a straight face for quite a long time but once in a while, I crack up and can no longer maintain control. Sometimes, Erik crosses his legs in mock seriousness, imitating me, and comes up with ten or more ways of pointing at me. Strange how a normal action, exaggerated and out of context, can not only become distracting but be considered blasphemous in a house of worship.

There's not a meeting that goes by without a disruption involving my brother. When we sing Kingdom Songs before and after a meeting, he deliberately croons off key twice as loudly as the rest of us. Last week, after we all bowed our heads in prayer, we opened our eyes to the sound of a single loud clap from my brother's hands—and we were sitting in the front row! That same day, after a speaker finished his talk, while the rest of us applauded, Erik, with elbow strategically placed on the chair beside him, clapped with his thumb and index finger in total mockery of the religious proceedings. While his actions are disrespectful, they are also hilarious. Tortured as I am by this unwanted attention, I'm envious of my brother's ability not to care what others think of him. My caring too much about the thoughts of others suffocates and paralyzes me.

Even though Erik is deliberately disruptive at home, in the hall, and at school, I recognize his intelligence, his wit, and his potential. I know he knows better but he continues to misbehave.

Elder Sandor chastises Erik.

"You're bad just because you want to be bad. You keep going the way you're going, you'll end up a delinquent. Sister Bataille, your son has his father in him."

Meanwhile, my friend Roland tells me it's because Erik doesn't feel loved.

"Erik needs someone to play with him, hug him, someone on his own level."

I'm sure there is truth in that, but I just can't. Although conflicts occur amongst us, we are unable to discuss feelings or express tender affection.

While the situation with Erik is difficult, he isn't baptized so discipline remains a family matter. This is not the case with Marina. As a baptized Witness, exemplary behavior is expected of her. If she gets into trouble, half the Kingdom Hall knows about it before I do, and the Elders will step in.

Marina will graduate from secondary school in a couple of months, but only at my insistence that she not quit earlier. I find Marina a couple of jobs. One is cleaning and the other is babysitting. Each job only lasts a couple of weeks as Marina finds ways of sabotaging them—stealing small amounts of cash from the first and food from the second. The problem is, both involve Witness families.

My siblings are having behavioral problems and I don't understand why. What's happening to them? Why is it both seem to have difficulty handling responsibility? I don't understand it. I'm working two jobs so that they have a better life, and they don't care to help out. They act much younger than their age in terms of maturity. How can children born from the same parents, experience the same upbringing and yet be so different?

I've tried to set the right example. Where have I gone wrong?

"Why don't we get an allowance? We're not working!" demands Marina.

"Allowance? You think I ever got one? I don't spend the money I make on myself. I buy you clothes, take you to movies, roller skating! You don't appreciate anything!"

I am to blame. I encouraged her to find these jobs and I pushed her to lose weight. Perhaps I encouraged Marina's commitment to our faith and her decision to get baptized because I was concerned with keeping up appearances as well. I chose to ignore her problems in coping with life.

It's not that I think I am any better. When I have stolen, I made sure I never got caught. Otherwise, what's the point? I just feel they are wasting their time and reputation on childish misbehavior and petty thefts. I would never steal from people I know and especially not the Witnesses. And if I was going to get caught, it would have to be something much more dramatic. A Bonnie and Clyde type of heist is much more my style. The difference is that I leave my thoughts of grand theft in my fantasy world and my siblings don't.

I don't know how to tell my brother and sister what I really think—"It's wrong to steal unless you don't get caught"—so I preach, "Thou shall not steal" instead.

The Sandors' initial elation at my siblings' progress is turning to disappointment and embarrassment, which adds pressure to all of us. Because I am receiving increased responsibilities at the hall, the contrast between Erik and Marina's behavior and my own is dramatic. The fact that I haven't been forthcoming about my knowledge of Marina's problems has placed me in a difficult position with the Elders. I know I'm supposed to report anything that might jeopardize Marina's position as a baptized member of the congregation, but I don't want my sister to get into trouble. I have had to weigh the embarrassment of disclosure against risking discipline for myself.

Since the Elders found out about the situation before Marina or I told them, a meeting is called. Because of Passover celebrations this weekend, the Elders have postponed it until next week. What's going to happen to Marina and me? We feel as if the label "sinner" is tattooed on our foreheads.

It's the most important event of the year—the memorial of Christ's death—but I am sick to my stomach. I don't feel like facing anyone. A third of the hall knows of our latest troubles. No one comes right out and says, "Those D'Haenes are at it again," but we believe they're thinking it. How could I let my personal feelings override my Christian duty? Of course, I can't and I won't. We arrive and find our seats just in time for the service. I experience an anxiety attack.

Beads of sweat run down my forehead. My face is burning up with heat. My heart is racing and my head is pounding so fast, I believe my temples will explode. My attack climaxes when Erik sniffs the wine that is being passed by the parishioners. I want to crawl in a hole and die. Why me? I care too much, while Marina and Erik don't care enough. Why? Things were going so well. What is causing us to have problem after problem? I want to help them, but I just don't know how.

I want out.

A couple of days after the Memorial, we attend an Elders' meeting. We are told Marina will be publicly reproved. I only missed getting reproved because I told them I was in shock about the situation and most definitely would have reported matters in the near future. Still this is an ugly blemish on an otherwise positive year. Things were looking so good. Obviously, there is something seriously wrong with Marina. I don't know how to help her. What could possibly cause her to be so self-destructive? She even fooled me into believing she was all right.

I would do anything for us to be accepted and loved, but I am definitely losing control of this family. This crisis is resolved, but what about the next one? All of us are healthy, I keep reminding myself, but are we happy? What is happy anyway?

Please God, show me the way out of this madness. I know there is good in each of us. Why do people only see the bad, not the good?

Although we studied scripture, we continued to blame ourselves for the overwhelming emotional difficulties we experienced. I trusted no one. I observed how my brothers and sister were punished when they confessed their sins before the Elders. I was not going to place myself in a similar position. They received no practical assistance or guidance. Without any comprehension of their trauma, the Elders viewed my siblings' acting out as sinful, period. I believed the Elders were right.

Chapter Twenty-Five

I cock one ear, thinking it might be the telephone, as I walk up the veranda steps. I rush to unlock the door and run to the kitchen phone.

"Hello."

"This is Inspector Norton Rhiness of the Toronto O.P.P...."

Drama. Ongoing, never-ending drama.

"I was wondering if I could arrange a meeting with you to discuss your father and his possible involvement in a murder investigation. Adam Sandor thought you wouldn't mind talking to me."

Inspector Rhiness is referring to that infamous chapter in our local history, the murder of Georgia Jackson, a case that has kept the rumor mill grinding for fifteen years. I've heard bits and pieces about it from listening to my parents' conversations with other Witnesses. Elder Sandor has himself questioned me about this case for several years, entrusting me with private information, believing that Daniel is somehow linked to the murder. Sandor is like a Jehovah's Witness private detective working on the Jackson case. He picked me to be his "deputy," a role I adopted willingly because I believed in his cause. It was God's will.

Just a couple of months ago, Sandor drove me to the Aylmer cemetery to show me Georgia's gravestone.

"Her blood is crying out for justice," Sandor whispers.

I don't know what to say, so I mutter, "How sad. What a horrible state of affairs."

"The truth must come out. Others were involved in this murder, or at the very least helped in covering it up. Did Daniel ever talk about the Jackson case?"

My senses are overloaded. Of course, Sandor is trying to encourage me to remember possible links I might know concerning Mr. X. Why do they want me to remember such things? Any talk of this murder disturbs me.

What explains their obsession with Daniel, I wondered, *and what could I contribute since I was only five years old the year the murder occurred.*

My initial distrust of the Sandors' motives in studying with my siblings seems justified. Is it just coincidence that a detective would ask to question me so soon after I enlist the Sandors' help? I cannot ignore the possibility that the Sandors helping us is a strategic move aimed at learning the truth.

Considering the police's apathy toward the Jackson case and the years of well-meant, sometimes misplaced energy, Sandor and Leder spent investigating people's lives, I am wary of this inspector from Toronto. As always, I keep my feelings to myself, never verbalizing what I am really thinking. This is how I avoid trouble. Oddly enough, I am intimidated by Rhiness' position of authority, not by the fact that a stranger wants to interview me about a murder. I don't want anything bad to happen to us, but my curiosity over why he wants to meet with me takes command.

"How soon would you like to get together, Mr. Rhiness?"

"Are you busy this evening, say around seven o'clock?"

"That will be fine. You might as well come here. That way we'll have some privacy. Do you know how to get to Spruce Street?"

"I'll be stopping at Adam Sandor's place first so I'll get directions from him."

"See you at seven then." I hang up the phone with a sigh. I have asked Rhiness to come to my home so he will be coming into my space. This will allow me to feel more in control and more relaxed. But I do wonder, *why now?*

"Hey, Mom, a detective is coming over tonight to ask questions about Daniel. Make sure you all are in your rooms," I command with authority. I am expected to call the shots, a role that comes naturally to me now. Rather than being nervous, I am eager to know what Rhiness wants from me. Anxiously speculating what questions he may ask, I watch the large hand on our old clock move at a turtle's pace.

Tick-tock, tick-tock.
I lie on my bed waiting, daydreaming...

Curtains are only drawn at night. A light remains turned on in the hallway to ward off our bad dreams and evil spirits. Other Donald dreams of a faceless man trying to grab him but never catching him. Other Donald is controlled by the man with no way of escaping. He is suffocated. He can barely breathe. Alone and cold, he fights to escape, to forget, to be free. Only Thinking Donald succeeds. Thinking Donald wakes up in a sweat.

Startled by a knock at the front door, I wake up. The clock strikes seven. I instruct everyone to keep quiet as mice as I answer the door. As always, I peek through the curtains first.

"Please, come in."

Rhiness is a tall thin man in his late forties. The gray at his temples betrays his true age. With his sincerity of expression and conservative dress, Rhiness reminds me of a modern-day Sherlock Holmes. He appears to be ill at ease. I wonder why, but my openness encourages him to relax. He accepts an offer of coffee. As I prepare the coffee, my back to Rhiness, I hear his deep voice begin.

"Where should I start? I've been working undercover on the Georgia Jackson case." Struggling in his choice of words, Rhiness continues, "Since the Elders told me what happened to you...."

Thinking Donald is always in the driver's seat and far more advanced than his chronological age. Yet, immediately my body adopts a self-conscious stance. What is this stranger talking about? God has helped me to forget the past. Only Other Donald knows about that. I can't believe I have to talk about that again. Other Donald knows the story, only too well.

Detective Rhiness is a friend of Leder and Sandor. Their united interest in Daniel's deviant sexual history has everything to do with their personal ongoing murder investigation and little or nothing to do with us as victims. Rhiness is direct and to the point. I wonder if I should respond in kind.

Feeling Donald speaks to me. *"Tell him! You know he's only using you to get information on the Jackson case. Don't let on you don't believe Daniel's involved. Turn the tables and use his interest for your benefit. You're just a pawn on a massive chessboard. You know sexual abuse is a crime, having stored this information for the appropriate time. Here's your chance. You don't have the money to hire a lawyer. Don't blow it!"*

"Do you really think my father could be involved in the murder?" Victim I may be, but innocent I am not.

"There has been so much deception, anything is possible. How did you all cope living with such a man? I just can't imagine—"

"Oh, we're managing just fine actually," I insist emphatically, again steering the conversation in a safe direction. "We are happy with Mom. She has always been good to us. And we have our strong faith in Jehovah God. He'll pull us through anything." I play my role well, but what else do I know?

"I understand better than you think," Rhiness responds. "Keep it to yourself but I'm also in The Truth. I don't tell anyone because in my line of work, it helps to keep that separate."

Rhiness' disclosure disarms me. Being in the same faith, especially ours, allows for a shorthand of language. Rhiness loves God, so he must be a good person. On at least one level, I no longer need to put on an act. He is a Witness working for our God, Jehovah, and the law of the land. I couldn't have wished for anyone better. I think this is a Divine sign.

The Lord must have sent him to me, I tell myself. *God does love us and cares what happens to us. Maybe finally something will be done, but what and why now? Perhaps God was waiting for the right time. Perhaps that time is now.*

Secrets. I am so used to keeping them. My parents taught me how. I appreciate this stranger's trust in me. He can trust me. Can I trust him?

For once in your life, speak up for your own rights. Ask him.

"Do you think...I mean, I was just wondering if...could we have Daniel charged for what he did to us?" I ask, amazing myself.

"Well...definitely," Rhiness manages, stunned that I would initiate the question. Gathering his thoughts, he continues, "But are you sure you'd want to go through something like this?"

"I'm sure it will help your Jackson investigation," I reply, convinced that's what Rhiness wants to hear. "I'll have to ask my sister, my brother, and my mother first. In the meantime, let me know what can be done."

I think whatever we kids have experienced is secondary, so I plug the Jackson case first. I am overwhelmed by his enthusiasm toward even a possibility of a case. Rhiness apparently decides this lends an angle to his investigation and delays questioning me any further about the murder. I have surprised him, though no more than I have myself.

Having gained courtroom experience when I testified for Mom's divorce three years earlier, relating my story was familiar territory. Consciously, this was not painful ground for me. I didn't hesitate in asking Rhiness about charging Daniel because I feared verbalizing my memories. In fact, our written statements, admitted as evidence at the 1978 hearing for Mother's divorce, were requested by our lawyer.

Yet now, three years later, I'm asking a stranger if I can have my father charged. My anxiety about asking stems from not knowing how Rhiness would respond. I am elated and frightened at the same time. My cousins were the first persons to express concern for our experience five years earlier. And now finally, someone feels that something can be done legally. Does it take a detective all the way from Toronto to recognize a need for justice?

My stomach churns uncontrollably. If we pursue this, our lives will never be the same. Is this desirable or harmful? Do we really want to do this? What motivated me to think of asking Rhiness if we should charge him? I have not willingly thought about the past for years. Well, not until this visit from D. I. Rhiness. Perhaps the fact that Rhiness is a detective triggers something within me. Detective Rhiness, working with a Crown Attorney, seems to be a good avenue to find justice. Besides, we wouldn't have to borrow money to pay a lawyer's fee.

When this opportunity arises to use the system to punish our abuser, hesitant though my request may be, I convince myself I finally have a hope for justice. More importantly, Rhiness' disclosure that he is a Witness momentarily relaxes me, allowing me to trust him enough to believe that a man who works for both the provincial government and Almighty God will be able to help us.

My beliefs inform me the world is coming to an end at any moment, so why waste time charging Daniel? Why not? With God's messenger leading us through the legal process, what do I have to lose? Testifying at Mom's divorce was a breeze. There is no question, I must proceed.

"I'll be in touch." With a handshake Rhiness leaves.

As soon as I shut the door behind him, Mom, Marina, and Erik come running out.

"What am I getting myself into?" I mumble audibly.

"What did dat man want?"

"What did he look like?"

"Are you okay?"

I take a deep breath, steady myself and answer, "Better than okay. I asked the detective if he felt we could have Daniel charged and he said, 'Yes.'"

Instantly and predictably, Mom's fear moves her to try to burst my bubble.

"Are you sure you want to do dat? It is de worldly system. I t'ink you should rely on God."

"A lot of good that did us all these years. Why is charging a molester not relying on God? And why, oh why do you always have to be so negative? Mom, the detective is in The Truth, but he told me to keep it to myself. So if he says we can put Daniel behind bars, why shouldn't we? Marina and Erik, there's one thing I need to talk to you about. If you are too embarrassed to go through the ordeal of a trial, I understand. I will not proceed unless you say it's okay."

"I'm behind you all the way. Let's go for it," says Marina.

"Me too," insists Erik.

"Okay, but Erik, I don't want to put you through this mess, so we'll keep your name out of it."

"That's a good idea," agrees Marina.

"I t'ink so too."

Protecting Erik is second nature to us.

In my bed that night, the peace of sleep eludes me. Am I really going to charge my father with something that isn't real to me? Life with Daniel seemed to last an eternity, but I cannot remember my father's face, how he felt, or the sound of his voice. I wished that I could force him out of my mind. And I did.

But why are the home-movie reels in my mind so vivid? How do I conjure up such images and yet feel nothing? It happened to my other self. I know it did.

Chapter Twenty-Five

Much of my existence is out-of-body. It is as though I am watching myself perform an action rather than actually participating in it. Why is it that Other Donald can remember minute details—what someone said or wore, the time of day, the temperature outside—yet block out whole sections of my life? Why can he relay the information while I, Thinking Donald, am not connected to the past? Why am I so numb, so emotionless? Sometimes I feel like a corpse.

Do people feel how cold my hands are when they touch them?

Chapter Twenty-Six

Early the next morning, I pull out our photo albums. I never leaf through these pages. There are holes throughout. Although someone has been cut out of several pictures, an aura from this ghost inhabits each photo.

I make a slow, deliberate movement toward the phone.

"Mr. Rhiness, do what you have to do. We're all for it, but we don't want Erik involved in any way. He's only fifteen."

"I understand."

"What's next?"

"We'll need written statements from your sister, your mother, and yourself. I'm sure everyone will feel more comfortable if you write them yourselves, instead of me asking embarrassing questions. Perhaps you could type them up for me, Donald."

"Sure, no problem. What style do you need them in?"

"Give your full name, date of birth, and a history of your family. Your mother should talk about how she met your father, her marriage, and what life was like with him. You and your sister will need to go into explicit detail about everything you can remember. I'm sorry you have to go through this."

"Don't worry about that," I answer with a conviction that surprises me. "We've committed ourselves. It's time something was done."

"I'm just overwhelmed by your openness. You're a very brave young man. I don't know if I would have your courage."

Courage? For Thinking Donald this is a piece of cake. I'm not even upset. No one asked me to have Daniel charged nor ever brought the possibility up for discussion. I didn't plan it. It just sort of popped into my mind.

I think about Rhiness' words. Is he really concerned about us? I'm not sure but I decide not to worry about the unknown now. Our statements are the foremost project on my agenda. I determine they must be open and honest. Aware that anger confuses the real issues, I determine to be truthful, yet controlled. The fact that I am not in touch with my anger on any level makes this goal effortless.

"When would you like the statements, detective?" I ask.

"I'll be in Toronto the rest of the week. Do what you can, and how about I come over next weekend and have a look at what you've got?"

"Mom is going to Belgium for a month, but I'll get on ours right away. I'll have as much done as possible."

I am excited by the thought of justice. I'm accomplishing something useful, something that validates my existence, *our* existence.

I had no idea how my family would react when I told them I was considering charging Daniel. I viewed their full cooperation as a sign that I should proceed and not let anything stand in my way. If Marina had not wanted me to, I would never have pursued this court case. I believed it was worse for her because she was a girl. My father didn't protect her, but I would.

It's amazing how society reinforces the idea that father/daughter incest is worse than father/son. Each time someone new found out about our abuse, invariably their response would be: "Boys can protect themselves but girls are weaker." In some ways the opposite is true. Because boys are not supposed to express emotions in ways that are encouraged in girls, young males often internalize the abuse, the psychological trauma, and act outwardly in destructive ways. Sadly, boys add to their pain by repeatedly telling themselves: we are bad and deserve to be punished. It becomes a vicious cycle—the real problem, that of abuse, is hidden deeper and deeper: For some, decades. For others, forever.

This pattern was definitely displayed by my two brothers, but I wasn't like most boys, and my sister wasn't like most girls. I was the feminine one in the family, my sister, the tomboy. I didn't worry about people associating sex with my father with homosexual activity as many male victims do. That fear deters many males from disclosing their experiences with abuse. Since I had been labeled with such terms as "faggot" and "gay" for several years at school, fear of being called a "homosexual" at this point carried no weight whatsoever. Marina had also endured ridicule for years. She had been labeled a "dyke" and "freak," so fear of being rejected because people would know her secret was never a consideration either.

Nevertheless, I was surprised to find Marina supportive of our case and willing to sit down and discuss her memories of the past.

"Marina, let's work on our statements together. I'll type while we talk. Remember, whatever we say will be used by the police and perhaps read aloud in court. We don't want any melodramatics. No Al Pacino histrionics like in *And Justice For All!* We'll leave that to Daniel's lawyer.

"I think we want to be a little detached while at the same time, truthful," I tell my sister. "So, I'll ask some questions I think they would ask in court.... Do you remember the first time F-A-T-H-E-R touched you? I do."

"I don't remember a first time at all. All I know is he played with me from early on." I start to type.

"I can vouch for that. I remember him bringing the two of us together with him."

"I didn't say anything because it was, like, 'Papa's teaching us new things.'"

"I remember him telling me, 'Touch Marina there,' and I said I couldn't. He told me at first everyone feels that way and that I would 'get used to it.'"

Marina remembers Daniel interrupting her bath. Mother told her to leave the door unlocked in case she needed help. While Mother was busy in the kitchen or outside, Marina continues, "Father would be busy with me. She never caught him—"

"Remember Marina," I interrupt. "Daniel said it was more exciting that way...because we might get caught."

"I didn't tell Mama because I was scared she would beat me, because that's what he told me. Later on, it was because *he* would beat me. I didn't think it was wrong, Donald. He told me everyone else does it."

"Right. He said, 'They do it, but people just don't talk about things like this.'"

"Sometimes he would finish it off if I got tired and my wrists hurt. Right in front of me. He'd have little pieces of paper with naked women tucked away in his clothes or wallet in case he ever wanted a quickie. He told me Mama and him had these fun play times in their room at night. He'd put his thing in the front of my vagina but never did he go all the way. He said I wasn't old enough but when I was, we could have, 'more fun with that.' He would show me a picture of a woman and say when I was that age we could have more fun. Also, he put his penis between my legs on the back of me as though he was entering my behind, but would only go between my legs. He said this was so I would get used to the real thing."

I tell my sister how petrified I became that Daniel might enter her private parts and how the words pregnancy and bleeding became alarm buttons for me. She knows I wanted to protect her and Erik.

"Sex became a terrible thing for me, Marina!" I exclaim. "I watched over the both of you, trying to make sure you weren't alone with him. So, I made myself available."

Marina meets my expression warily, then looks away. I can see her tears welling as I tell her: "I think I seduced him at times because of this, even though I hated him. I hated his looks. I hated his smell. I hated everything about him, yet I wanted that sexual excitement I could get and I was worried that you would want it too."

I draw a deep sigh. *How far should I, can I, go with this?* I feel both my sister and I need such a session to steel us for the trial looming ahead. I can perform, but can she hold up?

"I despised the earth he walked on, Marina. I was full of guilt feelings. He would say, 'You are like me!' That would scare the hell out of me. I got sick for days. He put ideas into my mind that I was the guilty one from the beginning. I'm the one who wanted sex with him and I should be proud of it. I almost gagged every time I had to touch him. I wouldn't sit near him, talk to him or do anything with him. How could he not figure out he affected us? Mom knew that when he got angry, he could kill us, so we had to be careful. The only reason I didn't kill myself was because of Mother. I just couldn't make her more lost than she already was. That kept me going." I know I am triggering Marina's memories.

"Oh, Donald, he so messed me up sexually. All he ever showed me was naked pictures of women so I began to desire the women in the pictures. I even fell in love once with a doll and on the day I turned 12, I destroyed it. Then I imagined myself to be in love with a make-believe pillow of mine. I treated it as if it was another person. I felt terribly guilty and felt sick inside." She pauses and I know she's mustering resolve. "*Good going,*" I say softly, "*build on this.*"

"One time," she continues, "Daniel came after me and I got scared and ran away, but I came back because I didn't want to leave Mom with him! I also suffered from bad dreams. One was about Erik and myself walking along the road calling Mom, but she didn't pay attention, and then a car came by and shot arrows at Erik's head and he was covered with them. I also dreamed about scissors coming after me and if they would reach me, I would die. I also dreamed that semen was on the shelves of Mom's bedroom which Daniel collected, and he would be trying to rape our cat in front of us, and I would wake up screaming to make it stop."

"Yeah...I remember, Marina, you screaming, in a cold sweat and not really awake, like you were in a trance. You looked as though you had been raped, crying for help. Mom would cradle you in her arms until you woke up."

I tell my sister I dream too, dreams so sick I can barely repeat them aloud: "Daniel is raping you or Mom right before my eyes and I am held back, sometimes by chains, other times by people. I wake up scared out of my wits. In some dreams, there's a light glaring in the hallway. A woman is calling out. Sometimes a man. But it's always the same beat. You know, in speech but in rhythm like an electric typewriter clacking away."

Marina's expression shows repugnance and yet there's a hint of resolution: "He did so many things, I just can't talk about it.... But...I want to charge him, Donald, for all the emotional stuff I'm feeling and what I'm afraid I'll face in the future—"

"You're feeling emotions? Marina, none of this is real to me. It's like a live dream!"

"What are you talking about? It's all real to me. I have all these memories and you know what? I can never live a normal life. Daniel gets off free of charge. No wonder he thinks he can get away with it. He shouldn't be loose in society. Think about him treating his second wife like he did Mother and having children with her! Imagine seeing those helpless kids go through what we had to. Dear God, it's so sickening."

I'm speechless. My sister is more articulate than I imagined possible. I thought I would have to coach her.

The month Mother is in Belgium is the first time we are apart from her for more than a week. Marina cooks and cleans as best she can, I continue working at the downtown car dealership, and Erik attends school. We maintain our schedule of worship and service in the missionary work. Most of my spare energy goes into preparing our statements for Rhiness and explaining our course of action to our closest Witness friends who question my judgment. Yet, stubbornly I press on. For the first time we will get justice, I tell myself. People will know the truth about what happened. I won't have to explain the unexplainable. My father will stop preaching to us through his letters about his born-again, convenient religion. More importantly, everyone who thinks we are peculiar and different will understand why this is so.

I have a habit of reading the mail first in our house. Today, I find two letters from Daniel in the mailbox. His continued condemnation of Mom and us children seems pathetic as we prepare evidence that will send him behind bars.

Dearest Jeannette, and beloved children Donald, Marina, and Erik: I want you to know how much I love you all no matter what treatment you give me. I realize you left me because of a meeting with your Elders in the supposedly Christian Congregation in Aylmer. Satan, of course, is working through The Watchtower Society to poison the minds of the unbelievers. Read without Watchtower glasses. Don't you realize you are children of Satan, my beloved ones? I am so sorry to write you that you will all burn in hell if you don't repent from your ways. Your Papa loves you all very much, my dear children, and can forgive you if you return to me. Jeannette, you know you had no Christian grounds to leave me. You left me because I changed my religion, The Watchtower Society having poisoned your mind. You copulated with me after what I did, so you forgave everything. Please pray to God asking forgiveness of your many sins. Always remember that I love you all very much.

Your ever loving, Daniel

P.S. Please read John 4:8 [God is Love]

We never correspond with him or acknowledge his letters. Years ago, I went to the police to see if there was a way to stop their delivery.

"Your only recourse is to mark the envelope 'return to sender' or file it under 'g' for garbage," an officer told me. He never asked me why I didn't want letters from my 'father'. We followed through on the officer's advice, but Daniel then stopped putting his return address on the envelope, and next had someone else handwrite our address to fool us into opening his letters. I think it's best to save the letters now because of the court case.

Each letter does make me acknowledge that there must be more truth to my movie reels than I'd like to believe. Something *did* happen to me. While Feeling Donald remembers the abuse, Thinking Donald rejects the intrusion of his space. While I detest Daniel for using God's name in vain, for blaming my mother for leaving him and for his hate-motivated harassment of Jehovah's Witnesses, I don't hate him for what he did to me. How could I? None of that is real to me. It's like watching a horror/supernatural scene on a television program. A viewer knows it's make-believe, but his mind finds it unsettling just the same. He has the choice to turn the TV off or change the channel. My movie reels are like horrific, vivid documentaries. They seem unbelievable but I know they are true. And although I can't turn them off, I definitely try to change the channel.

My brain tells me the scenes did happen. That message is verified when Marina and I work on the statements and she tells me that there were times we were abused together, when Erik remembers telling his Mama, and when Mom says she knows it happened.

Thinking Donald has to accept it must have happened, but Feeling Donald is never connected to this process.

Perhaps it is only Thinking Donald that can have his father charged. How else could I type up a report with detailed documentation of my life with Daniel and yet not feel anything? It's as though I am lying about having been affected by it all. How could I have been when I received pleasure from it? I feel I was responsible for it happening. I didn't say no. It didn't hurt me, but I know it hurt my brothers and sister. I have no answers, and I have no one in my life to give them to me.

Do other victims feel the same as I do?

Mr. Rhiness is coming to look at our statements today.

"Call me Nort, Donald," the detective requests as he extends his right hand, and Thinking Donald extends a hand in return.

"I've got quite a bit done. Mom is still in Belgium, so I don't have her statement yet."

"Donald, I'll have to speak to your older brother. Do you think he'd be willing to talk to me?"

I wondered when I'd be faced with this, another agonizing reminder of the past. I feel pain but cannot show it, least of all to this detective, cordial though he may be.

"I have no idea, but I'll give you Ronny's address. We haven't spoken in three years. He believes Daniel is a changed man. I don't understand why he sees him. Who knows what he'll do?"

I cannot associate with someone who would befriend the monster in my black and white movie, even if it is my own brother. My mind cannot handle Ronny visiting his father, our abuser. How painful it is even to think about my older brother, but I won't share that pain with Rhiness or anyone else.

"I have to ask you, Donald, other than your brothers and sister," Rhiness continues, "do you know of anyone else your father could have molested?"

"First of all, we only refer to him as Daniel. I never use the word 'father'—he doesn't deserve it. I do remember something happening with a landlord's son. He was a year older than me.

"I was eight. I'm pretty sure it only happened once. Maybe you won't be able to use that."

If our abuse was not important, why would a single incident with a neighborhood boy be important?

"Actually, the fact that abuse took place outside the family follows the profile of a pedophile. It will help your case. Can you remember his name?"

"Corey Smith. We were living in a house we rented from Corey's father. That was in 1969. I don't want to upset his family. I'm sure no one knows about it."

"Don't worry. We'll talk to the victim first. It will be okay."

Although I know the future is out of my hands now, I'm scared for Corey. We're used to this. Who has he had to talk to? How did it affect him? Does he even remember the experience? Maybe I should have kept my mouth shut.

"Before you leave, have a look at our statements. What do you think so far?" I ask, as though Rhiness was about to grade a book report. Rhiness makes notes in the margins using a yellow highlighter to mark sections while I pour another cup of coffee.

"I know it may be difficult, but you'll need to be more specific. We need graphic details. We have to assume Daniel's lawyer will go through this with a fine-tooth comb. There can be no innuendo. I'll mark spots where you need to clarify what you mean."

Looking over his shoulder, I scrutinize both the highlighted markings and the questions in the margins: "How do you know his tongue entered? In what room did this take place? What did he do exactly? What specifically did he say about getting caught? Explain what you mean by fear. How and when did Erik tell? What did your father say?"

I wonder what this would feel like if it were real to me. This statement business must be very difficult for people who feel pain.

"Your requests seem so impersonal." At least I must act like I feel.

"These are serious charges, and we don't want to allow the defense any window of opportunity to discredit your statements."

"I have total recall so that will not be a problem. Marina has blocked the early years but I have not. We'll do the best we can." I cannot tell Rhiness about my movie reels. He'll think I'm crazy. I must act like everything is real.

"And don't forget, I'll need your mother's statement as soon as possible."

"Yes, as soon as she's back from Belgium."

Chapter Twenty-Seven

While waiting for Mother to arrive at the Toronto airport, Marina, Erik, and I discuss the paradoxes of our life. Mom has just had the time of her life, seeing her mother, her family, and her friends. We were glad to be able to give this gift to her. Her husband, in twenty years of marriage, gave her nothing except a sewing machine.

During the car ride home, Mom shares many wonderful experiences of her trip. When we get home though, her elated mood grows somber.

"I don't t'ink you should charge Daniel. It's such a horrible t'ing, why not just forget about all dat?"

"How dare you tell me that?" I explode. "You go off and have a grand time, then come back and ask us to forget a large part of our life? Who are you thinking of, you or us? How convenient to tell us to forget about it now."

Mom sees truth in my response.

"You're right; I wasn't t'inking. I guess I want it to go away. Relying on Jehovah is what helps me. You don't know how I feel."

"I know God helps you, but you definitely don't know how we feel either."

Mother's constant referral to her reliance on God implies that we do not. Sometimes this gets on my nerves. Other times I let it pass. Although I never reveal myself to the outside world, my mother catches occasional glimpses of the real me.

What she sees scares her.

"Mom, Mr. Rhiness says he needs your statement right away. I'll help you. Tell me in your own words how you see the story of your life and I'll type what you say. I need you to speak slowly."

"I was born in Belgium. I first met Mr. X in 1955. We were married in—"

"Mom, you can't call him Mr. X in your statement. We'll have to use his name. You know, it's no wonder he's not real to me—we've even removed his name from our vocabulary. It's strange, I know, but we have to make him real."

"I told you so. We would be happier if we did not have to t'ink about him."

"Mom! I don't want to hear any negative talk."

"It is just dat he seems far away and I am happy he is too. But I do want to help you."

"Oh, brother," I sigh. "Why couldn't you have fallen for that short guy who had a crush on you? He would have been a better husband. You had to go for the looks, didn't you?"

"I told you Lecien was nice, but he just wasn't right for me. Anyway, I remember before we even married, Daniel asked me if I would listen to gossip about him."

"He only told you that to counter what must have been true stories. Did you hear stories?"

"Dere was some talk about Daniel getting a girl pregnant but I did not believe it."

"I'll type in the early history of your relationship later."

"Ronny is my firstborn. Donald, you were next. Help wit' de birt' dates."

"I know, you're always mixing them up. Marina is April 26, 1963, and Erik April 21, 1966. Now what?"

"I was never suspicious of him with anyone else because he had sex with me until I left him October 31, 1976."

"Mom, that's good. Keep going. Talk as if I'm not here."

"Right from de start, I was scared he would hit me. At first I fought back a little, but he would beat me. My place was in de kitchen and in de bed. For dese reasons, I did not have a life outside of de home and eventually got so used to it, dat I did not want to go out. De first years of our marriage were okay sexually. A lot of sex until Ronny turned five or six years old. From then on, your *vader* told me he was too tired to have sex, and I could expect it maybe once a month. When he came to me, I never said, 'No.'

"Remember Donald, you always said to me, 'I wish you had an affair so dat I would have a different *vader*.'"

"Yeah, Mom, you had to be a Christian. I think God would have understood your having just one affair, all things considered!"

"Oh, Donald. Do not say such t'ings. You know my fait' is the most important t'ing to me. I t'ought it was normal to have sex less often as de years went on so I got used to it and didn't even expect it more often dan dat. When Erik told me what your *vader* did to him, showing de motion he used, at first I t'ought dat he was confused, and I could not figure out what he meant. Den you explained it.

"Your Papa told me he stopped fooling around wit' you children."

"Remember, you're not talking to me. It's for the Court."

"Alt'ough I felt dirty when he touched me, and I told him to leave me alone, he forced himself on me."

"God, you didn't even own your own sexuality!"

"I tried to go on with my married life."

"I remember hearing you having sex, Mama. It disgusted me. I hated him for making you have sex with him whether you felt like it or not. My mind couldn't handle it, so I had to push it away completely."

"You and Marina told me on many occasions he did it wit' you again. Each time I would confront him. Daniel would admit it happened and say, 'I won't do it again.' I would t'reaten to tell de Elders and he would laugh at me. He knew I would never have gone. He said, 'Go ahead' once. I was scared to tell anyone. I t'ought, 'What can anyone do for us?'

"I try not to t'ink about it too much. It helps. The reason I never called de police was because I never read or heard dat it was against de law and he could go to jail. I t'ought once we left him, we should put it in de past and leave it dere. I didn't realize de total effect Daniel had on you children."

Tears glisten in Mom's eyes for the first time. Although I am infuriated just listening to her side of the story and remembering my own, I have none to shed.

"Don't worry, Mom," I say softly. "Daniel will pay for what he did to all of us."

"We have to leave it in God's hands. I'm giving dis testimony for you, but I don't t'ink we should trust de worldly court system."

"Well, maybe if someone had before, we would have had fewer years of abuse!"

"We can't change de past now, can we?"

"Wasn't that the same thing your mother told you when you confronted her about hitting for no good reason? It's always the same tune, isn't it? Forget the past."

"Oh well, let's go on with dis. I have to make de supper soon."

"Okay, continue."

"After we left him, Ronny got into trouble wit' de law and in relationships wit' girls. Donald was different and wouldn't talk to anyone except me and his *broeders* and sister. He was not a happy teenager and t'reatened to kill himself many times. I t'ank God he didn't. Marina was troubled too. Erik had his difficulty in learning in school.... All dese problems have been my punishment for staying wit' Daniel and not leaving wit' de children. I support charging Daniel because de children especially feel dat dey are de ones to blame for feeling the way dat dey do and dey are responsible for all de emotional upsets wit'in dem. Daniel took our four innocent children, molded dem, robbed dem of der normal childhood. He did not love dem. Also, Daniel is a dangerous man. To my kids and to oder kids too. I would feel more at ease knowing dat such a man was locked up and could not touch more children."

Mom's face seemed to grow older as she spoke of her feelings. This is the first time someone has encouraged her to tell her side of the story. Other than her children, no one ever asks Mom how she feels.

As I listen to Mother describe us, I realize that although I study Scripture, I do continue to blame myself for the overwhelming emotional difficulties I experience. I don't understand how my problems could have anything to do with the abuse. My struggle has become internalized. I trust no one. My introverted personality is often mistakenly labeled as shyness. Why would I open up to people I don't trust? Because my mother opposes this court case on some level, I don't even trust her. She wants me to be like her—pretend, forget, live for God. If we kids were abused for a longer period of time because of that belief system, how can I trust that faith? I want to believe her way is the best way. I just don't know if I can.

"So oder dan Daniel continues to bug us with his letter writing, de story ends dere. Did I leave anyt'ing out?"

My natural curiosity, the skills I developed during my secondary school education and my years as a Bible student contribute to my objectivity working on the court statements. I consider it a meaningful assignment. It is important that my contribution be concise, well written, and useful. Personal feelings and emotions, except for effect, cannot get in the way. I am obsessed with our statements, the upcoming charges, and the unknown possibilities concerning our court case.

Now that Mom is behind us, I can move forward and concentrate on my family's spiritual development.

Just as Ronny had been instructed by the Elders years earlier, I, too arrange for us to study as a family for each week's meetings on Monday nights. And history is again repeated as the combination of forceful personalities, sibling rivalry, and disrespect for Mom turns our weekly sessions into total chaos. As we each take turns reading paragraphs from Witness literature, the personality of each reader controls the direction of the discussion. We are lucky if we get through two pages of study material each week, and yet I refuse to give up. Every Monday, turbulent as our sessions are, I insist we study together. Quitting would be admitting defeat. Marina and Erik resent me, but respect my persistence, just as I recognized Ronny's sincerity and devotion. *This is God's will*, I keep reminding myself.

My family and I are doing the best we can.

Chapter Twenty-Eight

Approximately thirty people, including policemen, judges, attorneys, physicians, and the church elders, had been told of our abuse over the previous nine years. I wonder, if something had been done years earlier, how would our lives be different today?

Then I correct myself: "I must not waste my time playing the 'what if' game. I have a life to live, I have a family to support, and I have a Christian example to set."

Nort Rhiness picks up Mom's statement today.

He reports that everything is proceeding as planned. Rhiness tells me he met with my older brother and that he has agreed to support our case. He informs me that Ronny, "seems to be having troubles of his own and is a little insecure." Rhiness also found our former neighbor Corey who confirmed the abuse. When Rhiness told Corey's parents, they were appalled and furious. They support charging Daniel with the assault on their son. Corey had never told anyone about the abuse. Rhiness believes this corroborating evidence will help our case.

Part of me is surprised that Rhiness not only found a man by the name of Corey, but that this Corey also played The Game with Daniel. It remains one small reel in my movie. If that one is true, the others must be too.

Rhiness predicts Daniel could be arrested as soon as Wednesday. Events are moving more rapidly than I could have imagined. There is no turning back. Why would I want to?

Daily I check the newspaper for any mention of Daniel's arrest, but Wednesday comes and goes. Meanwhile, my life is filled with inconsequential events: writing letters to friends, giving a Bible talk at our Kingdom Hall, and going to see a sneak preview double-bill at the theater, *Arthur* and *The History of the World – Part I.* Mom, Marina, Erik, and I laughed all the way through the Dudley Moore movie, but the Mel Brooks film was so filthy, we walked out of the theatre. It seemed like the Christian thing to do. It's strange that while we are on the edge of disclosure, we finally are making time to enjoy some experiences together as a family. We're even planning a trip to the beach on Saturday.

Perhaps writing those statements purged us of a lot of bottled-up anger. I hope we're not experiencing a false sense of happiness.

Finally the charges are laid. The press is using Daniel's name but not ours, as is their policy. As our surname is uncommon in our area, we are immediately identified as the children of the accused.

I have a congregation meeting to go to tonight, but today my boss gave me four tickets to see Cleo Laine in concert at the Festival Theatre in Stratford. What a pleasant coincidence. I feel like I am sinning but considering today's circumstances, I tell myself, *"God will understand."*

My mother, Erik, Marina, and I hear the charges mentioned on the radio as we drive to Stratford. Later, as I am listening to Laine's angelic voice, I wonder how people will react. In one moment, I experience the best and worst of the human experience: the glory of art and the notoriety of disclosure.

The following morning, July 14, 1981, Daniel's arrest makes the local headlines:

London man charged with 10 sex offences

A 47-year-old London man was arrested by St. Thomas O.P.P Monday morning and charged with 10 sexual offences. Daniel Noel D'Haene is charge with four counts each of gross indecency and indecent assault, and one count each of buggery and bestiality.

The alleged offences involved three male juveniles and one female juvenile and occurred between 1963 and 1974 in the Aylmer area and other areas. Police received complaints from the victims, who are now adults, about one month ago. Investigations into the complaints were conducted by Det. Insp. N. Rhiness, of the Criminal Investigations Branch, O.P.P. Headquarters in Toronto, and O.P.P. Constable Pat Petz, of the St. Thomas detachment.

The accused was not arrested until yesterday because he was vacationing in Northern Ontario when the complaints were lodged. The accused appeared before a justice of the peace in St. Thomas yesterday and has been released to appear in St. Thomas provincial court today at 2 P.M. — *The St. Thomas Times Journal*

The London Free Press reported: "Daniel Noel D'Haene appeared in provincial court Tuesday...and was remanded out of custody until Aug. 11."

What a surreal experience to pick up the paper and read that the secret that I have kept for so long is finally being read by hundreds of thousands of people. I realize most people will assume that the three males cited in the media refer to my brothers and me. This is unfortunate, as people might view the situation as self-contained within the "family unit", and think that Daniel has not been a threat to their own children.

After breakfast, a sister from our congregation stops by. She swiftly hugs Mom and then me. She used to give us rides to the hall when we lived with Daniel after he was disfellowshipped. She is completely sincere in her concern, and her welcome gesture convinces me to relax my guard.

In the afternoon, Marina receives a delivery of flowers from one of her former teachers.

People will understand and show us compassion.

"You see, Mom, we were right to go public."

"I t'ink so too!"

Reinforced by these kind gestures, I convince myself I should conduct my life as if nothing happened. A couple of days later I nervously drive my family to our first religious meeting since the press release. We enter and sit quietly. No one mentions it. No one in the entire congregation tells us that they care. No one says they will pray for us. It feels as if I am living in the twilight zone. Are we being shunned because of Father's sin?

Or are they scared as hell of our circumstances? Do they not know how to act? I hoped that they would support our courage. I just want people to understand why we are different from everyone else and that it isn't our fault.

How predictable. I have been raised to live as though nothing happened and when the truth finally comes out, the majority of people behave as if nothing happened.

Yet people are talking about my family. I discover this reality in the most unexpected places. I take my family to see an elderly Belgian couple. During Mom's trip, someone asked her to visit relatives who lived in Aylmer. It is evident they are wealthy and it is obvious we are not, but they welcome us with open arms. Their daughter, Emily, who lives next door, arrives minutes after us. I wonder if her visit is planned, but I decide my energy is better spent turning off whatever upsets are ruling my world today and turn on the entertainer in me—a welcome escape and an effortless task as I truly enjoy meeting new people and I am fascinated with their stories.

Mom's habit of blocking out her history surfaces when our hostess reminds her that Daniel worked for her family in tobacco two decades ago. Emily recalls Ronny drinking oil from a stovepipe and being rushed to the hospital. She then states: "I recognized the D'Haene name in the newspaper. I plan on following the case closely."

I think it strange that she is so open about studying us so "closely" and so obviously. Did Emily turn up for a free freak show? Human nature, I suppose.

With my guard up and my radar on high, I sense she's dying to say something. She'll probably pretend to care. I decide to do the same.

"Daniel must be sick and needing help," she blurts out.

Hmm. Interesting that the first thing out of her mouth is pity for Daniel. No inquiry as to our health or whether we need "help."

"That's probably true. But he's never admitted to having a problem. If Daniel doesn't go to jail, how can he get the help he needs?"

I don't know why but this woman pushes all of my buttons. Although I am upset, I decide to leave a good impression on Emily and her parents, so I change the subject and focus on them. The evening is a success.

On the drive home, I reflect on this interchange. Why am I explaining anything? Daniel admitted "sinning" to the Elders, not to having a problem. Will I have to explain my decision to charge Daniel for the rest of my life? Now that the secret is out, will Daniel have to spend the rest of his life explaining why he abused us?

At moments like this, I do ask myself, "What have I done?" Yes, people are talking about us but how can I determine if their interest is genuine or self-serving fodder for the gossip mill. I don't know what to expect from minute to minute. The secret is out and our lives will never be the same. Will it be worth it?

Rhiness rings me, wondering if he can stop by.

"The courts really look for documented evidence, such as medical reports or psychiatric assessments. Have you ever spoken to a professional about what happened to you?"

"No, I've never gone to a shrink. I rely on God. He's such a tower of strength. You know yourself, we don't believe in psychotherapy."

"But it would help your case. Also, if there is anything else you can remember, I need you to write it down. You might think it's unimportant but it may be beneficial."

I was convinced, however, that Rhiness was less concerned about my well-being than he was about strengthening our case with documentation from a professional therapist. My response to his suggestion was a programmed recitation of my religious beliefs and fear of worldly therapy. I had never considered therapy for a moment, even at my lowest points. It's not that I didn't believe that there was something wrong with me. I just believed that if the Witnesses, God's chosen people couldn't help me, no one else could.

When I met sincere people, such as my high school guidance counselor, who asked me if there was anything I wanted to talk about, I really didn't believe there was anything to discuss. The layers of mistrust I'd cultivated over years of abuse also prevented disclosure. The only reason I considered Rhiness' suggestion was that I wanted our case to be a success. My religion told me it was dangerous to let worldly people look into my mind. I didn't let Witnesses in; why would I trust a non-Christian?

"Mom, Detective Rhiness told me it would help if I had a therapist's report."

"Why do you need dat? Dere's noting wrong wit' you. Is Jehovah God not enough?"

"Brother! There you go again. Negative as always. Marina and I do have problems you know."

What problems, I can't define but I know I have to sell this therapy to my mother.

"I do not t'ink it is a good idea."

"I haven't made up my mind, yet, but if I decide to, you have nothing to say about it!"

During the next couple of weeks, I continue my routine of work, worship, and home Bible study. Our daily life did not change with the public arrest of our abuser. In fact, Erik and I give Bible talks on a Thursday evening, a week after our father's arrest. There we are speaking of God's Kingdom in front of our congregation who have just found out about our secret life.

While Erik reads the notes that I prepared for him, oblivious to the larger drama unfolding, I concentrate on delivering my talk to the best of my ability, ignoring any disapproval or energy radiating to the podium concerning our court case. I'm sure I am the only one in the entire building who can concentrate on the material I am reviewing. I am emotionless as usual.

My ability to detach from reality serves me well. It always does.

To escape my obsession with the court case, I focus on my family's fitness. I decide a jogging routine will be the perfect exercise that the entire family can do together. Mom doesn't want to be seen so we have to wait until eleven o'clock in the evening. Marina and Erik think it will be fun.

Jogging is one of the few activities we participate in as a family where we never argue. Sometimes we laugh so hard at the sight of our mother running in the middle of the night, we have to stop to take a break and catch our breath. We have a cool mother who wants to join in our adventures. Some days, these good times fool us into thinking we are happy. Perhaps we are.

On the third night of our new routine, I set the clock for early in the morning so I can watch Prince Charles marrying Lady Diana. I love every minute of it. I know I'm not supposed to find enjoyment in the lives of worldly people, but I do. I think the fairy tale wedding is romantic and perfect in every way. I retreat from my real world into the world of television and fantasize about being a member of the Royal family. The television world of make-believe, even if it involves real-life characters, is so far removed from my experience that it offers me escape.

Even though I'm alone, I am not lonely. The people in the box with the picture tube are there for me when real people aren't. I fantasize about romantic, not sexual love. I can't imagine having actual sex with anyone other than myself, sinful as that is. Since I've always known I'd never marry, sex is out of the question for me. My faith won't allow sex outside marriage, and I refuse to believe that kind of commitment will be part of my life. I could never break my dedication to my faith, my vow of celibacy, my promise to serve God forever.

I decide it's time I discover the world around me and subscribe to *Rolling Stone*, *Time* and *Life* magazines. I have never been a fan of the Beatles, but since the hoopla over John Lennon's death last December, I'm spending this year rediscovering their music. What the critics have been saying is right—Paul McCartney was the poster boy while Lennon was the heart and soul of the group. But together, what a combination!

And the more I read, the more I find validation in my religious beliefs by glimpsing a world focused on success at all costs. This spirit of meism is as unattractive to me as the drug culture of the sixties and seventies. Still, and not for lack of trying, I do not fit into the Jehovah's Witness society I've inherited from my parents.

Always a visitor, never a tenant, I find no home in the real world. I am drifting, but I hide my confusion behind a controlled exterior. Control is the name of my game. Tobacco, alcohol, drugs, and sex hold no appeal to me because I can't control their effect on me. I avoid all situations where these lures may be offered me.

I don't know how to relax outside of my fantasy world. Whereas I am healthy physically, mentally and emotionally I am at a standstill. Unconnected to my past, I refuse to waste time feeling sorry for myself, and I won't let my family express self-pity either. They need me to be positive. They keep me going.

The more my fantasies takes over, the happier I think I will be. Whatever I am doing seems to be working. Mom is happy to see me taking her faith seriously. People respond more positively to a Donald unconnected to his past.

Chapter Twenty-Nine

There were times when I dissected my life, as if it were under a microscope and I was a scientist. *"Am I really okay or am I fooling myself?"* I'd wonder. We lived with abuse on a regular basis for more than a decade while trying to project to the outside world that our lives were normal. Our success only served to dissociate us further from reality.

I was beginning to question everything.

Why did Marina and Erik have so many problems? Why is it okay that I never see Ronny? Why could I not trust people? Why didn't I feel or show emotion? I was about to be subpoenaed to testify about experiences that didn't seem real to me.

How could I convince a doctor that I had been affected by the experience when I could not feel it myself?

Regardless, I convinced myself that I must do what I could to help put Daniel in jail. The challenge excited and terrified me.

To all outward appearances, I was doing fine. I had apparently transcended an insurmountable obstacle—sexual and psychological abuse, but herein lay my dilemma: as a victim of abuse, I was emotionally disconnected from that experience.

I had to unlock the compartment which held my memories and my torment! I didn't want to think of the past. I didn't want to remember. I preferred the movie reels. I believed I was functioning well. But I became committed to this case. The thought that Daniel would finally be confronted by his abusive actions was the only thing that kept me going. Otherwise, what would be the point of taking him to court?

Today the local papers report that Daniel made an appearance in court:

Man to elect trial on sex charges

St. Thomas (Bureau) – A London man charged with 10 sex offences will appear in provincial court here Sept. 8 to elect a trial, justice of the peace Daniel McGee decided in court Tuesday.

Daniel Noel D'Haene, 47, of 13 Lacy Cres., is charged… – *The St. Thomas Times Journal,* August 12, 1981

Man remanded

…the alleged offences involved three male juveniles and one female juvenile and occurred between 1963 and 1974 in the Aylmer area and other areas. – *The London Free Press,* August 12, 1981

"I'd like to make an appointment with Doctor Billingsley, please."

"What is it regarding?"

"A personal matter if you don't mind."

"Okay. What about 4:00 P.M., Tuesday, August 18?"

On a warm summer afternoon, I self-consciously shuffle down the sidewalk to the doctor's office, a four-block walk from my home. People can tell by looking at me that there's something wrong, or so I believe. Experience tells me I am not being irrational. I wish I could disguise my appearance, become someone else, and pass unrecognized.

Patiently sitting in the waiting room, I don't want to see anyone's face, the clothes they're wearing or the whiteness of any possible smiles. I wonder, *Is this another huge step forward to a new future?* I choose to escape my anxiety by focusing on an article I am reading, so much so that I am startled when the receptionist calls my name.

"What can I do for you, Donald?" asks Dr. Billingsley.

As usual, our family doctor's laid-back style is comforting, but I am so nervous and embarrassed I hem and haw. I have no idea how I'm supposed to approach this. Finally I blurt out words without taking a breath.

"I was sexually abused and I can't handle it!"

"You need to get it off your chest. I'll arrange for someone to talk to you."

"Thanks. I appreciate your help."

Within moments, my appointment is over.

"That's all? That's it? Well, that was easy," I whisper to myself as I leave the office. "Now I can enjoy the rest of this day."

The doctor showed no surprise, and treated my disclosure with calm detachment. Exactly what rational, emotionless Donald preferred. Perhaps Dr. Billingsley had read about my father's charges in the papers and had assumed the three male juveniles and one female were my brothers, sister, and I.

Here was the second person in an official position who acted on my behalf but at my request. There was an element of role-playing on my part when I told my doctor I couldn't handle my past. Having spent years studying people, their speech patterns, their choice of words, and their facial expressions, I knew how to act whatever emotion a situation called for. Rhiness needed corroborating evidence to substantiate my case, and nothing would stop me from getting it.

Deciding to dredge up the past was one thing. Dealing with my memories while functioning in the real world was quite another.

I am employed in an office right across the street from my doctor's building. As I walk over and sit down at my desk, I think it strange that my job is more real to me than the events that led to my disclosure just minutes ago. I keep to myself for the most part. Because I rarely talk, I must make it difficult for the other employees. Though I don't trust any of them, I try to be as polite as I can be. The fact that I work with thirteen men adds to the problem. I have nothing in common with these people, and they wouldn't be interested in what I have to say. I rationalize that anything I say could be used against me.

I never display emotion. I want to be left alone, unobserved. The usual chaos in the office means I don't have time to think about personal matters. I prefer it that way.

When I arrive home, Mom and I get into a long discussion. I resent her for not supporting us.

"Why charge Mr. X?" "Let God punish him!" "Why go for t'erapy?" "Isn't God enough?"

I remember her telling us to lie for Daniel. I love her, but right now I don't respect her. She is just one of a group of people who seem to feel that I should "let sleeping dogs lie." Why is every one of my independent moves questioned?

Of course, having to go back into the past means confronting demons I have buried. My resentment over my mother's role has lain dormant for five years. It is now brewing just below the surface.

I begin writing a diary five weeks after Daniel's arrest. With the goal of revisiting my past, I record my experiences to help our court case. I also have a secret yearning to make the movies real. Charging my father gives me the courage to do things I have never done before. I force myself to remember things that I have successfully blocked out of my conscious life. My first diary entry reflects an anger and emotional awareness Thinking Donald could never express.

> **Diary Entry, August 21, 1981. Who the hell does my father think he is? He wrecks our minds mentally and sexually, then demands his 'fatherly' right to a relationship with his children. The fact he never stopped demanding that right really affected me more and more.**
>
> **It's as though he's always lurking about, ready to pounce on me.**
>
> **I'm nervous walking downtown, constantly aware of his being on the loose, free to confront me. It scares me. Someone who has totally controlled my life for 15 years surely would generate fear even after a five-year separation. He owned my body and used it however it pleased him. This total submission has affected my relationships with most men. If they are at all aggressive or domineering, I go into a shell and don't come out until that person is gone. It is so much a part of me, I hardly realize I behave this way at times.**

I soon discover that writing down my thoughts and feelings provides a great source of release. It is also a place to rationalize actions and project positive thinking. Other than Roland, I have no one to talk to about my innermost thoughts. My diary proves to be a much-needed friend. My interpretation of my religious beliefs will not allow for displays of anger, hate, or dysfunctional behavior. So writing down my history while at the same time gaining acceptance for my developing "Witness" personality seems contradictory. I know God reads my diary and that writing such feelings down will make them real to a certain extent. So while truthful, my entries are religious and focused toward justice.

Diary Entry, August 24, 1981. I definitely want justice but is it there for me to get? I'll have to wait and see. I believe God will vindicate His name in this matter. We are his Witnesses and we are telling the truth. Although I have spent many years feeling worthless, I am sure He loves me and my family and is on our side. This keeps me going. I am only doing this because I want justice and other innocent bystanders protected from such an evil man as my father. Why doesn't everyone want the same thing? If they only knew how child sexual abuse affects their children forever, they would.

I feel better tonight writing my feelings down. Jehovah God, please help me.

I believe I was writing in an assured manner to convince myself we were worthy of justice. I had to project a dynamic voice—it certainly wasn't to be found in my surroundings. Where did my sense of justice come from? My diary was an avenue for working through my emotions and feelings, penned by a naïve and much younger version of myself. When I began to write my journal, I performed the adult male role, but was childlike in many respects, having only filtered knowledge of the secular world. Its contents initially exhibited my repressed anger disguised by a "Pollyanna" outlook.

The diary helped but I also received unsolicited aid in making the ugly past a reality. Even after my father's arrest, he constantly wrote us. I knew my father was engaged in psychological warfare. His words were as intimidating as he was in my memory. I had not seen him in five years. He had been a self-righteous, controlling fanatic. I had hoped his arrest would prove to be a humbling experience for him. I thought perhaps that once the truth was revealed, my father would leave us alone. Instead, he became outraged by the charges which he considered a nuisance, angered by our complete independence from him, and seemed to attack us in writing with renewed religious vigor. How dare we charge him? He was the Christian, we were not he constantly reminded us. I refused to give in to his mind games.

Meanwhile, Daniel thought of two ways of deflecting attention away from his crime. First, he told his religious associates that he had only committed acts of abuse during the time he was a Witness, implying he had this "problem" only during those years. Second, he would initiate a conversation on the case so he could influence his listener.

Informing a fellow worker, David, that there had been a story about him in the paper, Daniel warned, "My ex-wife is digging up the past to get me to talk about who killed Georgia Jackson." He told David he knew who did it.

Daniel was masterful at deflecting responsibility. He didn't believe for a minute that Mother wanted him to talk about the Jackson case, but he conveniently, albeit unwittingly, concurs with Rhiness when he suggests Bodemer's confession was inconclusive.

If David and his wife, Fran, had only known how I celebrated my tenth birthday in their basement, they would have bought the paper and followed the case more closely.

Daniel waged a propaganda war. His need to win emerged as greater than any issues of personal shame.

It is not surprising my father might think he was being charged to dig up information on the Jackson case. If it were up to Elder Sandor, Max Leder, and Detective Rhiness, he would have been correct. The truth was he never would have dreamed that his quietest son, Donald, might be the instigator of the investigation. I had never told him how I felt about him, not in word or deed.

He wrote us several times insisting the Witnesses had put us up to this. Nothing could be further from the truth. I became more determined than ever to let the world know what kind of man Daniel D'Haene was. No one could understand what it was like to live with this sick and twisted man. Would anyone even try?

Chapter Thirty

One week after my doctor's appointment, I receive a call from a social worker named Wilf Graham at the St. Thomas Psychiatric Hospital. Mr. Graham sets up appointments for Marina and me on Fridays, from noon to 1:00 P.M. I feel self-conscious as this stranger speaks to me through the phone. I know it is my introduction to someone who will try to figure *me* out. Marina and I are anxious to start our sessions. There is so much to talk about. Where will we begin? What will our therapists be like?

I imagine a yawning shrink in a suit and tie, asking me to lie on a couch while he fills out a myriad of prescriptions for medication to cure me. I put on all my armor before going to meet this imaginary foe. I concoct possible dialogue exchanges:

"I think you should try an anti-depressant drug."

"Oh yeah! I'm outta here."

"The problem is your religion."

"Good-bye."

"You should experiment with sex."

"Thanks, but no thanks."

To a Witness, a therapist represents the Devil in sheep's clothing. He will act like he cares about me, but he lives to take me away from my faith. He might even want to have sex with me. What if I don't say no?

Keeping my appointment this Friday requires more strength than the other aspects of preparing for the trial. From my perception of my experience with Mom's divorce hearing, the court system is an abstract process that does not require intimacy. With that experience behind me, I have had no intention of ever discussing the past with anyone, especially a therapist. But now, faced with a therapist's couch, talking about "it" yet again—and one-on-one at that—seems more daunting than anything I have experienced before. I only like having the focus on me if I control the direction of that focus. I fear this new unknown variable.

I leave work early to stop at home and pick up my sister before heading to St. Thomas. No matter how determined I am, half of me expects to find a reason to quit within the first session with Mr. Graham. I make myself view the meeting as I would a job interview — I want to make a good impression, but I might not take the job on.

During the car ride, Marina and I review our individual worst-case scenarios. We agree to walk out at the mere suggestion of drug therapy or condemnation of our religion. As I park the car, I notice the outpatient sign on the side of the hospital building. I carefully photograph each moment in my memory.

I have contradictory emotions regarding this experience. I love the fact it will be something new, fear the event itself, and hate the idea of physically going into a psychiatric hospital. *It's for the trial,* I remind myself.

Each step towards therapy seems overwhelming. Oversized doors, unfamiliar surroundings, the hospital odor, bright ceiling lights, and speckled tile flooring lead to a cluttered reception desk. Imagine my surprise to find a fellow high school student asking, "May I help you?" My anxiety is masked by a friendly but false demeanor.

"Hi. Haven't seen you in a couple of years," I remark.

"Well, I went to college...."

I smile, without really listening to what she has to say. Does she still think I'm a nerd? She never acknowledged my existence in school, why is she bothering now? *I know, she's only doing her job,* I tell myself.

"Good luck with your career. I have an appointment to see Wilf Graham."

"It will only be a moment. Please, have a seat in the waiting room."

Marina fusses with her permed hair while I fidget with my tie.

"God, I hate this, Marina."

"This place has a weird smell."

"Oui, Eau de Institution."

"I'm nervous, Donald, but I think I'll be all right."

"Remember, I'll be in the next padded cell."

A woman in her mid-thirties, with short black hair and a friendly face greets us both but her eyes focus on Marina.

"Marina? Hi, my name is Patty."

I quickly critique her appearance: wine-colored pantsuit, no jewelry, blunt haircut, attractive in an unconventional way. She'll be all right for my sister.

"Donald, Mr. Graham will be with you in a moment."

"I don't mind waiting, thanks."

The black-haired lady with the white complexion takes my sister away. I don't worry about Marina though, sensing she will be safe. I pick a *Maclean's Magazine* and read the theater reviews.

"Don?"

A young man, probably in his late twenties, who looks like a modern-day Jesus greets me with a soft voice. I'm shocked at this picture: jeans, rolled up sleeves, tie, shoulder-length hair and beard. My shrink is a hippy! Thank God, Jesus is not my type. I was expecting a man purposely flaunting his masculinity. Instead, I find a sensitive man perhaps in touch with his feminine side, extending his hand. I feel one wall come tumbling down. I might give him a chance, I tell myself.

"The name is DonALD!"

"Okay, Donald, call me Wilf. Unfortunately, it's quite a walk to my office. We take what we can get."

The idea of a therapist admitting his office won't be exceptional impresses me. I really like that I can call him by his first name. Still each syllable he utters is dissected, catalogued, indexed for return fire. He is a man after all, and a worldly one at that. Wilf unlocks the door to a hole of a room with two chairs and a desk. Because I know everything I say will be scrutinized, I choose my words carefully.

"What, no couch?"

"You've seen too many movies." He laughs warmly and sincerely I note. It's a good start.

"You're right about that. I love movies."

"Have a seat."

There are no visuals to distract me so my eyes focus on the renegade-looking social worker seated before me. I have seen him before. I was visiting Sister Jane from the Aylmer Hall here last fall. Who would have dreamed he would be helping me now? Wilf leans back in his chair, folds his legs, and starts intermittently playing with his tie and pen. Studying his face, I conclude there is goodness behind those eyes. I remind myself his eyes are still blind because he doesn't know The Truth.

"Your doctor set up this appointment for you at your request. Obviously you feel the need to talk to someone. This hour is your time. We can talk about whatever you want. I'm here for you."

"Did the doctor tell you why I wanted to see someone?"

"No. I think it's better I hear it from you."

Shoot. I know it doesn't make any sense, but I've been hoping I wouldn't have to talk about my past again. I really don't know what therapy entails. I'll tell him what he needs to know. Why waste his time? I've decided I'll never lie to my therapist. I know he can't help me if I purposely deceive him.

Editing is not lying, I convince myself. I'll just choose my words carefully. Eventually I'll inform him of the events that led to my visit. I do not need to tell Wilf the only reason I'm here is that Rhiness said it would be helpful to my case. I need this social worker's help. I also sense that I could grow to like Wilf, and I don't want to scare him off before I'm sure. I'll tell him when the time is right.

Right now, I want to avoid detailed explanation of the "acts." I don't know how I was affected by the abuse anyway. Instead, I will focus on my sexuality, my family, and my religion—anything but the abuse. I have to tell him something to start with. I know, I'll tell him my "reason" for visiting his office, using the same words I used at Dr. Billingsley's office. It worked then...take a deep breath...1-2-3...go!

"I was sexually abused and I can't handle it!"

Wilf looks at me in silence. *"You're supposed to say something,"* I scream in my head.

"This isn't easy, you know. I don't know what I'm supposed to tell you."

"Donald...." He says my name with warmth and kindness. "I know this isn't easy. You don't have to say anything you don't want to. Talk about something you feel comfortable with."

"Okay."

I test Wilf, setting my ground rules early. I need to know he isn't anti-Witness, wouldn't approve of incest, and that he would not do therapy on my molester. Most of all, I need to know he won't try to have sex with me. My feelings on these issues are black and white and not up for debate. I do not understand why my concerns are so important to me. All I know is that I will not compromise them on any level.

"I'm a member of the Jehovah's Witnesses. My faith means more to me than anything. We have very strict beliefs and there is no way I can go against what I believe in. I don't want to."

"You don't have to feel threatened by this institution. I'm not out to get you to leave your faith. It's very important to you and I respect that. I've known Witnesses in my private life, and they are very good people."

"That's good to know, because if you think I'll talk against my religion, you can forget it...."

"I don't expect anything from you, Donald. You came here by your own free will and you can leave at any time, but I hope you won't leave. It's totally understandable that you are wary of trusting me. Who am I to you? Nothing but a stranger, a man with the title, 'social worker.' But I do what I do because I really want to make a difference in people's lives. I want to help. All I ask is that you give me a chance."

Everything I have experienced up to this point tells me not to trust anyone, yet there is something telling me to try to trust this stranger. Even so, wanting to trust does not mean I know how. I am not relaxed.

Wilf is passing my inspection. I'm not prepared for this. I have to switch gears. I'll tell him what's going on in my life. Maybe he can figure out something from that.

"I admit, I do have problems. I feel disconnected from the real world. I question my existence. I know I'm under a lot of pressure. It's like there are two of me. Coming here I told myself, 'Is there something really wrong with me, or is it something in my head that I'm imagining?' Even you, sitting in front of me, are not real to me.

"My past is a blur to me. I've blocked out most of it. When I meet someone I went to school with, they always remember me. I rarely remember them. During those years, I lived in my mind. The external me froze in time. I'd write chapters in an imaginary story as it happened.

"Pretending things are all right, living in a fantasy world and not facing issues is easier than being honest with myself, with my family, and with my congregation. It's not like they'll understand when I don't understand myself. Sometimes I think I'm crazy, and other times I think I'm perfectly fine. This may sound weird, but it's easier being honest with you because I don't know you."

"Doesn't sound weird to me. Tell me what it's like being you."

"I spend most of my time taking care of my family, working, and in Witness activities. I don't date, I don't have sex, or do anything unchristian except I do practice self-abuse. I do it more as a chore than as a pleasure. It seems stupid because I always had that done by Daniel—and by the way, I never, ever call him f-a-t-h-e-r—that creep encouraged me to do it myself. That's the only thing he ever taught me. I hate myself for it though. I thought it made me like him. Sometimes I'm suicidal with guilt."

I amaze myself with my own forthrightness. Why did I know it was unwise to reveal myself to my spiritual family, yet feel it's all right to confess my mental processes to a complete stranger? Should I confess my sins to this stranger? Dare I?

"I do have impure thoughts, Wilf."

I look for a frown or a disapproving scowl, but there are none.

"I am attracted to certain men. Not many, mind you. For example, I'm not attracted to you, because you have long hair and a beard. No offense."

"No offense taken."

"I think I am a homosexual in many ways."

"How are you a homosexual?"

"That's difficult to answer. No matter, that kind of sex is obviously unnatural. God made men and women so that their parts would fit. I am attracted to men, but I don't know what I would do with them. I certainly don't want to have sex with them. I just want the affection that should go with it. It does go with it, doesn't it? I hate it. It's sick. I can't stop thinking about it though. I do something awful. Oh, I can't say—"

"You don't have to say...."

"Once in a while, I get porn magazines—oh, I can't believe I'm telling you this—but only since last year when I went on this trip to the United States, and I saw a magazine with a naked man on the cover and it freaked me out 'cause I didn't know such a thing existed!"

I stop for a breath, then ramble on again.

"Of course, I had seen naked women in magazines before, but men —I find it disgusting and stimulating at the same time. I only like men by themselves though. Not if they are doing something with someone else. Isn't that strange?"

"It's not for me to—"

"You know what else is horrible? I can't buy it but I can look at it!"

"How do you 'get' the magazines then?"

"I know it doesn't make sense, but I can't buy this filth—but I can *take* it, if you know what I mean."

"Oh, I see. You 'sneak' it out of the store."

"Yeah, sneak it and don't take it back. How could I buy a porn magazine when I am a Witness? Sometimes I do though, I mean, pay for it. Either way, I feel so guilty I want to die. Right away, I destroy the magazine…but not before I've looked at the pictures! I can't keep it in our house! It's a vicious cycle. Death is my only way out. I don't talk about this with anyone, even my friend Roland in London. But he does. listen to me talk about the past and my sexuality. He's married. He's happy. I will never marry. Sorry for rambling…."

"I'm not here to judge your behavior or what you say. Sounds like you have enough on your plate to deal with. No wonder you feel like you're living off and on in a fog."

Wilf's words are shocking and reassuring. He doesn't flinch at my scandalous stories of sin. If I had known therapy could be like this, I might have pursued it earlier. Why is it easier to talk about my sin than the past?

"It is important for you to decide what you want in life, Donald—to be a homosexual or a heterosexual—a very important decision."

"I wasn't expecting this. Wow. I can't decide that. How can I? I haven't even experienced normal sex with a man or a woman. There is no choice. I love God and he hates homosexuals. My religion will not accept homosexuals as members, but is willing to help those with such problems to overcome it."

Programmed answers for a serious question. I feel lost. Wilf believes as the Witnesses do, that sexual orientation is a choice. I am totally confused about my identity. I am incapable of deciding if I want to be homosexual or heterosexual. Acting out a variety of roles is definitely more comfortable than deciding which Donald I might want to be. In this, my first session with Wilf, I am faced with issues I cannot comprehend. My thoughts are consumed with the outcome of the upcoming trial and my recurring flashbacks. Deciding my orientation is the least of my worries, or so I tell myself.

There is something logical in the way Wilf talks. He has no reason to lie to me. I still don't trust him completely, but at the very least, I hope I will learn to. Regardless, Wilf thinks I should look at my sexuality. The fact that he confronts me with this head-on scares me, but I decide to try. I don't want to be a homosexual, but I cannot deny certain things: my sexual confusion, my attraction to male figures, my need to be loved by a man.

I am surprised how open I am with Wilf. I feel comfortable with him and at the same time anxious. My problems are confusing me, and I'm very upset as I notice Wilf look at his watch. I don't want to crack up and be sent home.

"Thanks for seeing me, Wilf. This is new to me. I'm having a hard time but I am trying."

"I know you are, Donald. I look forward to seeing you next Friday."

Wilf extends his hand. I find it more difficult to shake his hand saying good-bye. I could care about this person and I hate that fact. He firmly grips my hand. He is warm and alive. I feel dead inside.

What I thought therapy was and its reality are two completely different things. I am glad I like Wilf, yet at the same time, I fear what lies ahead.

I mouth the word good-bye. I walk the long corridor to the waiting room to find Marina. Something is starting that I do not want to end. A window to a world outside my own?

Somehow I know I will never be the same.

Chapter Thirty-One

"For the first time in your life, someone was focusing on the real Donald. How did you feel?"

"Overwhelmed, Maurice."

* * * * * * * * * *

On a humid August evening, I travel to the home of a new acquaintance in London. We have planned a weekend get-a-way for some time, and I look forward to some rest and relaxation.

Driving to Steve's place, I have to pass by the factory where Daniel works. Out of nowhere, I experience a panic attack, imagining my father jumping into my car and assaulting me.

Are objects closer than they appear?

This is ridiculous. I'm driving fifty miles an hour. It's impossible for Daniel to reach me. Yet I'm shaking and my eyes water. By the time I arrive at Steve's house, I recover enough to be polite. But as we talk about impersonal things, I feel terrible pain inside, overwhelmed by my problems.

That night I write in my diary:

Diary Entry, September 1, 1981. I want to be a member of my faith and I want to have a normal sexual relationship with a woman. I want to desire a woman, but I want the love of a man, too. I want to be kissed, touched, and loved by a man—for me, and me only. I think I am seeking a father in a man, the love instead of the sex, sex, and more sex that I received and gave to my real father. Because I think I have

experienced love of a man only through sex, I can only think of men in those terms. I hope Wilf will understand who and what the hell I am because, right now, I sure don't.

To me, there are two sides of me. One is dictated by my mind, the other by my heart. My brain tells me the kinds of things that can happen because of homosexual relationships, but my heart tells me that's what I want. The next time Wilf asks me to decide, I still won't be able to give him an answer.

I think I am scared of sex itself. I have read about what men do with other men and it is revolting to me. I feel like throwing up thinking about those acts. But intercourse with a woman seems dirty to me too.

To me a life ahead of me like this seems quite empty and lonely.

My journal continued to be a strong tool in dealing with my conflicts. It became a healthy space to work through my problems and reflect on events and people in my life.

The diary entry conveys the confusion I lived through. Although I had just experienced an anxiety attack related to my abuse, I focused on my sexual dilemma. In my mind, it represented the lesser of two evils. I was taught from birth that homosexuality is wrong. For non-believers who study with Witnesses, once you find "The Truth," you're supposed to quit the practices. Of course, as I was celibate, I didn't have to make that choice, but my memories of The Game, my confused sexual identity, and the many role reversals in my family all contributed to my internal struggle.

The sexual confusion I felt is common among male abuse victims. I have found that this confusion is played out in both young gay and straight men who were abused. There were no books at the library saying, "It's okay to be confused." A person cannot go through this experience and not be traumatized. The questions, "Am I gay?" and "If so, is it because of the abuse?" are universal. The quest to change sexual orientation is also a classical theme among victims. Sexual abuse is in no way a form of education as my father suggested. It takes the normal human self-discovery process on numerous detours.

The Donalds were called on to handle this dilemma. Rational Donald follows the Witness and societal party line. Feeling Donald feels the need for male sexual contact. Rational Donald protests, "I do not feel guilty." Feeling Donald says nothing regarding the guilt. Did he even feel it? It was left to Rational Donald to decide, but decide what?

How naïve and innocent of me to believe I could possibly decide my sexual orientation from one therapy session to the next.

And once again my actions were full of contradictions. I was a close-mouthed individual, yet I discussed my sexual confusion with a stranger. My faith disapproved of therapy but I initiated the experience. Left on my own, I wouldn't have pursued counseling. Although I was strong-spirited in some ways, in others, I was craving direction and leadership. I had been self-reliant for several years; to pursue this court action required trusting others. Trust in a doctor, trust in a legal authority, trust in a social worker, trust in the whole judicial system. I did not trust them, but I had to force myself to go through the motions in order for our case to progress.

The following morning, Steve and I prepare for our trip to Kleinburg to see the McMichael Collection. I can't wait to see the works of Emily Carr. There is such passion screaming from the broad strokes of her brush. My world is expanding and I find the road of discovery wonderfully enlightening. My life is changing and it is difficult to understand. More and more people are responding to The Donald I present to them. They appear to like him. How could so many people not like me before, and now I find it difficult to accept any intimacy or invitation of friendship? Do they feel sorry for me? Although my distrust of their motives prevents me feeling any intimacy from these new friendships, I do not wish to deny myself the experience and I won't.

In Kleinburg, Steve and I stop at a gift shop. I notice a young man in his early twenties staring at me. At first I assume he is looking at someone behind me, until I actually check to make sure. Embarrassed, yet pleased at this attention, I smile shyly back. I think he might be one of those homosexuals. I find this a strange predicament. I like the fact he might like me and at the same time I know I'm supposed to feel guilty. I certainly don't want to be with this person. I'd freak out if he so much as touched me. I can't mention it to Steve because he's straight, and he'd never understand my conflicting feelings about this attention.

When I get home, I telephone Roland and tell him about my great weekend trip. Roland always encourages my interest in the arts, and I know he will be genuinely happy for me. I also mention the stranger's flirting with me. He points out that in the world of the gay community, flirting in public places is a common way of meeting new people.

"You never associate with the world, and you've lived such a hermit's life. You're innocent about a lot of things, Donald."

I know I have lived an isolated life, but innocent?

"I never knew that went on. It was an extraordinary experience. But Roland, I have to be honest. Although I would have walked away if he had come up to me, I liked the idea he was attracted to me just the same."

"We're all human. Remember to pray to God to resist temptation."

"Oh, I do. I feel guilty so I know that's a good sign. You know I'd never do anything."

That night, Mom, Marina, and I watch two television programs on homosexuality.

"God hates t'ose acts!" Mom preaches. "How disgusting."

Marina and I remain silent, hugging our pillows extra tight. What a coincidence this happens so close to my Kleinburg experience, or is it? I don't hate the homosexual people on the television program, but I don't understand why they perform those abnormal acts. I'm attracted to the relationship aspect of two men together but the sex scares me. Why am I experiencing all this gay stuff after Wilf asks me if I want to be a homosexual? I'm sure it's the Devil trying to tempt me.

Just before we go to bed, there's a knock on the front door. Since we don't expect a visitor at this late hour, I marvel at how scared I feel—it might be Daniel!

"Oh, it's you, Brother Smith."

No one can fully appreciate what a relief it will be when Daniel *is* in jail.

Chapter Thirty-Two

It's therapy day again. Even though I look forward to seeing Wilf again, I hate the thought of driving to the hospital. *"Crazy people live there,"* I tell myself, but as soon as I'm sitting in the warm atmosphere of Wilf's office, I willfully replace my anxiety with positive thoughts.

"Wilf, I've been feeling better the last couple of days because I've tried to put the trial out of my mind. It feels good just sharing my problems with you, having someone to talk to. This therapy thing is nothing like what I expected. I thought you would tell me what to do."

"My role is to provide a listening ear. I don't have a lot of experience working with victims of sexual abuse, but that doesn't mean I can't help you. You have the more difficult position because you will have to do the work. You've taken the first step in reaching out to someone."

"I'm just amazed how many things I still have to overcome, things which I've accepted as part of my existence."

"What do you mean?"

"Well, I feel weird, abnormal."

"How are you so different from everyone else?"

"My experiences have somehow made me different in a negative way."

"Donald, you're not responsible for what happened to you."

"That's so strange to me. I don't know when I began to feel this way, but I thought I was very low to have those relations with Daniel. However, by the age of ten, I wanted those practices and he encouraged this feeling in me. I felt like a prostitute. Since I hated the sight and touch of him, the only way I could have relations with him was to make myself think I was dirt. Then I could enjoy my satisfaction in the relationship in certain ways, without feeling too guilty or getting too sick of him. Later on, I would never touch him unless he satisfied me first or at the same time. This happened especially in the last three years. His touch disgusted me so much that I would leave myself."

"How so?"

"Well, it's like although my body was there and I was experiencing it, I removed myself from the situation, like I flew away to somewhere else. I can't tell you what it felt like because I wasn't there. The Donald sitting before you now was not in *his* room, ever. I feel like I'm telling you about scenes from a movie. They're black and white, in clear focus, but it's not me in the frame. I've never cried because of what happened. I'm angry for what happened to my brothers, my sister and my mother though."

Wilf has such a kind face. I think I can tell him anything. I hope he'll never want to have sex with me. I'd be so disappointed.

"I think all men are perverts. I hate men. I pretend I don't, but I do. I freeze around males in my world who are mean to their wives and their children. There is shame attached to anything masculine. I never wanted to be masculine. Daniel is and I never wanted to be like him. I also don't trust men, perhaps anyone. I don't know how anymore. I just know how to pretend I do. It's like there is more than one of me. A body is sitting here in your office, but I'm somewhere else. He relays information to me. Sometimes I think I'm just crazy. Oh, my God, I must sound like it. What do you think?"

"You are not crazy, Donald. You've experienced very traumatic things, and separating yourself from the abuse was your way of surviving."

"But it wasn't traumatic. I can't lie and say it was! I don't feel anything about what happened. I have hazy memories of a Donald who ripped an emotional cord from his soul, but for reasons unrelated to the abuse. I hate Daniel for everything else he was. Oh, I just had a flashback...the past...I can't believe all that happened. Even though we don't talk about the past, we sure remember things in detail. Some of it seems hysterical in retrospect. The day we left Daniel, we were scared to death of him. And what did he do? He called the police to tell them Mom stole his sewing machine! A *frickin'* sewing machine! He is an evil man and I've always known it. I think I hate him because I figured out he was lying about Mom. He made her out to look like the bad one...."

"Donald, I won't ask you to talk about things unless you are ready to."

"Don't worry, I can talk about it without feeling anything. I could tap dance while I tell you my story."

"That's one of my concerns. I don't think you should reveal things until you feel you're ready. I notice you've brought a writing pad."

"I've been writing stuff down on paper. I can write more openly than I can talk things out. I wondered if you wanted to read it. It might help you understand me better."

"I appreciate your gesture of trust in me, but as this is only our second session, I think you need to really reconsider your willingness to leave something so personal with me. You don't know me and I don't know you. I haven't earned your trust yet."

"Hmm. I see what you mean."

"I also notice you're using an old notebook for your diary. We have to appreciate personal feelings and experiences, Donald. You're really cheapening your experiences and expressions by using an old notebook. I'll bring a book from home for you to write in."

"You don't have do that but thanks. I just thought it would be easier to have you read how I feel than for me to tell you."

"Easier for you, you mean. It will be more helpful for you if you tell me when the time is right."

"I'm afraid, okay? Afraid of many things, some of which I'm not consciously aware of. Others, I know about—I am afraid of commitments. I don't want to get hurt so I avoid close relationships. I'd rather kill the closeness before it gets to that stage. Even though my mind tells me I am only hurting myself by doing this, I still do it. Is it a sick desire to hurt people because I've been hurt? I'm not sure. I think I feel commitment in a friendship means changing myself to suit the other person. I've done that a lot and ended up a mess.

"I can't stand being touched by men or women. Especially if someone comes from behind and touches me before I know who it is. Oooh! It makes my skin crawl—I don't know why. Is that sick and stupid? I try to forget it as much as I can. The fact that I don't like being touched is so sad to me. I am missing out on so much. You know, just talking about problems honestly and talking about what I'm thinking helps me. Other than with my friend Roland, I never reveal what I'm really thinking."

"That's what I'm here for. Confidentiality is an important part of building trust. Before we end our session today, I want to ask you a question. Do you want me to go to the trial?"

"I…ah…I don't know how to react to that."

"You don't have to give me an answer now. Just think about it. I want you to know you don't have to be alone. I'll be there for you if you want. Well, we have to wrap things up for this week…."

"I hate having a timer on our meetings, Wilf. There's so much more to say. I hate good-byes."

I planned topics I wanted to discuss with Wilf, but our conversation flowed in unpredictable directions. I could have reacted to Wilf's questions by what I thought I should say, but he wanted honesty from me. I felt sorry I told him I had to think about whether he should go with me to the trial. I didn't want to hurt his feelings, but I also hesitated because it meant commitment to something, to someone, perhaps even to this therapy. I was afraid that after I committed myself, Wilf would himself back off and I'd be hurt again. At the time I wasn't ready for anything real. I lived in the world of the abstract.

It's such an obvious contradiction to me now—while I admitted I hated being touched, feared closeness and the unknown, and I mistrusted everyone—I didn't think the sexual abuse affected me. Of course it did and Wilf knew it. He listened and listened as I recounted story after story.

He helped me see there was no level of my existence that had not been tarnished by my father's touch.

Pedophiles who develop relationships with their victims are calculating and manipulative. They are able to abuse for longer periods of time and are able to brainwash their victims. Although they are obsessed with committing their crime, they are also keenly aware of the need for self-preservation. Over a period of years, my father successfully convinced his children that we were equally responsible for The Game. Hence, disclosure became less likely.

Displaced anger is a trait common to victims. We hate and distrust people who are "guilty" of nothing more than offering us a sympathetic ear. Such is the extent of the damage caused by child abuse.

Sometimes we hear only what we want to hear. When Wilf said he didn't want to read my diary because it wasn't the proper time, I only heard, "I don't want to read your diary." In hindsight, I know that if Wilf had read my journal, I could have avoided having to discuss my feelings. Wilf didn't want to give me the easy way out. I was impressed that he caught on to a couple of my games so early on. I thought I used an old school book for my diary because I didn't want to waste paper. I was shocked that Wilf would connect the tattered book with how I felt and thought about myself. He was right.

When he asked me how I thought I felt different from other people, the real question was, "Is there any way you are the same as everyone else?" Besides dealing with the abuse and the sexual confusion, I also belonged to a sectarian faith. How could I not be different?

During the first two decades of my life, I never questioned my faith. As a teenager, I hadn't planned on becoming a devout Witness, but I did not doubt my mother's "Trut'." I was drowning in a sea of self-hate and depression unable to make even simple decisions. My religion seemed to provide the life preserver I needed.

Jehovah's Witnesses believe the world as we now know it is coming to an end. Only a relatively few who are faithful up until the end will survive the future Armageddon.

In that sense, life as a Jehovah's Witness is comparable to being on the Titanic in its final hour. Some passengers are aware that the ship is sinking and are getting into the lifeboats, but most are either oblivious to the fact they will soon perish, or remain skeptical, so they keep singing songs and sipping champagne. Those fortunate few who make it to the tiny lifeboats are secure, knowing that they have been chosen. They live with the stench of death permeating the air, as mankind drowns all around them.

This knowledge gives one an incomparable awareness. Since so few people are to survive the final days, when you believe you have The Truth, a sense of superiority is inevitable but seldom acknowledged. I always felt like an alien sent from another galaxy and plopped on earth. *Why me? Who was I to be in the know? Was I being tortured now as penance for a future reward?*

Being considered a freak became overwhelming. But the reality of being viewed as odd by my fellow Witness survivors felt like being on hallucinogenic drugs—how do you make sense of the madness? *Why bother surviving? Why would I want to live forever with people who don't really know me?*

Initially, my naïveté carried me through some turbulent waters. I didn't feel I had a choice. Why reject a life preserver when the other options equal death? I experienced a measure of happiness knowing that the boat I had climbed into might make it to its destination. I couldn't foresee the future, but my religion did provide temporary sanctuary.

Chapter Thirty-Three

"How could you go to church with all that was going on?" asks Maurice.

"Are you kidding? Without my religion, my beliefs, I would have gone mad, as bad memories were becoming reality more and more. I remember I would drift off, then pop back into reality."

I told him my faith was a great source of strength. Religion played a role in explaining my survival. Belief in God gave me the stamina to go on. Throughout my parents' marriage, there were Witnesses who recognized the control my father had over my mother as unchristian behavior. As far we children were concerned, when Witnesses expressed their empathy about our mother's situation, they were setting a Christ-like example.

"Many Witnesses helped my family, going beyond the call of duty, and we understood that as long as we remained Witnesses, that help would be forthcoming."

"But at what cost?"

"Well, believing the Witnesses were the only Christians did confuse me. These were imperfect men and women who were good people, but no better or worse than 'worldly' people I knew. And when I reviewed my situation, I recognized that although I was part of this faith, more fortunate than the unbelieving world surrounding me, my family definitely had more than its share of problems. I wondered, *How could second-rate Christians, which was how I considered us, be better than non-believers who were kind and good-hearted despite what I had been taught?*

"My religion held both comfort and confusion."

* * * * * * * * * *

Rhiness and our therapists came into our life at a time when we needed them. No one from the Kingdom Hall encouraged us to initiate a conversation with a detective, let alone a psychiatrist. Marina and I consider ourselves fortunate that Rhiness needed a therapist's statement. In light of our religious environment in 1981, it was a brave move for Marina and me to seek out therapy.

Initial reaction from acquaintances was, as we had expected: "If you have God, why do you need therapy?" I was a Witness asking a worldly, "non-Christian" for support and advice. What if we caused our therapists "to stumble" from seeing "The Truth" by talking about our troubles? We aren't supposed to leave a negative impression on worldly people. The possibility that our problems stemmed from the abuse was never acknowledged or understood. Some believed we didn't love God or study our Bible enough.

Seeking therapy and charging our father were considered selfish actions by others. It is important to note that these messages were delivered by a vocal few, and it is safe to say none of these people have had experience dealing with the complex issues involved in sexual abuse. Unfortunately, I felt a need to explain our choices, and unwittingly opened the door to more disapproving comments.

I continued my therapy, even though I too viewed Wilf as one of Satan's disciples. After all, if a person wasn't serving God, who else was there to serve?

I've met loving people in my life before my therapist, but the contrast between Witness help and that of my therapist is that Wilf supports me without expectations as to my behavior, and his help is unconditional.

Wilf sees me as a wounded soul and only wants to help in any way he can. With his patience, his caring, and his nurturing, over such a relatively short period of time, I seem to be progressing swiftly. In Wilf, I find someone who admits his imperfections, someone I trust as much as I can, and someone I believe won't lie to me. I know my mother loves me, but I know everything she says to me is to maintain me as the Christian son. I trust her love for me, but not her judgment.

All the manifestations of help I have received before beginning this therapy were designed to make me not feel pain, to help me deny my feeling self and instead, rely on God to solve my problems. That makes intellectual sense to me, and it is a path I easily gravitate to since everyone surrounding me validates this road to denial.

A Witness friend invites me out for coffee.

"Do you think you're special, Donald?" asks Jody.

"Well, I ...I don't know."

"Well, you aren't. Here's a book for you to read, *Your Erroneous Zones* by Dr. Wayne Dyer. It really helped me."

I really like her personality and spunk, but Jody's insinuation hurts deeply. I am only twenty, she, thirty-eight. Her message is sincerely delivered but I hear: You, Donald D'Haene, are not worthy.

After the two decades I just survived, feeling special is a comforting concept.

I appreciate the book, though. I devour it with a passion and it sends my life in a completely different direction. I'm now a believer in Dyer's philosophy. The problem is, I am too successful. I use the information, compute it in my brain, and print out a new "Donald."

My friend in London notices my extreme change.

"You need to feel some of the steps along the way," Roland warns.

"I don't know what you are talking about. I am feeling better. Isn't that the most important thing?"

Of course, I don't listen to him. I don't know how to stop the process. I have found a new obsession. As a new convert, I buy another book by Dr. Dyer, *Pulling Your Own Strings*: I learn no matter what circumstance you are in, you can take control of your life.

I have never read self-help books before. Most of my reading time is dedicated to Witness literature which provides positive spiritual food and wonderful examples of what a normal family life is. The problem is I can't see anything remotely resembling my life in them. I have tried to make my family fit the model of Witness behavior and I have failed miserably. That doesn't mean I will ever quit trying, but I am searching for direction. I am a student craving information. In Dyer's book, I read about dysfunctional people that somewhat resemble me and my family. I realize that whatever past you have experienced, it is only by living in the present that will improve your quality of life. I become the master student.

This escape conflicts somewhat with my therapy. Wilf wants me to feel. I think it is better if I feel nothing, a choice that is validated by most people in my life. Nothing I have experienced has prepared me for the sincerity, encouragement, and determination of my therapist.

Consequently his messages are repeated again and again: feel, express, let go. I try, but I cannot. I progress intellectually. I am developing awareness, understanding, and an ability to express the hitherto unspoken in words.

"Donald, why don't Witnesses encourage therapy?" Wilf asks.

"They disapprove because they believe that members would be inviting worldly, satanic thinking into their lives."

"But what if therapy is a life-saving option?"

"Even though they discourage it, they don't forbid it. Obviously not, I'm sitting here right now. There are two kinds of people in my life. Witnesses say, 'Stop blaming Daniel for the problems. Face them and accept full responsibility.' What they are telling me is if I don't turn out right, it is my fault and my fault alone. You say, 'Stop blaming yourself for your problems and feelings. The problems and feelings you have are due to the things Daniel did to you and are a result of the environment you grew up in.' I know you don't pity me."

"But I am concerned about you."

"I'm trying to figure out why. Marina says her therapist helps her because it's her job and she's paid to do it. I'm not so sure. I want to believe you are my friend. If I can't believe that, I wouldn't let you in. Ever."

There were subjects I avoided with Wilf, such as the real reason I sought therapy, but I longed for our sessions. I wasn't used to having someone center his attention on me. I was the one who focused on other people: on my family, on Roland, and on people in my religion. It was such a new experience.

I found myself thinking about my Friday appointments more than anything else. It was becoming yet another obsession. They became more important than my Witness meetings, or even the trial. Everything I experienced, I related in terms of how Wilf would respond to my telling him about it. Going to work or to the meetings was just putting in time until I saw Wilf again.

If I had believed that Wilf was helping me only because it was his job and that he really did not care about me, I would not have made the progress I did. He knew that too. Since my experience with Wilf, I've heard of some terrible experiences other victims have had with therapy. I know how fortunate I was.

I realized a therapist's role was not that of a friend. I did not expect to see Wilf outside of our roles as social worker and patient.

On some level though, the relationship between a victim and his therapist is more intense than that of a friendship. At the time of our sessions, I certainly viewed Wilf as a friend. No one had listened to how I felt with such loving care up to that point. He was the first person outside my family to not only witness the "Donalds," but to acknowledge their existence.

Although my appearance was that of an adult by this point, I needed to be parented in healthy ways, as though I were a child. My therapy became an important first step towards emotional recovery. I so craved and needed the unconditional love that Wilf was showing me. There are victims who progress with other forms of therapy. But I wouldn't let a therapist scale the walls that my survival had required, had he not shown an interest beyond the limits of a sixty-minute session.

Diary Entry, September 7, 1981. Now I know more than ever the reasons I had to seek help, and I'm glad I did. I just wish something was done years earlier. Better yet, the abuse should have been prevented. We don't have to give up though. We have no right to give up. To give in to people. To give into the past. No way. I feel I want to make something of my name. My family doesn't have the same goal. We should be like faceless people in a large crowd, they feel. They have no respect for our name. I resent that. I try so hard to make something of myself, practically against all odds. But the failures and letdowns make me try so much harder.

Wilf is my friend. He cares about me and finally I care about him. I felt the need to reach out to somebody so I called Wilf at home. He said he didn't mind. I believe him. That was very important to me. Wilf said I was a nice person. I want to believe him.

Chapter Thirty-Four

As I continued the journey of examining my problems, my home life became a battlefield. Marina and Erik, both extroverts like their eldest brother, were expressing their true feelings. They showed disrespect towards authority figures and hatred for conventional behavior, attire, and manners. Their abuse was real to them. They hated living in Aylmer as much as I did, but they knew they had to escape.

Today, newspapers report another court appearance by Daniel.

Jury trial sought in morals case

St. Thomas (Bureau) – A London man facing 10 sex-related charges chose to be tried by judge and jury when he appeared in provincial court Tuesday...Daniel D'Haene...is to appear in provincial court Nov. 26 for a preliminary hearing. – *The London Free Press*, Sept. 19, 1981

I delivered *The London Free Press* for three years to make extra money. I think it is time Erik contributes to the household income and convince him to take on a route. At first he likes the idea, but within a few weeks, he balks at the early morning trek.

This morning the big blow came to set today's tone. Erik has only pretended to deliver his newspapers. Several complaints to his newspaper representative leads to an investigation. Erik has taken a food cart from a grocery store, dumped his papers into it and set them on fire. The cart was found in a nearby ditch.

The Aylmer police and our congregation will be involved with us again. Although I will see him through this once more, I feel very depressed right now.

"Why did you do this?" asks Erik's newspaper representative.

"'Cause I did," answers Erik with a smirk on his face. "I don't want to do it!"

His boss is understanding. He knows Erik has other troubles and is willing to give him another chance.

"Well, you're just going to have to," I tell my brother. "Everyone has to help out the family."

No sooner does he restart the route and there are more complaints.

"Sorry about that. I'll bring a paper right over, Ma'am."

When I arrive, Mrs. Smith asks me in. She seems to have something more on her mind than the fact Erik failed to deliver her paper.

"Is Erik giving you other problems?" I ask.

"Yes, and our neighbors too! Your brother delivers Mr. Wilson's paper as well. He took his milk bottles three days in a row. Mr. Wilson caught him and tried to scare Erik from doing it again."

"Erik told me a story about finding milk tokens and giving them to the milk man. He was trying to help us by giving us milk. I'm sorry he did this, but I know in his mind he meant well."

"I understand. Just from listening to Erik talk, I knew there was something wrong with him. The neighbors and I figured out Erik was one of the abused children from the clippings in the paper. It's understandable the way he's behaving. Even Mr. Wilson understands. He was just trying to get Erik not to steal anymore. Are you all getting some kind of psychiatric help?"

"Yes, we are."

"That's terrific. Nothing to be ashamed of. I sympathize with your family's situation."

Here a complete stranger acknowledges the trial and shows empathy for our situation. This effort to try to understand is appreciated.

Erik explains things so well. He can act to a "T," and almost convinces himself he is lying for a good cause—to help the family out. This is another sign Erik needs more help than Elder Surin or I can give him.

Later in the evening, we missed our Witness meeting because Erik, Mom, and Marina argued until it was too late for us to go. Then, when I don't feel like going, Mom says, "You're giving up again."

Because Elder Surin expected us to be at the meeting, he stops by afterward.

"Erik, you'll have to explain yourself 'cause I'm not doing it for you anymore."

Erik tells the story.

"Well Erik, I think you're going to end up a delinquent but that's because this is what you want."

"I don't believe that," I interject. "I don't know why he's doing it, but I think it has something to do with everything he's experienced and witnessed growing up."

"You're using the past as an excuse, and Erik more than any of you. Discipline is the answer."

Although I agree with him, I get the feeling we are again ranked as nothing. Why is every decision by a D'Haene reflective of the entire household? We have the problems we have because it's our fault—we didn't bring Erik up right, or he is following in the footsteps of his father or his eldest brother.

I feel terrible. I try so hard to keep going but I always get kicked in the face along the way. I have enough problems, yet I can't back out now. I believe Erik would have a better life in a foster home away from us!

Erik is so stubborn that any request for help is refused, every suggestion scoffed at, every meeting attended disrupted. Wilf has encouraged me to break out of my role as disciplinarian, but that's easier said than done. What's going to happen to Erik if I let him do what he wants? How can any of us feel safe?

It is obvious to everyone that Erik is a disturbed child.

Mother is helpless. "I do not know what I am going to do wit' him."

Witnesses are judgmental.

"He just needs a swift kick in the behind."

Wilf is understanding.

"Obviously Erik is rebelling against rules because he is in pain."

I don't know what to do or who to believe.

A guidance counselor from East Elgin Secondary School calls to tell Mom that Erik is having difficulties. They feel he needs special help since, "he is obviously disturbed in some way." It seems every day I come home, Erik's into some problem. I refuse to blame myself for this anymore. I'm trying my best, and as his brother, I can only do so much.

What a day! Marina and Erik reject everything I tell them. Although I've kept them from running the streets, they're going to have to learn that life could be equally difficult on their own. We should save all our strength to survive the trial next month.

Later in the day, Erik kicks me but I refuse to fight back. I am trying not to retaliate, but then there is no order in the house. I know I need outside help.

I schedule a meeting to talk with Erik's new counselor, Lance Batram, to take place right before my appointment with Wilf. I am there for an hour and I feel better, focusing on Erik's problems.

I discuss my dilemma with Wilf.

"Wilf, I've been a little better, but I'm feeling the pressures of raising Marina and Erik more and more, especially when they get into trouble. Erik tried to pick a fight and Marina swore at me. I just told them to leave me alone. Things are worse for us than people know. People don't want to hear how it really is living in our world. They think we're complaining, pitying ourselves. There isn't time for that. I hope Batram can help Erik, but I still feel responsible. I am sure they take me for granted. I know they rely on me to take care of finances, and they are content living that way. Although they have struggles and hurts, they don't know what responsibility is. All they want to do is play, have fun, and sit around doing no work. What a life!"

"That sounds normal for teenagers, though, doesn't it, Donald? When do you have fun?"

"I haven't got time for that. My siblings are so immature. If it isn't one creating a problem, it's the other."

"Why isn't your mother the one who is the disciplinarian?"

"Oh God, that's a long story. The short version is that Marina and Erik don't respect Mom."

Wilf's countenance tells me he is more interested in the long version.

"Well, Mom...she has no control over them. She hasn't since we left Daniel. So a long time ago, I thought: Am I going to let this family fall apart, or am I going to take control? I decided to take over. I want them to have a better life so at least they can find a happiness that I haven't found. The problem is they haven't learned anything by having me do everything for them. They haven't matured as I have, because they were not forced into that position."

"You have to let them have responsibility too, allowing them to learn from their own mistakes. You're not doing them a favor by bailing them out every time they have a problem."

"Marina and Erik want out of the house because things are so terrible for them. Well, they also make things difficult for me. I often tell them I just want peace and quiet but I never get it. Actually I believe it would be better in some ways, but their reasons for leaving are not mature. They are common to teenagers who want their independence. Would Marina really be happy on her own? Everyone tells me she doesn't act like an eighteen-year-old—more like thirteen. So how could I let her leave without feeling guilty?

"How can I do things for myself when it takes so much time to handle Marina and Erik? They don't want me to give them advice, yet they want my money, food, and home. Altho ugh something terrible might happen in the future, I can't handle things too much differently than I do now. Marina and Erik want me to move away and take them with me to find some place where we will be wanted and loved. I just won't let myself even think of leaving until after our name is cleared up, and I won't run away from problems. Marina and Erik say if something they do is wrong or goes wrong, it will be because I didn't move away. Either choice I take, people will disagree with it. I am determined to stick to my decisions no matter what!"

"Perhaps they're just being normal," Wilf suggests, "and you're the one with too much on your plate."

"I know that, but I can't help myself. It hurts too much to see them suffer."

"What about your own pain, Donald?"

"I don't like talking about negative things. Pain is a negative."

"I understand. Last week you talked about feeling 'weird and different.' What was school like for you?"

Why is Wilf changing the subject? I want to talk about what's bothering me today, September 28, 1981! I stare at Wilf in silence.

"Donald, are you okay?"

"I'm remembering.... I don't like talking about it. School was the most distressing part of my life. It's a difficult thing to talk about. The D'Haene name sounds like a swearing word just as the word 'Papa' does. We were always called 'D'Haene' at school, but it was always said with a sneer in their voices that expressed disgust and hatred toward us.

"I wish I was kidding but I'm not. Actually I think I'm describing this too sweetly. People cringed when they saw us. It was very painful to take but I did. I know I should have fought back but I didn't.

"Those were very lonely years. I grew up eventually hating everyone, especially men and male students. Sometimes, the guys would hug me in front of their friends, either in the halls or even in the washrooms. I was the fag joke of the school.

"I now see the reasons are many why this happened to me. I was different. I never swore, smoked, acted-up. I was never any good at sports, which made everything worse. I had what I have read are called a 'substantial buttocks' and a slim waist, so people said I had a 'girl's body.' I had a high-pitched voice and long eyelashes. Once I was voted 'the second longest eyelashes on a guy' at school. Thrill of my life. I felt cursed." Wilf does not interrupt me. Nor does he take notes.

"Our pants and shirts were so outdated it wasn't funny. Actually, it was funny! I wore every color of the rainbow until I managed to save enough for my first pair of blue jeans. The only masculine thing about me then was my name and my crew-cut." Wilf and I share a laugh, which breaks up the tension.

"I have to laugh at those things now, or I'd jump off the bridge down the street. How could I face those things? I couldn't talk about them. I thought I hated everyone except my mother. I only thought about suicide!"

I am not entertaining Wilf with my story now. I see in his eyes that he wishes I had not gone through the things I did.

"When people hear me mention I felt that way, I get some strange reactions. For some it's shocking. Others say, 'Them's the breaks, kid,' or 'You didn't appreciate all you had in life.' I agree. I didn't appreciate the fact that I was alive and how precious life is! Here I go again, explaining away a very painful part of my life. What a life to appreciate! I am only telling you this because it's you. I can't talk about this anymore—too much pain!"

"You are a strong person, Donald. But you have suffered and should be allowed to feel, express the pain for all your experiences. Kids can be very cruel."

"I was easy to pick on. I blame myself more than them."

"You don't have to rationalize others' behavior. You didn't deserve what happened to you. You were feeling different because your life experiences were not normal. It's not your fault. Your father having touched you sexually robbed you of anything approaching a normal childhood. A father is supposed to teach his children principles of right and wrong and demonstrate a normal love for his children. Instead, your father destroyed his relationship with you. You needed counseling when you were a child."

"I hear the words you are saying and I want to believe you, but I've separated the two—I am a freak, and then there's this abuse thing."

"It's common for abused children to blame themselves for their negative feelings. You are not alone and not to blame—"

"Words, words, words! Just more words. They don't change the way I feel."

After leaving Wilf's office, I try to re-charge my batteries before going back to work. I am very late but no one says anything. Everyone is very quiet—almost too quiet. I wonder what that means.

That night I write:

Diary Entry, September 28, 1981. My eyes hurt right now and I feel a pressure on my heart. The present is too difficult for me to try to remember any more of the past today.

People wonder why I try to forget the past. It's the only way I can bear the present.

Chapter Thirty-Five

Life is complicated for all who look below the surface. Wilf knew this but was willing to go that extra mile with me. During each visit, he chose his words carefully at all times, trying to get me to feel the pain, or at the very least, acknowledge it. I told him tales he labeled "horror," but it was impossible to go there with him emotionally, and although Wilf, in typical therapist mode, always expressed an interest, I avoided discussing my dreams and nightmares with him at all costs. I feared that talking about them acknowledged their validity. What if they recurred—or worse yet, came true?

Wilf helped me see the levels of my dysfunction were so multi-layered that more than a few sessions of weekly therapy would be necessary to break down the emotional walls to reveal the damage. What proved most helpful to Wilf was that I always sought honesty and truth, no matter how brutal. I openly disclosed what my experience had been to the best of my memory. Ultimately, I hoped Wilf could provide a cure for surviving sexual abuse. Wilf often pointed out that the ramifications of my past were made manifest in my subconscious. At the very least, I acknowledged the abuse happened to my other self. I had to. Otherwise, why was I in therapy?

For weeks now, I wonder, when is Wilf going to ask me questions about 'it,'—s-e-x with P-a-p-a?

One Friday, I sense the conversation is heading in that direction. I won't bring it up first, maybe never. I'll talk about anything but that. It's not something I ever want to talk about. It's embarrassing because I don't remember the sex as an attack. I remember it as a learning experience, something new, different, and exciting. It is upsetting to talk about because I know how far-reaching its effects are.

Wilf finally blurts out, "What happened?"

I can't look at him. I keep my eyes focused on the tile floor, counting the spots while Thinking Donald relays the story. No emotion. No tears. There never are.

"Seventeen years ago now. That first occurrence is as plain as anything I can remember.... I was four years old. I know because it was before Mom taught me how to write my name on my pink piggy bank when I turned five. As I have different moods in my life now, I recall different things according to those moods. I don't flash back chronologically. Too many major things have happened. I've stored away a lot of the events.

"In the real world, I didn't have any chores. Just sex with 'Papa.' Sex was never mentioned in my 'Papa's' house. It was never given names. It involved a look, a nod of the head, a motion, a touch. Daniel never said, 'Let's have sex,' or 'Do you want to have sex?' I was naïve about sexual terminology because of this. I was doing it before I knew what 'it' was!

"As The Game grew tiresome, Daniel began to bribe me to get what he wanted. The non-verbal communication far surpassed any dialogue. The question, 'Do you want to go to the sales arena?' meant, 'If you want something, you're going to have to have sex with me to get it.' Sex was always understood to be the bartering tool. You know something? I don't even think I thought it was sex. I think 'sex with Papa' is only an expression I've coined as an adult because I never used that term while I lived with him.

"Sometimes I considered The Game a chore and a command performance. Now I call it 'fist-fucking,' because I had to make my small hand into a fist. I often found it quite boring, and my wrist would hurt from being tired out."

"What was your relationship like?"

"What relationship? Daniel never talked to me outside of sex. Never! During The Game, he would tell me I was 'special.' I believed him.

"Daniel encouraged us to try and fool around with kids at school. I never did. I had so much sex at home, why would I need to do it at school? On the other hand, Daniel never wanted us to experience 'bad influence from the other children.'"

"The contradictions started early then," suggests Wilf.

"Yes, contradictions all right. That's part of the reason Daniel has not been punished yet. He is one of the most believable professed-Christian men one could come across. Yet sexually, one couldn't find a man more deviated or unbalanced. I compare him to that Reverend Jim Jones. A man who used some form of faith in 'God' to twist many of his people. They were so changed by their blind faith, they would act against the laws of the land for their power-mad leader.

"If people knew what Daniel has gotten away with all these years, it would shock their little tootsies off. If it comes out during the trial, it will be for some, the latest gossip. For others though, an education. Daniel uses religion as an excuse for breaking laws. A person who was truly sorry and had repented wouldn't fight against truth. Or would he?"

"You wouldn't think so."

"Yes, on the one hand we were Christians and on the other hand I had regular 'sex with Papa.' But I remember I felt shame, especially of my body. Only two or three people, my parents being two of them, to this day have ever seen me nude."

Wilf listens to me intently now. He jots down a few things. I pause as I sense he wants to suggest something to me. My instinct proves correct.

"Donald, even though you rationalize that the abuse did not affect you in a negative way, your issue of personal shame is directly connected to the sexual abuse. You believed your 'father' knew what's best for you—he was okay but you weren't. It happens in many cases of improper sexual relationships. The victim feels the shame and the guilt."

"More WORDS! How can I feel like a victim when none of it is real! I can say I see what you are getting at, but that's only because I know that's what you want to hear. You want guilt—I feel guilty because I was born different. Fate has dealt me an original deck of cards. The combination of my parents' genes has much to do with it, but I had completely androgynous looks as a child. Up until puberty, I was often mistaken for a girl. It was hell—'cause I was born a freak. This fact did not escape Daniel's notice. He thought so too!

"I wanted to be a woman so much that it consumed me. Did people know I was different because of what was happening? I didn't. I thought I was a misfit, that I'd been given the wrong sex. I felt like a woman because that's how I was raised."

"How could you not have sexual identity problems, Donald? The truth is, perhaps you are innately full of both feminine and masculine aspects like many men, including myself. It's unfortunate that you had to spend so many years without having someone to confide in, someone to tell you, 'different is okay.'"

"Well, I sort of did.... Mom and I were close. I remember I loved pretty things and tended toward feminine manners because I didn't like what I knew to be a man was. After Erik disclosed the abuse, Mom and I talked when Daniel was at work, openly discussing sex—maybe because we both slept with the same man!"

"It's unusual for a mother to discuss sex with her child. Didn't it make you feel uncomfortable?"

"It wasn't me that was uncomfortable. She was. I know that sounds weird but I was no normal child. I asked too many questions. Mom never discussed her feelings or life with my siblings. They never questioned her like I did and she never initiated the conversation.

"It was more like an interrogation. 'Why did you do this?' 'How could you have done that?' I think I wore her down. Under normal circumstances, she would never have discussed adult feelings with a child, but there was nothing normal about our house or her second born. I believe if she had never opened up to me, I would never have taken her on as my obligation. Her honesty fed my desire to free her....

"Oh, gee. What was I talking about...I went off on a tangent.... Oh yeah, outside the home, I was not emotionally or mentally equipped for the world. To me a man was someone who had sex with children and mentally abused his wife. I didn't want to become that. Consequently, I didn't want to become a man.

"Outside of The Game, I never initiated a conversation with Daniel my entire life. I was completely indifferent to him. I loathed his touch and avoided any physical contact whatsoever. Much of that was below the surface. I never showed him I hated him."

Nothing I say shocks Wilf. He always listens, reflects, and speaks softly.

"Sometimes you say you enjoyed The Game and other times, you hated it. Daniel never cared about how you felt, Donald. Creating The Game was his way of maintaining control over you. If this was the only way he played with you, of course you would think you wanted to play. Pedophiles count on such confusion to prolong the abusive relationship."

"I want to believe you.... Oh, nothing makes sense. I wish I could cry. My mind and heart are hurting but I can't cry. I haven't cried in such a long time even though I've had more reasons to this year than in all the years before. I have to let go of my feelings sometimes, but I'm afraid to do that. I don't want to reveal things people can use to hurt me."

"Donald, you don't have the feelings you think you have."

"What do you mean?"

"You are a good person. Don't take this the wrong way, but you've disconnected yourself from your feelings. With everything that's happened, how could you not?"

"But it's not my fault! I had to cut them off to survive. I would have killed myself if I had to feel the pain."

"Donald, I understand. I'm not saying you did something wrong. You did what you had to do to survive, but to really enjoy your life now, you'll need to feel again."

"I don't know how, Wilf. I can't all of a sudden feel at the drop of a hat. It's like I can't get back to the time when I felt. I don't remember what it was like."

"You live in your mind. That's why you write down what you think, why you can talk about what happened with your father without emotion."

"I know...I use my mind more than anything else. It's like my brain has its own identity. *He* inhabits the body sitting before you.... Still I try to help people, brighten their day, encourage them. I don't have great feelings of love for others. I knew it was important to forgive people who've hurt me, so I got rid of them and what they did in my mind so that I could."

"Don't you see, Donald, you intellectualize everything—'My religion says I must forgive, so I do.' You don't let yourself 'feel' the pain of your experiences."

"Why would I? Who would want to hear me talk about my pain?"

"I do."

I leave Wilf's office feeling disoriented, confused, angry, and hurt. My face is burning. Have I wasted time avoiding feelings, acting on how I think I should behave? Am I a phony?

How do you measure the psychological pain imposed upon a victim by his or her molester?

Sexual abuse within families has its own unique effects. How does one unravel the layers upon layers of damage? Wilf was trying to steer me in the direction of "dealing with the incest." I'd often ask him, "What the hell does that mean?" I had no idea. He recognized a well of emotions in me that I was unwilling or unable to express. Up until I began therapy, I had only received intellectual help. Although I believe I'm genetically inclined to be a "thinker," the social world that surrounded me also feuled that inclination by their input: "Rely on God, read the Bible and our literature, and stop feeling sorry for yourself!"

An endless parade of non-feeling statements crossed my way. How could I know that a good cry, an expression of anger, or a scream or two might have been more helpful to release what was inside of me? How could the people around me, uneducated in matters of abuse, have known any better?

I had become skilled at pretending I had no feelings by creating an expressionless face. I developed this ability in order to survive my social interactions at school, at the hall, and at work. The lines between acting and reality were beginning to cross.

Because Wilf pointed out that I did not have the feelings I thought I had, I questioned the importance of everything, especially writing my diary. Sometimes, I'd skip writing any entries for a couple of weeks, then make up for it by writing a ten-page entry. I wondered if I'd be spending my life writing my feelings away. I was the child who never acted out because I did my acting out in my head. Writing came naturally to me. As Wilf pointed out, I lived through the words I wrote. I felt anguish at hearing Wilf's observation, but I knew I would return to his office.

The hours spent with Wilf were very productive. When he challenged my rationalizations and decisions, I would debate what he said, then spend the rest of the week either trying to disprove him or discovering that he was right. I wanted to understand what had happened to me. Here was someone validating my worth, and I appreciated his caring way of reaching out to me.

Diary Entry, October 4, 1981. I am not sure whether I have feelings of 'love' for Wilf but I do trust him. Why? His personality for one. He is soft-spoken and doesn't pity me. He talks kindly to me. He doesn't make fun of me or joke

about my personal or strange feelings. I am naturally drawn by such character in a person. I do not mean 'love' as in the sexual relationship I had with my father. Even from the first meeting I had with Wilf, I thought of him as a doctor. I just cannot see a sexual relationship between a doctor and patient.

I am trying to honestly describe how I feel about things in my life. Although I sense something emotionally for Wilf, that is one feeling I cannot describe, so at this point I will not try.

Chapter Thirty-Six

When I realized, with Wilf's help, that the years of self-hatred were a waste of my energy, that my sexual confusion was normal, and that I wasn't a "pervert," I channeled my anger and resentment into making changes in my way of interacting with the world. If I was normal and not a bad person, then this must have been true all along. When I understood just how much I had let other peoples' projection of their negative feelings of me influence my state of mind, it created a force or energy that enabled me, an introverted young man to speed up the work of recovery. Giving up wasn't in my vocabulary. I wanted to be "normal," and I wasn't going to wait until I completed therapy to get there.

The truth was I wasn't "normal"—I was in an emotional time freeze. I wasn't human—I thought I was superman. I became fearless. Nothing would stand in my way. I discovered that I was not as weak as others had led me to believe.

I began gathering the strength to look at my sexuality.

I rush to get to my session with Wilf after work.

"Do you believe me when I say I won't hurt you?" Wilf queries.

"I trust you, if that's what you mean."

"I think you should make up your mind whether or not you want to be gay."

"Want to be gay? Who would? No, I don't want to be gay, but I want to express the loving part of my feelings for a man. If that part of me doesn't get fulfilled, I will still feel that something is missing. I want people to let me be me. I want to be strong enough to fight back against people who try to make me into something I'm not."

"Maybe you fear something—men, perhaps."

"Yes, in many ways I am still afraid of men. You could say I'm just a 'scaredy-cat,' but it goes much deeper than that. I've been afraid of getting in the position where a homosexual experience could occur because I know that I would not say 'no' unless the person was real ugly. Even then, if I was forced, would I fight back? Sometimes, I think a man could do whatever he wanted with me. I might hate what was happening, but I might like the relationship aspect, the control he would have over me as his sexual slave. Perhaps I don't want to be strong in that sense, but I'm not sure. I am not attracted to men who are physically stronger than me. Mentally strong men, definitely. I am drawn to intelligence."

"What role does pornography play then?"

"I think it keeps me in a fantasy world, and men at a distance. A world that is safe like my black and white TV friends were when I was growing up—"

"And like your black and white movie memories that keep your past at a safe distance?"

"I think so, but I don't know how to change that."

"Well, are you strong enough to be different, to choose a life that you want?"

"I can't! In the past four years, I've fulfilled a man's responsibility: as breadwinner, leader, disciplinarian, and organizer. I've had to give parental discipline to Marina and Erik like a father would, not like a mother. The feminine approach does not always work. Although I hate to admit it, I have mentally supplied what a husband would give to his wife as I did with my mother. Ronny did when we left Daniel, and I did when Ronny left us. So I have been acting as a man would be expected to act in a family relationship. I've tried to give security and direction to my family."

"Donald, may I suggest your taking care of your family is not altogether altruistic. It's helped you avoid dating, experimenting, socializing…all things natural to growing men."

Only within the safe atmosphere that Wilf's office provides, is it possible to hear the truth.

"I realize Mom feared being alone so much that she didn't mind me being introverted. She could have me as a companion. She was alone most of the time, so I was the friend she needed, which explains why we're so close now. Too close! I've had no freedom until this year. Maybe you're right. Maybe I didn't want any freedom. When I tried to have some for the first time this year, she made me feel guilty. She admits it and realizes she was scared I would eventually desert her. I don't want to hurt her, but she is getting hurt and will more so during the trial. In the end, this pain will work out for the best, I'm confident."

Wilf taps his pencil on the yellow pad, weighing his next comment.

"There's a lot of turmoil in your life right now. Just because I say, 'you need to decide if you want to be gay or not' does not mean I think you are gay. I want you to look at yourself instead of focusing on your family."

"Okay. Look at me. I have many male and female characteristics. That wouldn't be so bad if I was satisfied or knew what I wanted sexually. Although I want a relationship with a man, that does not mean I am gay. I never realized this until this year. Although many people feel and believe that homosexuality between consenting adults is okay, does that make it natural? If a person believes in God, is it not obvious the creator made Adam and Eve to fit one another sexually? His intention is two-fold. First, as companionship for one another, and secondly, to fill the earth with their offspring. That makes a lot of sense to me."

"I know that's what your religion teaches, but what does Donald really think?"

"My needs sexually for men are natural to me because I was trained and conditioned that way." My honesty shocks me.

"I definitely do not feel guilty about what I've become anymore. You've helped me see that it's not my fault. It is people who have made me feel guilty to a large extent anyway. It wasn't something I dreamt up!"

I can only slip out of Witness mode for so long.

"Another reason homosexuality does not deserve acceptance is found in the importance of family relationships. We live in a society so different from centuries ago. Yet homosexuality goes back to Sodom and Gomorrah—those sexpot cities. No rules or decency, just sex, sex, and more sex. How could homosexuals raise children? Have they the right?"

"I know homosexuals who have raised children, Donald, and their children aren't gay. How do you explain that?"

"I don't know any homosexuals, so I can't answer that, but let's say I am a homosexual. Although I may be, I certainly have helped Mom raise Erik for five years and no way have I affected him that way. And although I may have feminine traits, Erik is definitely heterosexual. I would feel very bad if Erik went into that homosexual way of life. I was glad Ronny didn't. But Marina is more mixed up about sex than Ronny and Erik were. I really want to understand why, though. Ronny was sexually abused and taught homosexual practices. Erik was introduced to them for a short time, and they both turn out straight. Marina and I though seem to be in reverse roles. We were both abused the longest, and we lived with Daniel while Ronny was mostly outside the house. And Erik, he was only ten when we left so maybe that helped him. Do you think that has something to do with it?"

"Might I suggest you consider two points? One: You weren't taught homosexual practices. Sexual acts between a father and son are sexual assaults. I believe that when the Elders referred to the abuse as homosexual acts, this added to your sense of guilt and confusion. They should have labeled the acts a crime, not a sin. Two: Some researchers are starting to think that you can't teach another human being their orientation. It's inherent, innate. Sexual abuse of a child confuses the process of a victim's developing sexuality."

"I 'know' what you are saying is correct, but it doesn't make it any easier to deal with."

"You are right about that. Well, we have to end today's session now."

Today's discussion was difficult. I sense a lack of love and touching, kissing, and hugging in my life. Just because I want that from a man, does that mean I'm gay? I seriously wonder whether I want the homosexual way of life, but I can't say I want the heterosexual way of life either. Yet, I am aware I can attack some of my problems immediately. I wonder if most of my problems are not in my head anyway. My homosexual conflict is only inside my mind. Until I tell someone about it or act upon it, it is totally within me. It is my problem. I must deal with it. Wilf disagrees with my theory that I became homosexual because I sought a father image to replace the love—not the sex—I so much wanted from a father figure. It started out as wanting love, then hugging and kissing, then finally I couldn't break the association of love with men as including a sexual relationship. It also has to do with hating men and identifying with women, including Mother and Marina. Wilf wants me to come to terms with myself, with my position in my social and religious life. He wants me to try and look at my sexuality. From now on I'll try.

Since Wilf and I had just been discussing my sexual problems, I try to see men as sexual partners. Although I desire men in some ways, I can't really picture myself in a sexual act with anyone I meet. After five years of celibacy, I guess I feel like a virgin, and I'm apprehensive of a sexual encounter. Sounds funny! I wonder what I would do or feel. I want to feel love for someone, and be willing to accept love too!

To that end I accepted an invitation to visit a friend in London this Saturday. Although I am scared to get involved, I'm going to because I want to change. I want to be happy.

Luke is a new Witness acquaintance who lives in London.

"Sure I'll spend the weekend, Luke. It will be nice to meet your family and get to know one another better."

During my visit, I go through a familiar dialogue: "You'd really like my mother...and my younger brother, he's so much more fun than I am.... Marina's so warm and outgoing...and my older brother, he's so sporty and likes to hang out with the guys." Blah, blah, blah...same old crap. I put myself down to get out of feeling uncomfortable. I lack confidence with new people.

Wilf says I should be honest about what I feel and what bothers me. This guy does not want to hear what is bothering me.

At one point during the weekend, Luke states, "If you want to tell me your problems, I'll listen."

It sounds as if Luke will bring himself to my level, if I want him to. "Thanks, but no thanks."

I'm not going to be someone's evening entertainment. Give him a sob story and he does me a favor by listening. God, who needs that? I spend the rest of the weekend focusing on him. He likes that. So do I. I try to ask him questions to bring him out of *his* shell. I think he will feel better. I am not sexually attracted to him, but I do want to feel loved by him. If he touches me, I would *let him*! I want him to hold me and tell me he cares, or hug me even.

That's something at least. I feel so empty without a father's love, hugs, and kisses. Those things that a boy needs from a man when he is young and growing up. Mom always hugged me and kissed me goodnight. I felt secure in her love. Our women friends always loved me too, and I kissed them good-bye freely.

Although this weekend I obsess over being gay, I enjoy the break from my world.

We receive an invitation to my cousin's wedding. This will be the first marriage ceremony of a relative I attend, and another nice break from our problems. Ronny got married last year and even though we received an invitation, we didn't go because it would have been hypocritical to show up when we weren't speaking. More important, we knew Daniel would be there.

My cousin and I have not seen much of each other over the years either. My parents' messy separation and divorce pretty much ended any regular communication. Aunt Simonne and Uncle Achiel didn't want to get involved.

I remember my uncle telling me: "Every man's house is his own business. I am responsible for my own house. At least your father always provided food and shelter for all of you." I knew such logic was convoluted, but I didn't know how to explain why, so I didn't voice my objection. My uncle had a difficult childhood himself and altho ugh he was bitter about his past, he remained proud he became a self-made man. I admired him. Even though he never cared for his brother-in-law, he suffered Daniel's company so the two sisters could visit each other. My uncle and aunt were always positive role models in my life.

I help my mother and sister pick out new dresses to wear at the wedding. They will look smashing. I will wear the suit Brother McTavish bought me for my graduation a couple of years ago. Marina and I have to figure out who to ask to the wedding as dates. I know Luke likes Marina. I'll ask him for her if she'd like. I think I'm going to ask Marina's friend, Peggy. She's a lot of fun and she's so pretty. I'll make it clear to her that I'm asking her as a friend. I wonder if she'll go with me.

Peggy and Luke accompany us to the wedding. We have a wonderful time together. On the other hand, we feel like strangers at our own relative's wedding. Nevertheless, it is great to experience something normal for a change. When I make it clear to Peggy that I just want to be friends, I can tell she would have considered dating me. She too was raised in a dysfunctional family, and we have a lot in common. But I know dating is more than I can handle. She seems to understand. She is another person who looks beyond my physical appearance and really tries to connect with me. She has a tremendous impact on me. I am attracted to her beauty, her warmth, her sense of humor.

Yet my attraction to Peggy confuses me. If I am a homosexual, how do I explain this? For a fleeting moment, I feel normal, but Wilf is right. I have to find out who or what I am. Maybe I should talk to someone who is homosexual. I call Information, determined, yet nervous, and ask for any number that represents a gay organization. They give me one.

"H-e-l-l-o." The tone and level of the voice paints a picture through the phone: an unpleasant woman.

"I think I might be gay and I want to talk to someone about it."

"We're closed right now. You'll have to call back."

"But, I...."

Click.

So much for that part of my discovery. I won't be doing that again. Sometimes it's easier staying confused.

Chapter Thirty-Seven

Today is my eighth appointment with Wilf.

"I thought I'd tell you a bit about *my* history today...."

As Wilf talks about his family, I listen intently. My therapist talking about himself makes him more real to me.

"Do you ever get freaked out listening to patients' problems all day long?"

"Sometimes I do, but I try my best to keep a balanced life outside of these four walls. You know, Donald, I must keep my limitations in mind. The trust you put in me places me in a powerful position in your young life—a role I never want to abuse or take for granted. I care about your feelings. That's why I think it's important you keep in mind the possibility—you should be prepared—that Daniel might get off with a light sentence, or perhaps none at all."

"I can't think about that. I agree that possibility exists, but that's negative thinking. The difference in my case is that although I started the ball rolling, the Crown is charging Daniel. Something like, 'Her Majesty the Queen vs. Daniel D'Haene,' the inspector told me. The pressure of losing is not as great as if I hired a lawyer to represent me, but when the Crown charges someone and we are subpoenaed as witnesses for its case against the accused, I feel confident they will not lose without putting up a strong fight."

"You've watched too many courtroom dramas in movies and on TV. They are based on the American model: District Attorneys grandstanding for the cameras. In Canada, Crown Attorneys are appointed, not elected, and there are no cameras in the courtroom."

"That sounds like good news to me."

"Okay, I won't belabor the point. Donald, I've been meaning to ask you, why did you have Daniel charged?"

I explain the roller coaster of events that transpired immediately following Rhiness' initial visit.

"Depending on the nature of each of those events, my motivation changed. If I received a letter from Daniel telling me I was going to hell, I wanted to silence his religious hypocrisy. If I watched my family's dysfunctional interaction, I wanted to send the message that my father brought us into this world, abused us, and left us to pick up the pieces. On a day when I wanted to commit suicide, sometimes I felt he was responsible for my unhappiness. Is that revenge? Is it hate?

"God, maybe I'm just naïve! If I wasn't, I probably wouldn't have chosen to charge my father in the first place."

"Donald, it required a great deal of strength. There is a certain amount of risk-taking involved."

"Perhaps I felt I had nothing to lose since I had lost so much already, or is it just that I am unable to look at the risks? Perhaps Mother's divorce and my testimony left me with a false sense of confidence. After all, I only testified for a few minutes. No one questioned my honesty. Things worked out in the end. Regardless, I am not going to consider the possibility of losing our case."

"Whatever your initial motives were, the real issue concerns a crime that was committed against you when you were a child. You shouldn't have had to decide whether or not to press charges. There had been numerous opportunities for responsible people in your life to go to the authorities. That didn't happen, so it was your choice as an adult to inform the authorities."

"Thanks for saying that, Wilf. My early fear was that every one would ask me why I charged Daniel and you know what, countless people *have* asked me! You just did yourself. Other than Mom, I don't know a single person who has asked my father why he chose to abuse us."

"Donald, we live in a victim-blaming society. When you decide to make your story public, you can expect public scrutiny and judgment."

"I really didn't know what to expect, but I didn't think people would be so negative. Perhaps we don't look enough like victims. Or maybe we're too good at acting. For a period of time I wanted to change my name. The four of us kids wrestled with the idea when we were teenagers, but as time went on, we became aware that once again negativity directed at our name was not our responsibility. Our peers were superimposing their own feelings on to us. We resolved to stick to our surname.

"I recall Elder Sandor and his wife telling me, 'You should definitely change your name.' Even while I outwardly considered it, internally I knew their comments were a projection of their own personal feelings. They seemed to be unaware we might have feelings too."

"No wonder you have problems with self-esteem. Even your church has let you down."

"I don't think so. It's not the religion. I think it's the imperfect men in it. This therapy is helping me develop confidence in my personal self-worth."

"Donald, my research on abuse has taught me that victim self-hatred is common."

"Well, I look on this surname issue as a challenge. My quest is to create as much positive publicity regarding our family name as is humanly possible. If I had a crystal ball, I might decide to change my name, but I don't so I won't."

"I understand, Donald."

"I brought the journal you gave me. Do you think you'd want to read my diary now?"

"I would like that very much."

As I'm about to leave Wilf's office, I remember something.

"Wilf, I found out two Elders received subpoenas last night. They offered to be witnesses for the Crown. I can't believe it, but I'm scared to go to court. I'm not doubting its importance. I just realize that I have to reveal my personal feelings publicly. I've always survived on my strength from the God I believe saved me from committing suicide, but now I feel I am alone. There are people out there who support us, but they are out there and I am here. I'm kind of scared."

"I know you are. Just remember, I'll be there for you."

"Thanks, Wilf."

After dinner, I sit down to write.

Diary Entry, October 23, 1981. Because ours is a harsh reality, many refuse to confront and deal with it. They avoid it and anything that has to do with it. That includes us. Daniel wrote our relatives informing them they would

receive news from us that he would be going to jail. He wrote that they shouldn't believe it. He and his second wife are feeling just terrific and nothing is going to change it. Is he crazy to think that he will get away with it? He's gotten away with it for over seventeen years. It is hard to believe we will get justice at last.

We had Witness friends over for supper. Of course, the conversation eventually turned towards Daniel. They changed their minds about our past and now think it's good we are charging him, stating, "We admire your strong spirit of wanting justice and not giving up."

They still don't really know the effect on us. Marina said she was surprised how frank I was. I feel better, now that I don't care what people think of us. People still rationalize their past bad feelings about us and the mistakes they made in their judgment of our situation. After the trial, I will have to continue living with these people in my social life. I genuinely want to forgive them, because I have made mistakes too.

Later in the evening, another Elder calls to tell me he has received a subpoena. Elder Surin wants us to go over and discuss the case with him. I said we would, but I dread talking to him.

"Why didn't you go to the police when you first heard evidence we were being abused?" I ask.

"If we get asked that question in court, I will state, first, we didn't know it was against the law, and second, that we handled it the best way possible by removing Daniel from the congregation."

"But why didn't you try to help us get away from him?"

"I don't think we should have taken you away from your father. Why? Where would we have put you?"

Marina pipes up, "Foster homes perhaps?"

"It would have been worse than living with your mother and father because the children's agency would most likely have divided you up, and you wouldn't have been a family."

I cannot believe what I am hearing. My face is red. I'm angry, self-conscious, and very hurt, but I refuse to remain silent.

"I don't agree."

"Donald, you're the one who is wrong. Your anger is affecting your judgment. Why are you trying to make us feel guilty for something that happened so long ago? Especially your Mom—why make her feel guilty?"

I change the subject. I can't express my anger or feelings. What else is new? I decide to press on.

"Brother Sandor said it would be a good idea to change our name. I don't think so. I think people will think of us as Daniel's victims."

"You know, it would be better if you did change your name. There is a bad sound to that name now. It's connected to Daniel. People will think of him and it will reflect on you all."

Too bad Wilf isn't here to listen to this. Yet another person thinks we should change our name.

The rest of the evening is spent debating which one of us kids looks most like Daniel. "None of dem," says Mama firmly. Yet Erik wins the most votes. Poor Erik.

On the ride home, I promise Mother: "Until the preliminary hearing, you won't hear me blame you or anyone else again!"

I am upsetting myself and everyone is getting annoyed with me. I am sick of this bullshit, but even more determined to see this through. God is on our side and although people may make mistakes, He is the only one we can totally rely on. I must believe the Elders are convinced they acted in good faith. Still, I think they should have tried to help us. I can't do anything about that now. I must accept what happened to me and that there is no justice in this life.

I call Wilf about what happened tonight.

"I knew you would support my feelings, Wilf. I feel better, thanks. I've made up my mind that Mom has paid for not doing something about the abuse, and I have no right to continually make her feel guilty. If something were to happen to her because of this case, I'd never forgive myself, no matter how I justified my role or actions."

"Donald, remember there is no right or wrong here. You are expressing feelings. That's the important thing. We'll talk about this next Friday."

Before I try to sleep, I write:

Diary Entry, October 23, 1981. Although today I did not feel well, I'm surviving. I just take deep breaths and go on!

Now from three sources, I have been told to prepare myself for the fact we might lose the case.

Although I express confidence in the trial and that we'll get justice, I know nothing is certain. I have waited almost seventeen years for justice. I can wait as long as it takes.

I think I'm going crazy, nearing a breakdown even, yet I always make it. I have strengths I can't believe I have. If I let go, everything I've worked for goes down the drain. But the pressures are getting to me. I've become mean and full of hate. Everyone is telling me this hate will destroy me. In many ways that's true. Yet I told Mom again, hate keeps me going to a great extent.

People are just waiting for us to leave our religion, to give up, have a nervous breakdown, fall into immoral practices. Then they'll say either, "I told you so!" or "I knew he was going to end up that way too!" It's like they want us to leave so they don't have to face us D'Haene children.

Oh I think all of this is almost too much!

Please someone help me know what to do. I think I am what I am whether I change my name or not. If I run away, I'm running away from myself—fleeing reality! I should be thought of based on what I am worth, what I have accomplished. These people are putting actually what they feel about the name D'Haene and Daniel into the conversation. If I listen to these kind of people I would go crazy. I am coming closer to the point I don't want to discuss our life with anyone.

God, help me to keep love in my heart, not hatred.

Please, please someone love me for what I am, and allow me to love them too.

I must accept the fact Daniel might get off on probation or such a light sentence that justice won't be done. With our society the way it is now, I shouldn't be surprised. Most people don't receive justice. I shouldn't expect more than the average person. I'll just have to wait and see.

I try to go to sleep, but I can't. Everything rolls over and over in my mind. The memories plague me. I just want to sleep! I want to force *him* out of my mind.

Chapter Thirty-Seven

I finally nod off.

Daniel comes into our house and forces himself upon me, raping me, taking control of me against my will. I feel cheap, dirty, worthless, low. I have to commit suicide to escape. Although I'm an adult, I can't hit Daniel because I feel helpless like a small child. No strength. I have no right to fight back. "Papa knows what's best." He gives my sexual desires satisfaction. It is my fault. I want that satisfaction from him. I go to him.

I bolt upright.

That's why I feel I'm to blame for the sexual relationship. That's why Daniel knew I wouldn't charge him. He knew I felt responsible.

Not wanting the dream to be repeated, I reach for my pen.

Diary Entry, October 23, 1981. I'm so mad I could scream. At who? Almost everyone in my life, past and present. Everyone tells me what to do, what to feel, who I should be! I am SICK AND TIRED of it! Why can't I just be me? The hell with other people's ideas from now on. I have got to do what I've got to do. I don't need anyone's opinion or approval. Mom says, "God will punish Daniel at Judgment Day." I believe I am charging Daniel as part of God's Judgment. God will be victorious and he will get his long overdue punishment.

Chapter Thirty-Eight

At 6:30 P.M., the next day, Constable Larry Nickson hands us our subpoenas to be witnesses at the preliminary hearing, November 26. It feels very strange. The reality of the trial is drawing nearer. I don't want to think about it much because I still want to live in the present.

As I drive to work, I reflect on our situation. *Would we be happier in St. Thomas?* I wonder.

Marina is branching out. She's gone back to high school, but in St. Thomas this time. She's meeting new friends and seems happier now. The guidance counselor at East Elgin Secondary School suggested she transfer to a school there because of the pressures that lie ahead.

We seem to be having tremendous struggles in coping with life in Aylmer, not to mention our financial difficulties. We have nothing but hope in God to keep us going, but how I appreciate that hope! I would not be alive today if I didn't have faith in a future.

I love the movie *Gone with the Wind*, especially the part where Scarlett O'Hara resolves, "As God is my witness, they're not going to lick me. I'm going to live through this and when it's over, I'll never be hungry again. No, nor any of my folk." Whatever it took, she was determined to reach that goal! Her spirit is a strong influence on me.

I have actually taken over her attitude in many ways. I am not going to live poor for the rest of my life, no matter how hard it will be, no matter what sacrifice I have to make to that end—including friends and entertainment. The only ones I really care about are my family. I have given my strength and hopes to them. Although, I do not get appreciation now, in the future, Marina and Erik will realize what I did for them. Though I've made mistakes, I've kept them from totally giving up, and perhaps ending their lives.

With this positive frame of mind, I walk into the office.

My good mood doesn't last long. My boss hands me two letters containing pamphlets against my religion that Daniel has sent in care of my employer. This is so wicked and cruel. It breaks all my privacy rules, my need for control. I'm more scared now than ever. I am sick and tired of having my "father," the hypocritical "disciple for Christ," condemning my family and my religion. Although I consider this a test and a training period in my life, how much more pressure can I take? Is there a breaking point?

Daniel is continuing his attempts at control by writing to our friends, our relatives, and the Witness congregations in the area. He has attempted communication with these people since his conversion in 1976, sending religious pamphlets and the like, but he has laid low for a couple of years. Perhaps had I not charged Daniel, he would not have renewed his campaign to convert Witnesses.

When I arrive home from work, I discover Daniel's second wife, Marsha, has sent Mother some religious material. Is Marsha a naïve woman brainwashed by her husband much the way Mother was? I vent my frustration through writing.

Diary Entry, October 29, 1981. Mr. X is the main reason we've suffered so much unhappiness. Yet, I am strong enough to fight to keep going, making the best of my life while I can. At times I almost think I won't make it. Who am I fooling? I want to make Mr. X pay for what he has done. I want revenge. I want back what I lost—my innocence, my youth, my happiness! And why shouldn't I? Who will do anything if I don't? No one. I can't rely on any human to seek vengeance for me. Should I expect or demand people's support? I have to live with and do what I feel is right in spite of what people think or say.

Later that evening, an elderly Witness gives me yet another letter Marsha sent. This one states that the Witnesses are persecuting her and Daniel, and she is soliciting prayers of support to fend them off. Later, at the Kingdom Hall, we discover that Daniel has written many others as well. He's on one of his crusades again. He's probably angrier than ever now that the trial is pending. He thinks the Witnesses are behind it, though few of them understand why I'm charging him.

Chapter Thirty-Eight

I want this more than anything, yet I'm scared my mother will go through hell again.

The Elders think justice should be left to God. The "born-agains" say we're out to damage Daniel's credibility as a Christian. They seem to think the fight is religion versus religion, not Daniel versus the Crown, not a perpetrator facing justice. Maybe they are right.

An omen of things to come?

Chapter Thirty-Nine

Feeling unusually optimistic, I enter Wilf's office. I'm beginning to be myself with Wilf. I joke, laugh, and at times express sadness and anguish as well. I want to tell Wilf something: I now want to feel something when I'm touched. That's a step forward I hope. It took me twenty years to feel nothing. To go back and reverse the procedure will be difficult. I want to take time to recover. I don't want to close the open wounds. I want those wounds to heal. I want to tell him...but I don't.

"Wilf, although it appears that I'm the one who receives acceptance, I certainly don't feel accepted. How can I? People don't even know who I am."

"Something tells me having your father charged will change all that."

"I don't believe anybody even remotely respected me until I made decisions independent of my religion and Witness friends."

"Going to court is definitely a choice completely contradictory to the weak persona people have labeled you with. The truth is you are not weak. You've chosen to live, despite abnormal, cruel circumstances."

"And Wilf, I've decided to make some assertive moves in my life as well. It's not easy but I've already begun. At the Kingdom Hall this week, I had a red-hot flush in my face for two hours just because I had made up my mind that I didn't want to have any Hall responsibilities anymore. It took all that time to get my nerve up, but I said it honestly and straightforwardly: "I'm not doing it anymore." They accepted it because they do realize I'm under a lot of pressure.

"And Erik's new counselor came over to discuss with all four of us what we can do to become united as a family. I believe he said a lot of positive things that certainly will help if we apply them. There is a lot to work out but things are better by far.

"Erik passed all his exams. He's getting help from Lance. I'm not as involved as I used to be. After all, I'm only his brother, and besides, I've got problems too. I'm not responsible for him.

"Marina and Erik are old enough to make decisions whether they are good or bad. They must face the consequences of their decisions. I am not going to feel guilty when they make mistakes anymore. We are separate human beings. Marina can now arrange to go anywhere she wants and eat anything she wants. She has to look after herself. Mom seems to be supporting this arrangement."

"I think those are healthy decisions, Donald. This will lighten your burden. You've focused on your family, their problems, and their feelings enough. I think it's..."

"I'm not done yet! I think we should stop discussing Daniel and our life with him with other people. We should find things that interest other people and somehow give them a lift. And why do we keep saying 'Hi' to people who feel we are nothing and make darn sure we know it too?"

"Why do you?"

"Well, it's the Christian thing to do. You know what? Mom and I are alike that way. I've let people run my life just like Mom does. That's not helpful to my situation and feelings, but no matter—Mom has been a great example in not giving up! She didn't want to face our sexual problems, but she did tell us that we were special. She always said we were worth something, even if other people didn't think so."

"I still think you harbor some resentment toward your mother."

"I have a lot of bitter feelings concerning my mother's role in our past and present, but they are more than compensated for because of what she's done for us and the love she has shown. I cannot blame Mother for not understanding what happened to us. We never told her how we really felt. I don't think we even knew. It's just as well we didn't tell her though. She wasn't mentally prepared to understand what happened to our minds. Coming to these conclusions can't be all bad if they allow me to live and keep going, can they? I want to be happy even though I have to remember the past for the trial. Is that too much to ask?"

"Donald, you really have a survivor's mentality. You're dealing with very difficult things, but you know when it gets to be too much, so you pull back."

"Yes, although there are times I have to think about the past—to try and remember various matters I've stored away—I've finally snapped out of dwelling on the subject to the extent that it controls and clouds my mind. I hope this lasts anyway. I realize now, more than ever, people do not understand the damage sex abuse does to children, as well as later on in the adult years. I can't explain to every single person why we are the way we are.

"I'm glad to be alive. I'm not as obsessed with the trial as I have been the past few months. I've decided to take charge of my life: doing what I want to do—not because other people require it or demand it! I am more determined than ever to go ahead with my court case. I shall not solicit opinions anymore from friends and relatives. I trust you, Wilf, and God. That's it! I love many others but that doesn't mean I trust them."

"It's amazing how far you've come."

"Certainly I am making a lot of mistakes but at least I'm alive. And I know I'm extremely stubborn in my baby-step decision-making. I have to be—who can I trust? Every choice is trial and error, but I learn the ropes of survival quickly. It is sink or swim!

"Oh, and Wilf, I've decided Nort Rhiness and Constable Petz can't have my journal. I don't want them using my personal thoughts in the way I think they would."

"You seem to be at some sort of turning point," Wilf says. "I'm glad you're feeling better, but just remember that if something happens that dampens your spirit, you always have someone to turn to."

"I don't underestimate the help you've given me. I am trying to make new friends. I have a weekend invitation to visit Toronto with a friend from London. I look forward to getting away, even if it's only for two days."

"Getting away will do you a world of good. Oh, before you leave, I want to return your journal. I was deeply moved by what you've written, and I really appreciate your sharing your innermost thoughts with me. I cried at times."

"I tried to forget you were reading it. I'm sure you understand me better now."

It's strange, but my first visits with Wilf left me with the feeling he thought I was crazy and unlikable. Now I can tell he likes me and thinks I'm a worthwhile person. This has built up a little confidence in me. I am starting to feel more like a human being and less like a doormat.

Even though I understand why he was moved to tears by my writing, I am envious. Why can I not feel my pain?

Finally, the weekend is here.

"Would you like to walk down Yonge Street?" my new friend asks. "Since it's Halloween, people will be lining the streets dressed in costumes."

"I've never seen that before. Sounds like fun."

Even though I believe that the celebration has evil origins, I love watching the people pretend to be anything but themselves. Oh, to experience such anonymity. In Aylmer, I'm constantly aware that I am being watched by people who know me. The more people who know we have been sexually abused, the more self-conscious I become.

I have not been ridiculed since graduating high school. The metamorphosis of my physical appearance took on many stages. As a teenager, life post-Daniel, I bought modern, unisex, often unflattering clothes with money I earned from my part-time jobs. When I took my religion seriously, I became much more conservative in appearance. I purchased ties, white shirts, and jackets. Out went the platform shoes and the loose-fitting clothes of the seventies. To progress in the Witness faith, one automatically chooses modesty in dress, hairstyle, and appearance in general.

It also became a convenient way of making myself invisible. The more reserved my appearance, the less I was noticed. There arose a satisfaction in anonymity, but there was a performer inside screaming to get out.

My thoughts return to the Toronto street scene. I don't know why I'm attracted to this bizarre world, but I refuse to dwell on my curiosity. I have to focus my energy on my family, their problems, their looks, their feelings, and the trial ahead.

From my motel room that night, I place a call to Inspector Rhiness.

"I am realizing more and more how much I'm fighting a losing battle staying in Aylmer. I've been trying to believe I can hold out long enough because I'm strong, but I'm tired of this crap. You'd think we D'Haene children had done something wrong. I am not some super human being who can go through what I've gone through and come out unscathed. I'm seriously thinking of leaving this hall."

"Like I told you before, Donald, I don't know how you've survived staying in Aylmer. Moving would be the best thing that ever happened to you. You take care of yourself. I'll be praying for you."

As I replace the receiver, I vow never to walk into the Aylmer Hall again. For some unknown reason, I also know Nort Rhiness will never question me again about the Georgia Jackson case. Strange that. I wonder if I will ever see him again. Perhaps at the trial. God must have sent him to me—an angel sent to help us and vindicate His name.

Diary Entry, October 31, 1981. I'm not going back. I won't either! No matter what anyone says. No matter how bad that makes me or my family. Because of my therapy, I do not accept what happened in my life as one of those things. I have felt guilty for things that were not my fault. I am not alone. In just ten weeks with Wilf, I have come so far. I've been trying to please everyone but myself. The hell with that. There is so much to live for. I will choose my friends from now on. I will like myself.

Chapter Forty

Unfortunately, just as Marina begins feeling better about life and meeting new people, her therapist, Patty, moves to London to start a new job. Marina feels abandoned, but Patty is quickly replaced with a new, more aggressive therapist, Mandy.

Marina wants out of this house. She is right to want out. She's eighteen and she doesn't want to be told what to do. Mom is upset and worried for her, but I tell her, "You have to stop protecting Marina." Marina would benefit from living elsewhere. She would become more responsible, independent, important, and free. Her constant battles with Erik would end. The noise level would drop, and I would be able to read and study in peace for a change.

Marina arrives home.

"My therapist has helped me come to the conclusion I should move out and soon," she shouts as she enters the house.

"Marina, I understand, but maybe you don't have to. I think we should all move to St. Thomas."

"Really?" Marina says, shocked at my change in attitude.

I'm not surprised at my sister's bold statement. Her new therapist is helping her as much as Wilf is helping me. I've attempted to help her, but I'm learning the hard way, I can't. I have to leave her alone.

Marina keeps her true feelings to herself, nursing her thoughts for a time, then blurts out how she really feels. This is our fault, not hers, she says, because she can't talk to Mom or me. I'm "superman." I haven't time for "feelings." Mom only wants to hear about positive matters or Witness concerns.

Marina knows I care about her, but I don't know how to show it. We all know there is so much that isn't said. It's too painful to discuss, and too difficult to express.

That's why I am glad we have our therapists. I don't think it is a coincidence that Marina and I both consider moving at the same time. We've both heard an outside voice, opinions not connected to our faith, our town, our family or our history.

Moving to St. Thomas seems to be a natural progression. So why have I kept going faithfully where I didn't feel appreciated? Until now, I believed it was God's will, but to stay here is to continue under telescopic pressure and microscopic scrutiny. How can we serve Him when we have so much standing in our way? Perhaps to feel God's love, we must spread our wings and fly.

I really tried to make a go of it, but I am working toward an impossible goal: acceptance, love, and happiness in Aylmer. There are many people who care about us at the hall. I hope they will respect our decision. We've felt like caged birds long enough. I don't hate the Witnesses here. I hate what the Aylmer Kingdom Hall represents in my movie reels: a windowless, claustrophobic crypt of unhappy memories. Although I hated going to the Aylmer Hall the most, I was the last of the D'Haene children to admit defeat.

But how will I sell the idea to Mother?

"I think we should move to St. Thomas, Mom," I declare. "At the very least, we should go to meetings there."

"Oh, we cannot do dat," insists Mom. "You cannot go to de meetings if you do not live in dat area."

"Do you really think God wouldn't understand? Marina and Erik want to. We must."

"Maybe it is for de best."

How is it that I am displaying strength in my life right now? Witnesses are under obligation to attend meetings within a certain jurisdiction. It is a bold and independent move to make such a decision without seeking approval first. No matter what the consequences are, I must proceed. I am searching for my rainbow, where tranquility, security, passion, and fulfillment are in my life!

Diary Entry, November 4, 1981. Thanks goes to Wilf for helping me see strengths in my character I never knew I had

and for helping me use those strengths in accomplishing a great deal.

It's my first meeting in the St. Thomas Kingdom Hall since I was here as a boy. Many of the members are strangers but that doesn't matter. It's the first time I feel relaxed in years. Midway through the service, an Elder walks to the podium and makes an announcement, "If anyone has received a letter from Daniel D'Haene, please give it to the Elders." It feels weird, but I don't let it bother me. "*They are talking about someone with my last name, but he's a stranger from years ago in my bad dreams,*" I tell myself.

The contrast between the two halls is so great, I am energized by the positive display of Christian goodwill—people who have no prejudgment of our situation. Just the fact that we are attending meetings in St. Thomas is the boost I need. Even though we still live in Aylmer, our escape is halfway complete.

Diary Entry, November 15, 1981. I'm trying to live my life with some brightness. Whether I win the case or not doesn't seem all-important. What is important is that I survive and that Mom, Marina, and Erik do too! The inner peace of mind I have experienced these last few weeks is beyond words—due in a large way to the change in halls to St. Thomas. It was necessary for my survival. Somehow through the unreality of living this year, I am seeing some things in perspective and I am coming back to earth slowly. If I had gone further into the unreal world, I know I would have cracked up.

Chapter Forty-One

I had been a puppet for so long, I didn't realize the strings everyone else pulled actually belonged to me—until I received the objective help of Wilf. Although I had been a victim of circumstances, I now began to pull my own strings. These strings, invisible to the human eye, were connected to my low self-esteem. The more confidence I built up, the more decisions I made independently. Since there were so many levels to this process, progress was slow, and my failures overwhelmed me at times.

Because I had spent a life cowering to men's demands, instructions, and wishes, my therapy helped me face my issues with men in authority and my fear of them in general. As Thinking Donald, the insignificant pawn on this massive chessboard, continued to grow in independence and intelligence, the men in my life balked at my every move.

Yet, the obstacles in my path were formidable. I believed completely in my religion without doubting any of its doctrine for a minute. My closed frame of mind hindered my therapy. I entered therapy believing the Witnesses and their Elders were infallible. A lot of time was spent during my sessions determining what outside controls influenced my decisions. I had been unhappy with my life, and assumed I was helpless to change those circumstances.

Now I knew better.

Mom and I are called to attend a meeting at the Aylmer Hall with Elders from both congregations to "decide" which hall we will attend. I have to break my promise not to enter Aylmer's hall, or the St. Thomas congregation won't let us attend their meetings. It's a big deal to switch halls with all the tension in the air.

At the meeting, the tone and manner of the four Elders strongly suggest that in the future, we should say we felt supported by the Aylmer Hall. Our attending meetings in St. Thomas has created a big stir between the two congregations. I have to explain why we're moving and changing halls, but I will say whatever they want to hear so that we can leave Aylmer.

I can't believe they even have to ask! Are we not preparing for a trial that everyone knows about? They hear me out and agree it is best that we switch halls, but the four of them determine the Aylmer Hall did not act too badly with us.

On the car ride home, I express my anger to Mom.

"Can you believe how that meeting went?"

"I know, but you did handle de situation well, t'ough."

"It's called acting, Mom."

"Well, it all worked out in de end."

Mom believes these men are infallible. I'm not so sure anymore. I will discuss this at my next appointment with Wilf.

"Because of the changes I have made in my family, the spirit in our home is getting much better. We will make it if we stick together. Wilf, although the Elders didn't do anything about our sexual abuse, they did help us. The Elders thought they were doing the best at the time. Although I was nervous at the meeting—I couldn't eat for two days prior to it—it wasn't that bad. I remained calm and spoke firmly."

Even though I realize the Elders have made mistakes, I am a Witness speaking with an unbeliever about God's chosen people. I don't want to paint all Witnesses with the same brush. I always remind myself not to "stumble" Wilf from seeing "The Truth."

"I think you're more afraid of men than you realize."

"Well, I don't want them to feel badly about me. I want their respect and approval, but this therapy is helping me to make assertive decisions. I know I sound like a broken record, but that's the last time I'll walk into the Aylmer Hall. I went back on my word once, but no more. It's not so much the people as it is the memories associated with that place. Daniel sat with me in that hall. He abused us and faked Christianity. There is so much pain connected to that place. The memories are more hurtful than the people are."

"You rationalize the Elder's role in your family. Are you positive you're strong enough to stand firm in your convictions, such as your vow not to enter the Aylmer Hall again?"

"If I make up my mind, I can remain firm. I was cornered into this situation, but next time I'll be prepared. I know I must take action to control my life."

"Do you think the Elders and the Witnesses truly supported you? And if so, why?"

"Until this year, I believed they had. Now I can't believe their reaction, but they are still God's Elders."

I decide not to discuss this situation anymore than I have to, so I change the subject.

"You know, I have never felt like a human being, not until I came to see you. This feeling is quite new. I am very optimistic about upcoming events. May sound strange considering the preliminary hearing is this Thursday."

"I've asked you before, but I want to ask again. Why did you seek out the help of strangers, going to your doctor and telling him you need help, and then coming to see me?"

I can't tell Wilf the truth. I don't want him to kick me out of his office. I don't want this therapy to end. I'll tell him what I discovered my real need was.

"I was headed for a major crack-up, and I had all these responsibilities with my family. I couldn't afford time off work. I needed answers. What does it matter now? You are helping me. The movies are becoming reality more and more. Once I have reached the point where the dream is no longer a dream, but total reality, I will have made even greater progress. I'm even feeling a little better concerning 'Am I really here or not?' I know it's because things have been so unbalanced in my life, because of so many changes and developments and the pressure of becoming public information. Sometimes it gets too much to think about."

"Yes, it does and you need your strength for the preliminary hearing tomorrow. Of course, you know I'll be there for you."

That evening, Detective Rhiness calls.

"I wonder if your therapists would be willing to talk to me."

"I'm sure they would."

"Do they feel you were affected to any degree by the abuse?"

"Of course they do!"

Rhiness is in objective, detective mode.

"Fine then, could you and your family come down to the St. Thomas O.P.P. Station tonight? Constable Petz and I want to discuss tomorrow's preliminary hearing with you."

Rhiness and Petz suggest we have to prepare ourselves for the possibility that Daniel may change his plea to guilty at the last minute. When I ask why, they tell me Daniel's lawyer probably recognizes there is sufficient evidence for a conviction, and he may be working on convincing his client that it's best not to have a long, drawn-out trial. They ask us questions that could be asked during the hearing.

Constable Pat Petz shows me my father's mug shot, which was taken at the time he was arrested and fingerprinted. The look in his eyes is of sadness, surprise, and shock. It is as if he never even considered the possibility that he could be arrested. He looks stunned at the idea that he's done anything wrong and that he might be called to account.

We take home our statements to read over, and we're told to add anything else we can think of. As we drive back to Aylmer, exhausted, disturbed by the unknown possibilities facing us, we only voice confidence and optimism.

When I think back now, I can understand Daniel's surprise over his arrest. He had gotten away with a crime for years. He had support from his Baptist brethren who were unaware of the abuse. The Witnesses hadn't reported him to the police. His wife and children remained silent. Having the police show up on his doorstep must have been a gigantic shock. I find it amazing that I did feel sorry for him, though. I wonder how many tears he has shed in regret for what he did to his children. I remember staring at that photo, mesmerized by a look I had never seen before in his face.

Today, we are headed to St. Thomas for the hearing. I think my abdomen is going to burst. I just don't know what to expect. I am nervous and frustrated by the unknown factor. Our therapists are here and two Witness friends from London. We are hidden in a room without windows so Daniel can't disturb us. Constable Petz enters the room.

"Daniel is in the east hallway, but he won't bother you here."

Chapter Forty-One

"I wonder if Ronny is here today," I inquire.

Suddenly, a bearded, blond-haired man opens the door.

"Is this where I'm supposed to wait?" Ronny inquires. The timing of his entrance is startling. Marina's therapist speaks up.

"Do you want Ronny to leave the room?"

"Yes!" we say in unison—after all, Ronny is disfellowshipped— but a second later, I change my mind.

"No! I want him to stay," I state forcefully.

I just can't bear hurting his feelings. He is obviously extremely nervous about seeing us in these circumstances. It is all so bizarre. Ronny is shaking as he begins to speak.

"Why did you charge him? Who put you up to it?"

"Ronny, I found out that sexual abuse is a crime and asked a detective if he could pursue the matter for us. No one ever told me before that I could charge Daniel. The Witnesses are not behind our case. They'd prefer no publicity at all."

"If you say so, I believe you."

Nevertheless, I can only let down my guard so much.

"Daniel's been writing, and he led us to believe you'd rather be sitting with him today."

"Well, if he did, he's lying. When I left bible college, I tried to believe he'd changed and told him I had forgiven him. But that wasn't enough for him. He said I had to forgive him for what he did to Mother and you guys as well. I couldn't, and I wouldn't! Daniel couldn't stand that so we parted ways."

"How long ago was that?"

"Two years ago. He called me recently and asked me to lie for him for this case...."

"Lie about what?"

"That we had regular communication in the last two years. I want you to know, I don't have the strength to do what you're doing, but I'm in support of this. In the time I did see Daniel, I never saw one ounce of repentance, none, zero. He's never once acknowledged any wrongdoing, and he's never owned up to his actions to me, you guys or anyone else. That's why I came here today. He didn't deserve my forgiveness."

Ronny understands what Daniel really is, and not what he had hoped his father would be.

Although Ronny presents an air of physical strength, he doesn't fool me. He seems quite vulnerable and innocent. I'm sure it's been hard on him these past four years. I have no physical strength, but mentally I am strong. I want to make something of myself, and I believe Marina, Erik, and Ronny do too.

Three hours, waiting and waiting.

"You won't be called to give testimony," says Constable Petz. "The judge has determined there is enough evidence to go to trial."

Even though I am satisfied with today's development, my thoughts concern Ronny. I can't get over seeing my brother after so long, but I'm glad I did. How he left was so painful that I wanted to forget it. I didn't think we would ever see each other again. Not until this year did I realize I felt anything for him. Before I thought he was bad for leaving our religion and because of his attitude toward us, but this year— hearing Marina and Erik condemned, and finally even myself—opened my eyes to the destructive power of letting other peoples' opinions rule my life. Too much condemnation and not enough encouragement to stay in Aylmer. There is no question Ronny is a troubled man who made mistakes. Is that a crime?

My second concern is that there are people who support our case, but they seem to be Witnesses from outside of Aylmer. This realization hits me like a ton of bricks. I have to change my acquaintances immediately. I have to sever ties with people who have too much influence on us. I must cut Elder Sandor and his wife out of our lives. Even if I am strong, I can't let these people destroy us. Yes, they care about us, but only as long as we do what they say.

I have to quit my role as Sandor's "deputy" in the Jackson investigation. I am being used because I was Daniel D'Haene's son, and because I believe in the cause so much, I can be counted on to pass on the truth. I still support "the cause." Anyone involved in a murder should have to face the consequences. "Everything covered must be uncovered," the Bible says, but I have enough to deal with. I hope God will understand.

I will be marked by the Sandors for avoiding them, but I want my freedom. I want control of my life. I'm bothered that I thought this couple was so smart and knew what they were talking about. I now realize that they are human like everyone else. They're so obsessed with "the cause," that they forgot their friends are equally fallible.

Finally, that they influenced my opinions of others is heartbreaking and something I find shameful. Because of this harsh lesson in life, I think I can forgive others for hurting me. They are human too.

The following day, the newspaper reports on the court appearance.

Hearing waived in 8 sex counts

ST. THOMAS (Bureau) – A London man facing 10 sex-related charges was committed to trial on eight of the charges Thursday when he appeared in provincial court here before Judge Alan Baker of London.

Daniel D'Haene, 47, of 13 Lacey Cres., waived his right to a preliminary hearing of the eight charges which include buggery, bestiality, three counts of indecent assault and three of gross indecency.

D'Haene was remanded to Jan. 29 for a preliminary hearing of the two remaining charges of indecent assault and gross indecency.

D'Haene was charged in July after provincial police from Toronto and St. Thomas investigated reports of incidents in Elgin and other Ontario counties between 1963 and 1974.

At a court appearance in September, D'Haene elected trial by judge and jury. The trial is expected to be in February. – *The London Free Press*, Nov. 27, 1981

At my next session with Wilf, I plan on discussing my feelings concerning Ronny. I've decided I want to renew my relationship with my brother. I know he will tell me to wait for the right time to reunite. I want the family to get together once Daniel is in jail. I want to talk about this, but Wilf throws me a curve ball.

"Donald, before we start, I want you know that Detective Rhiness has spoken with me. Before you leave today, I'm going to give you a copy of my assessment for the trial that I've already given to him. There's nothing in it that you don't already know."

"So much has happened since I starting coming here. I haven't really thought about your assessment. I am afraid to read it though. Will it help to make something real to me?"

My session is lost in a haze of fear. All I can think about is that assessment. The written word has always had a great impact on me.

Verbal communication is different from reading a confidant's analysis of my character and past history.

How strange that I've gone from a private individual who never discussed personal matters to someone who's opened up to a detective, a doctor, a therapist, the police, and now the public. Yet even my feelings on this subject are contradictory, for, on one hand, I want a big explosion of facts, but on the other, no publicity at all.

So much has happened since the arrest was published, that my expectations have changed. Although people are concerned about us, I don't expect them to show it anymore. Nor do I want them to. People find it difficult to approach the last taboo—incest. Some feel they must be careful not to say the wrong thing, so they avoid us altogether. Others feel we will be a bad influence. Perhaps it will rub off on themselves or their families. Human nature, I suppose. Somehow it doesn't seem to matter anymore.

Sitting in my car in the hospital parking lot, I pull out Wilf's assessment from the envelope.

"Each time Donald trusted someone, it led to some form of abuse....In the final analysis, one can describe Donald as having been robbed of his childhood.... Where other children had outside interests and activities, Donald only had church, school, and sex with his father."

I read it over several times. I know I'm late for work, but it shakes me up, startles me. *"This 'Donald' must be very sick. Everything negative has happened in his life,"* I tell myself, as though I am reading about someone else's life—perhaps Other Donald.

When I arrive at work, my supervisor asks, "Donald, how many more weeks ، are you going to be taking time off for these appointments?"

"I don't know."

His frown and furrowed brow tell me he is not happy. What am I going to do now?

The following week, I come down with the flu. I send Marina to pick up my paycheck. There is a lay-off notice in my pay envelope. I know it's because I have been taking Friday afternoons off for therapy. I'm shocked and happy at the same time: no good-byes, which I prefer, plus this will give me the incentive to start a new life in St. Thomas. Meanwhile, what am I going to do financially? I am worried that with all this time on my hands, I'll have too much time to think. Will the vacuum that remains suck up my spirit, my sanity?

This unexpected turn of events is the best thing that has happened to me. I find a part-time job cleaning an office, and I am busier than ever. I spend time reading, writing, and I take up painting. I devote many hours to studying scripture, and corresponding with friends and relatives. After six years without pets, a Witness family from St. Thomas gives us their poodle. I'm amazed how much love and la ughter Buttons brings to our home.

While we still have our struggles, we seem hopeful that a happier future is at our door.

Chapter Forty-Two

"At least you had some relief for a time."

"Yes, it was great, having moments of 'normal' existence, but it proved to be short-lived. Everything seemed to be unraveling. I tried not to blame myself, yet once I proceeded with the court case, Erik got himself into more and more trouble, and Mom—well, she looked as if she had aged ten years."

* * * * * * * * * *

Erik thinks up new ways of creating problems. He skips classes at school, citing his therapy as the excuse. He claims to be selling dope and using it. He even brings three shady characters to our house, one of whom takes an egg out of the fridge and drops it on the floor, for no apparent reason. Another takes some change I had laid on top of the refrigerator.

The worst bomb bursts when the police arrive at our door to report Erik stole money from an elderly Witness, Sister Ruth. She hired Erik to clean her driveway, and Mom let him spend this money. Erik claims he stole about $40, while the woman says $178 is missing from her house.

The policeman asks Erik to leave the room so he can talk to me.

"I know about the trial that your family is involved in, and I wonder if charging Erik with this offense will harm him."

"If you don't charge him now, he'll never stop stealing. It will just get worse."

After the policeman leaves, I visit Ruth to apologize for Erik's behaviour and find her to be very understanding.

"I'm sorry Erik did this," Ruth says, "and I'm sorry for your whole family. I know how hard you've tried to keep things going."

"Every time things seem to be going well, something goes wrong."

"You're the only one who has kept a good name!"

Although Ruth means well, and I could take this as a compliment, I don't. My only thoughts are, "*this is putting the full burden on me again. What if I make a mistake? Everyone will probably crucify me!*"

After these latest incidents, with Erik once again in trouble with the law, Wilf, Mandy, and Lance come to our house. They suggest family therapy may help, with Wilf and Mandy acting as facilitators. Lance will continue to meet with Erik alone. Their goal is to remove me as disciplinarian, with the expectation that Mother would take over and encourage Marina's and Erik's independence. I do want Marina and Erik to be more responsible, but I don't know if this is going to help. Do the therapists really know what the solution is? More than anyone else, I welcome the intervention, but I have little faith in the process.

So much is happening, my mind is spinning. We have to go back to court on Friday, and on Tuesday, Ronny and his wife are visiting with their children for the first time in four years. I also obtained a second part-time job in St. Thomas and found a place for us to move to next month. Then we have our first appointment for "family therapy."

Our first session proves to be a disaster. By attacking the only remaining authority figure in our family—me—the therapists unintentionally leave nothing to replace it but chaos and anarchy. As if that weren't enough, my honesty about our family situation leads Elder DiAngelo to call.

"Because of Erik's problems with the police, we are going to have to call an Elders' meeting on Tuesday."

"But, Brother DiAngelo, Erik isn't baptized!"

"He still associates with other Witnesses, and he could be a bad influence on the younger children in the hall."

Because Erik has been charged by the police and is showing no signs of repentance, Erik might be publicly reproved or worse, disassociated. Because he isn't baptized, he can't be disfellowshipped, but this is only a technicality. Since there really is no difference between these two terms, he will be excommunicated either way.

The day before the meeting with the Elders, we receive a call from Erik's school. They had to contact the police because Erik stole once more. He's in trouble yet again. People know about it. We're moving and we have to leave Aylmer with this send-off. Now Erik is charged a second time for theft under $200. The policeman drove Mom and Erik to the station, and then took Erik to the St. Thomas Elgin General Hospital overnight for a few days of observation.

The Elders went ahead with their meeting the next day. Since Erik was in the hospital, he couldn't attend. On the other hand, he wouldn't have gone even if he were out of the hospital. Afterwards, Elder DiAngelo went to see Erik in the hospital to tell him he was going to be disassociated, but Erik refused to see him. The Elder considered this rebellious move a sign they were justified in reproving Erik. "He must have had a bad heart all along."

When you make mistakes, people rewrite your history.

Wilf and Mandy are upset at this turn of events. It looks like Erik may be placed in a foster home. Things have gone from bad to worse, and they feel partially responsible. With everything falling apart around me, it is decision time: 'NO MORE THERAPY!' The Witnesses might have been right all along. I'll rely on God from now on.

"It's not your fault, Wilf."

"Donald, I think we've made a big mistake. We tried to fix what was unfixable. You and your family developed your own coping mechanism. You learned over the years, how to survive as a family unit. With the best of intentions, we came into your world and tried to change things. It's totally backfired. Good intentions don't excuse it. I feel responsible."

"You really did help us. I think therapy just spearheaded the inevitable."

"Won't you reconsider placing Erik in a foster home?"

"But, Wilf, you said yourself, I'm too involved in the decision-making in this family. Everyone must be responsible for their individual choices and face the consequences. I give up control of the family and all hell breaks loose. I told you; Mom has no control of any of us, especially Marina and Erik. Erik might be better off out of the home. Maybe things will work out in the long run."

"Erik feels very unloved and not appreciated," Wilf says. "He needs understanding, love, and attention."

"I wish I could express love to him by hugging him, but I find it extremely hard to do. It tortures my mind. Thinking about having to play, hug, or kiss as a father would with his children gives me great anguish. I just can't, okay?"

Nevertheless, I visit Erik in the hospital. Of course, I am the good Witness and tell him he is being punished by God.

"I do care about you, Erik. Don't you see if you don't stop this behavior now, things are going to get worse?"

"I don't care."

"I don't believe you. I know you care. I just don't know what to do to help you."

The next day, a policeman drops off a summons for Erik to appear in court. Later in the day, another officer hands me my fourth subpoena.

Wilf, Mandy, and Lance feel we should let Erik come home because he deserves another chance. The St. Thomas Elders tell Mom that Erik is just playing games with her. If she can't handle Erik, then he should live somewhere else where he'll get proper discipline. Mom's hurting right now and Erik is going to hate her for agreeing to a foster home. Does she love him enough to let go? Did she ever have him? I admit Erik has gone through a lot. He will feel rejected for this, but he certainly will not appreciate Mom for letting him come home. I love Erik very much. I want what's best for him, but something has to happen to change things. We can't go on like this.

The next day as I'm working my regular shift at the variety store in St. Thomas, Mom shows up. She had a friend drive her to my work to tell me that Erik has to come home. Administration said they would charge us $104 per day to keep him in the hospital.

I pick Erik up in the late afternoon, but only after calling everyone: our therapists, the police, the Ontario Hospital, the Mental Health Association, friends, even Ronny—no one can help us. The reason Erik is in the hospital in the first place is to give everyone some breathing room until a foster home is found. It's not the right time for him to come home. Things are not resolved and I fear something explosive lies ahead.

And so, not only has my individual therapy ended, but so has therapy for all of us. Therapy has helped me personally, but it has disintegrated this family. No one is happy. Wilf and Mandy regret stepping in, Erik will end up in foster care, Marina is mixed up about her feelings, and Mother feels like a failure, afraid for Erik's future.

Now that Erik knows we have to take him home, he thinks he can do what he wants. I'm sick and tired of the games he's playing. Either he listens to us or out he goes.

"We don't have to feed you unless you cooperate."

"We'll see about that. I'll just call Lance!" Erik sneers, laughing in my face.

"Dis is what comes from de t'erapy! I don't want any more part of it!" yells Mom.

"Neither do I!" I agree. "I've had it with people telling me things contrary to the Bible. God's Word has a superior way of handling matters. I've let it play second fiddle and look what happens to us!"

Erik has no intention of listening to any authority or rules. I ask him to come downstairs.

"No!"

I can't leave the house with Erik in this angry frame of mind. He might hurt Mom or Marina.

"You can't stay in our room forever. Come down!"

"Make me."

"All right, I will."

I proceed to try and drag him downstairs. Then Mom joins in the fight. For twenty minutes, we push and prod to no avail. This is insane. Erik's fists are flying. Mom grabs a broom. I grab my belt. No one wins. No way will Erik budge. We stop fighting.

"Okay, if you're not going to abide by the rules of this house, you won't get your supper."

It's 4:00 P.M. the following day. Erik still hasn't budged. We didn't feed him. Erik calls his therapist. "I told Lance you abused me. He's coming right over."

"You were extremely cruel to Erik!" says Lance. "Now I believe Erik would be better off outside the home for a while."

An appointment is made for 6:00 P.M. with a worker from the Children's Aid Society. Does it take something this dramatic to get attention?

"Yes, I know we 'abused' Erik," I confess to the Children's Aid Society worker. "Don't you understand? It's an impossible situation. You can't tell a kid that big what to do. We can't leave him home alone. We're being held hostage by a fifteen-year-old. This whole thing wouldn't have happened if we weren't forced to take him home from the hospital in the first place!"

I see the absurdity in this situation. We were all abused for well over a decade, and we couldn't get anyone to notice. Now Erik cries abuse, and everyone comes running! This is a nightmare. I don't want to take care of anyone, but I don't want to abandon them either. Now it looks as if they would have been better off if I had left. Introduce three worldly therapists into our lives, remove any sense of order, and all hell breaks loose. Once again, Mom and I are to blame. I plead temporary insanity. I don't want to make Erik do anything. I don't want to be his father. I'm not his father!

No one realizes how manipulative Erik is. He's calling the shots, but he doesn't realize he's not winning. He didn't want to go to a foster home, yet he has to go to be "protected" from us. Erik knows we're not abusers. If he had been spanked for all his misbehavior these past years, he'd be black and blue!

On the car ride home, I tell Mom and Marina: "I don't know what the answers are. I just know this is it for me. I can't play 'father' anymore. I'm going crazy. Two days before the trial!"

"This doesn't solve anything," says Marina.

"I know. Why did Erik steal? He's been breaking the law for the past year, and he never got disciplined by Mom or me. We hoped that The Truth would help him. Is he doing all this just to get attention?"

"Told you, you should have left Aylmer earlier!" says Marina.

"It breaks my heart to see Erik like dat!" cries Mom.

"I know, Mom, I know," I sigh.

Lance took Erik to the Children's Aid Society. Erik will stay for four weeks in a St. Thomas emergency foster home. An impossible situation led to this. It seems like a healthy solution for Erik, for us.

I can't believe this! The trial is tomorrow and the St. Thomas congregation will probably announce Erik is disassociated at the Thursday meeting. This is too much. Daniel will probably go to jail the day before his son is punished by the Witnesses. It is possible the newspapers might report both father and son have a date with the courts on the same day.

I am responsible for this train wreck. By the time I decided we had no choice but to move from Aylmer, it was too late. The damage had been done. Too many years of scorn, explaining ourselves and living in denial. We have no idea what to expect from the trial coming up. Marina has no confidence in it at all. She seems to feel it would have been better to have dropped the issue. I am trying to keep my head up in this sea of criticism, but this past week I've actually questioned if sacrificing privacy is worth it. Definitely, I conclude, if it changes the family's situation. *Isn't it?*

I am the only one in my family who hasn't been publicly reproved. I can't let down my faith, my peers, my family. How could I live with myself if I failed?

Like Scarlett O'Hara, I tell myself, I can't think about that now. I'll think about that tomorrow.

Sometimes my movie friends do provide relief, for I'm going to need every ounce of strength I have to survive the trial. Being responsible for Erik and Marina has given me four years of heartaches. At the same time, it helped me escape and avoid having to face my own problems. I can't undo the past, but I can change the present. Before I go to bed, I write a prayer in my diary:

> **Diary Entry, March 15, 1982. I'm weary from imagining Daniel's appearance. I can see the slave role I had with him as a reality more and more. No way will I give up my fight for justice, whether or not I get it in the courts. God, please help us to never give up and forgive us for our shortcomings. Help us to forgive others and be patient with friends. We need you more than any human could possibly help us.**

If there are people who believe that sexual abuse of children is wrong only because society has dictated that norm, how would they explain my family's disintegration and dysfunction? Back then, we had no knowledge of its devastation. Each of us was coping the only way we knew how, and not doing a hell of a good job of it! Living under the scrutiny of the Jehovah's Witnesses did not help. How could we err without it making table talk headlines in the local congregation? What should have been classed as normal, expected, confused behavior became labeled sinful, selfish, and wicked instead. Our not being able to live up to the ideals and expectations held up to us aggravated our low self-esteem.

As much as was possible at that time, I let Wilf into my outer world, but emotionally I kept him locked out of its inner sanctum. During our year together, I never cried, lost my temper, showed the spectrum of feelings I would have possessed, had I been in touch with my feelings. It was Thinking Donald who progressed by leaps and bounds. I suppose it was necessary for me to keep it together for my family, the trial, and appearances. Just because I wanted to feel emotion did not mean it would or even could happen. I wasn't ready.

Our individual therapists had their work cut out for them when they took us on, and although mistakes were made, they hadn't failed us. Initially, I went to see my therapist for all the wrong reasons, but a survivor's journey doesn't include a map of healthy choices. My brothers had chosen to fight the system; I chose to manipulate it. This course of action changed the direction of my life forever. Through the process, I discovered our family's dysfunction had everything to do with the past. Faced with this reality head on, I had to admit it to myself, if not to others. At least I admitted this truth to Wilf. Despite the pain of having to face the damage and the unfortunate transition to group therapy, the positive aspects of my therapy far out-weighed the negative. I was beginning to experience a few real emotions—anger, fear, sadness—not in terms of the past, but in real time. I was also becoming more assertive, learning to look at how I felt about a situation instead of heeding everyone else's wishes first.

Our therapists not only helped us open Pandora's Box, they permanently removed the lid.

Chapter Forty-Three

"How did the preliminary hearing go on the charges involving you and Corey?" asks Maurice.

"Well, it was the first time we had seen or talked to one another in thirteen years. It was very difficult for Corey. He was an emotional wreck. He told me how much the incident with Daniel had affected him all these years. I thanked him and his fiancée for supporting us. Unfortunately, the charges in Corey's case were dropped because he was molested outside Elgin County, in another jurisdiction."

"That must have made Daniel's day!"

"You should have seen Daniel, his wife and their supporters cheering on the court house steps. It made me nauseous. Unfortunately, Daniel was never recharged on those counts. As far as evidence for the trial, the Court wouldn't hear testimony that Daniel sexually abused a child outside of our family. Our only hope was the remaining eight other charges."

"Still, seems like one thing after another," says Maurice. "How could you handle it?"

"The pressure was beginning to take its toll. I couldn't control my feelings or thoughts. No matter where I was, my mind would dart from the past to the present, and even to a fantasy future. It was frightening, but the physical effects of the stress scared me more. I even made an appointment with Doctor Billingsley because I was experiencing chest pains."

"With so much going on, I don't doubt it. It's no wonder you blocked out the past."

"Call me 'Sybil by choice.' I not only blocked out the past, I blocked out the present too. As events happened in real time, they were immediately transferred to my movie reels."

"You do have moments of great escape."

"Sometimes I blanked out by choice. Other times I had no control over which memories or events were sent to my movie reels. Both past and present experiences became part of my fantastical world. I needed them to."

"I know you did."

"Well, good-bye, Aylmer. It's a quiet, sleepy town, don't you think? At least for most people here, I'm sure."

Maurice and I are off again, to what I had hoped would be our last destination. This is one time I don't mind looking in the side view mirror.

"Donald, how far is it to St. Thomas?"

"About twenty minutes," I tell him. *"This time."*

*   *

Traveling west on Highway 3 between Aylmer and St. Thomas, I find the silence unbearable.

"Ten minutes to 'show time'!" I announce from behind the wheel.

"You know, Donald, I'm not as nervous as I thought I'd be," states Marina confidently.

"It's so quiet without Erik."

"I hope he is okay at de hospital and dat foster home will treat him right," sighs Mom.

"At least it's better than the constant fighting, isn't it?"

"I know, Donald, but I miss him. He is my son."

"Remember, Mom, we didn't want Erik to have to go through this or hear our testimony. He's too young," Marina reminds her.

I am not apprehensive as I approach St. Thomas's oppressively grand Wellington Street County Court. *"It is just a courtroom,"* I tell myself.

"At least we know our way around here, eh Mom?"

But this time around, I feel more like a visitor than an actor in an ongoing saga.

Walking up the sidewalk leading to the courthouse, we pass by two large, decorative cannons placed strategically on the lawn. Three over-bearing, arched pillars loom ahead. We enter the building through relatively plain doors and, searching for a familiar face, proceed to find our way through a maze of corridors. Everyone is in a large waiting room, not far from the main chamber. Nine Witnesses from St. Thomas, Straffordville, and London are here to support us. The fact that not one member from the Aylmer congregation is present does not go unnoticed.

"Hmmm. Mom—Marina, I thought the Witnesses who were subpoenaed to the preliminary hearing would be here by now. I wonder what this means."

"Maybe dey have to work," says Mom naïvely.

"Hi, Mandy. Nice to see you," says Marina.

"Thanks for being here, Wilf. I appreciate it."

Since I had stopped therapy, I wasn't sure if Wilf would show up. I consider his presence a sign of his caring, and that he is a man of his word.

Suddenly, I see Daniel walking by in the hallway. He casually nods his head as he passes by Mom seated on a wooden bench. He acts as though they are old friends. He looks as if he's taking mental notes about Mother. We notice his hair is dyed. I whisper to Mom, "Don't you think the red hair gives him the look of a natural harlot?"

Hey, this is different. A sepia movie for a change. I'm a fly stuck in a web. I spy with my insect eyes all the living things below me. It's dark and I'm cold. Only a flash of red hair adds color to this picture.

Constable Petz walks in to provide an update.

"On March 6, Daniel fled the country to Belgium."

"But we just saw him walk by, hair and all!"

Petz explains that Daniel left his wife a note stating that as a result of receiving death threats at work, he was leaving the country. He also told her how much she should sell the furniture for. Marsha called their lawyer, Joe Feinstein, who in turn contacted the police. Daniel's parents pleaded with him to return to Canada, telling him he would probably be deported. On March 11, Daniel returned to London. A warrant for his arrest was issued and he was picked up yesterday, March 15. He was held in custody overnight, and released early this morning.

"Isn't that good news for us?" I ask.

"I think it certainly could be construed as a sign of guilt."

Considering these events to be a great development, we believe it will help our case. Just the shot of confidence we need.

"Don't get your hopes up too high, Donald," cautions Wilf, ever the voice of reason.

"Oh, I know. You're right. I'm just trying to think positive."

The court officer approaches.

"It's time to enter the courtroom."

"Let's sit over there, okay?" I suggest, pointing to the back rows of seats.

The room is nearly empty, except for a few gloomy-looking people scattered about. Today's drizzling rain and fog probably add to my perception. Thinking Donald photographs the interior: brown paneling, brown benches, brown chairs. Ugly, dull, dark. Three expressionless reporters take up residence in the front row.

Marina, Mom, and our supporters surround me. It is nice having them present, but I thought Ronny would be here today. He was subpoenaed.

From my vantage point, I scan the courtroom. I watch the Crown Attorney, Harold Greenfield, chatting with the clerk. Greenfield is a short, pudgy man with spectacles. He seems friendly with everyone in the courtroom—everyone but us. I think it strange that he neither speaks to us nor acknowledges our presence before the trial begins. He could trip over us and he wouldn't know who we are. But he does have our statements; perhaps he doesn't need to talk to us just yet.

"He knows our names. He'll just call us up on the witness stand when he needs us," I think to myself.

I spot Daniel's wife, sitting in the second row. Marsha looked happier at the preliminary hearing. A minister and one other supporter sit with her.

Marsha looks older than her years, wears no make up or jewelry, is poorly dressed, and needs a hairstyle better suited to her. Her appearance cries out for a makeover. In many ways she reminds me of how Mother looked when she was married to Daniel, all those years ago. Mother looks younger, healthier, and prettier now than when he last glimpsed her. No wonder he glared at her in the waiting room. He was probably shocked at her weight loss, makeup, jewelry, and modern hairstyle.

Marsha must be ignorant of the truth. Otherwise, I am insulted by her presence here. Does she really believe that Daniel is one of God's disciples? Does she think all three of us are lying? *"Must be a case of blind faith,"* I tell myself. I do pity her though. She has to sleep with Daniel. We don't.

An elegant man enters the courtroom wearing the same style of robe as Greenfield. He stops and talks with Marsha. It must be Daniel's lawyer, Joe Feinstein. He's tall, distinguished-looking, and appears animated in both gesture and conversation.

Greenfield approaches Feinstein. They shake hands and exchange words. They laugh and pat each other on the back. *"Something is definitely wrong with this picture,"* I tell myself. A shiver runs down the length of my spine, and I feel a knot form in the pit of my stomach.

A police officer accompanies Daniel into the courtroom, and leads him to the docket. Daniel is holding a small red Bible in his left hand.

I have no connection to this stranger whatsoever.

The ghost of my dreams, the man in my black and white movies appears before me. He doesn't seem as threatening in living color.

As soon as he is seated, he starts jotting notes on a pad of paper. He looks back in my direction.

"Mom, he still looks over my head, just like he did when he used to be upset with me. Guess I've given him good reason, this time."

But he looks more proud than ashamed. He even seems confident. Does he know something we don't? The knot in my stomach tightens.

"Everyone rise," states the officious clerk, his voice resonating. "The Honourable Judge R. L. Bannister presiding."

I don't believe our luck. Judge Bannister, who had granted Mom her divorce, is presiding over this case. As Bannister briskly walks to his seat, the knot in my stomach relaxes. Four years later, his face is still as handsome and kind as I remember it to be.

"Mr. Feinstein, is this Daniel D'Haene?" the clerk continues.

"It is, sir."

"Daniel D'Haene, please stand."

Looks like Feinstein will be addressing the Court. I thought the Crown would present their case first.

"Before Mr. D'Haene is arraigned on this charge, he was taken into custody just yesterday which made it difficult for me to see him this morning. I have not been able to see Mr. Greenfield. We'll need a few minutes to agree on a few matters."

"In that case, we'll have a short recess. Advise the clerk when you're ready—I assume fifteen minutes?"

Does Judge Bannister know that Daniel had fled the country? And Feinstein's choice of words is a bit strange. *Agree to what?* I wonder, as I feel my stomach knotting once again.

"Wilf, they just get going and they're already talking recess!"

"That's the way these things work sometimes, Donald."

"I need some fresh air."

"Oh, Donald!" calls Mom. "Dey are starting."

The clerk asks Daniel to stand. He begins to read off a long list of charges—section this, criminal code that. Daniel is charged with indecently assaulting and committing an act of gross indecency on Ronny, Marina, and me. The seventh charge read by the clerk states Daniel is charged with committing an act of buggery between 1974 and 1976. My mind drifts off.

It's so highly impersonal hearing your name called during an arraignment. And it's so foreign to me to hear The Game called "an act of gross indecency," "indecent assault," or an "act of buggery." No wonder Daniel called it The Game. How would have I reacted if he had said, "Do you want to play 'Gross Indecency,'" or "Do you want an 'Indecent Assault?'"

I'm in the audience of an X-rated, late night game show. I hear the announcer proclaim, "Donald, come on down. It's your turn to play Buggery!"

"…committed the act of bestiality with a goat, Section 155," the clerk continues.

"What? Did I hear right?" a voice whispers, startling me out of my daydream. The clerk's reading of the last charge is a shocker. It certainly wakes up the onlookers and the Witnesses who surround me. Even the reporters appear to be intrigued.

I cringe lower and lower in my seat. This is more embarrassing than I thought it would be.

Daniel had elected to be tried by a court composed of judge and jury, but I don't see a jury come out. Daniel must have been advised that juries can be much tougher than judges in cases of sexual assault.

"Do you now elect to be tried by a judge without a jury?" asks the clerk.

"Yes, sir."

"Is that with the consent of the Crown, Mr. Greenfield?" asks the judge.

"Yes, sir, it is."

The clerk proceeds to repeat the litany of charges in reverse order. After each charge is read out loud, Daniel is asked how he wishes to plead on each consecutive count, guilty or not guilty. The clerk reads the three indecent assault charges first, followed by the buggery charge. For each, Daniel pleads, "Not guilty." Next, the clerk reads the three charges of gross indecency to which Daniel pleads, "Guilty." Finally, Daniel pleads, "Not Guilty" to the charge of bestiality. I'm not surprised. But why would anyone make something like this up? Had it not been for his admission to the Elders, no one would have been the wiser.

"Wilf, why the different order? Why is Daniel pleading guilty to only three out of the eight charges?"

"I don't know, Donald."

"Are you ready for your trial?" asks the clerk.

"Yes, we are," states Feinstein.

"Your Honour," says Greenfield, representing the Crown, "I have the facts with respect of those counts on which the accused has pleaded guilty. I'm offering no evidence on those counts on which the accused pleaded not guilty."

"Those charges will be dismissed, the Crown offering no evidence," decrees the judge.

The knot in my stomach bursts into frayed ropes. Dismissed! I can't believe my ears. Why is the Crown Attorney not offering evidence on the "Not Guilty" pleas? Earlier, two charges had been dismissed because the acts had taken place in Middlesex County. Now this!

Daniel is only pleading guilty on three charges of gross indecency. The maximum sentence for gross indecency is five years, for indecent assault, ten. If Greenfield proceeded with the indecent assault charges, it might produce a longer sentence. We gave Rhiness pages and pages of written documentation. We could verify each other's testimony.

And why drop the buggery charge? I am fully capable of testifying to my experience. Something smells fishy.

Outwardly, I am the epitome of control. Inside, I am seething with anger and emotion.

"Please God help me. All I want is justice. What's wrong with that? You and I both know Daniel is evil, that his claim of being born-again is a façade. What more can I do?"

Greenfield begins his address by recounting the events that precipitated the charges, stating that a police officer commenced the investigation on May 31, 1981, in Aylmer, where Marina and I said we were both sexually assaulted for "some seven to eight years."

The Crown should have taken the time to interview me. I certainly never said I was abused for eight years. I told Inspector Rhiness, it was a period of eleven years, from the time I was four years of age to when I was fifteen. It was my sister who was abused for eight years. Greenfield must have misread his notes. I do hope Inspector Rhiness gets here soon.

Greenfield continues: "By way of background, the accused was married to the parents of these children in 1956—I'm sorry, the accused was married to the mother of these two children in 1956. The fourth and last child of that marriage was Erik D'Haene. He was born February 8—it must have been 1970 that child was born. That child has nothing to do with these charges."

What *didn't* Greenfield get wrong? Though Erik may not have anything to do with these charges, he has a lot to do with our being here today. He was the first in our family to break the code of silence in 1971. And Erik was born in 1966, not in 1970 as Greenfield claims, otherwise he would have been a one year old when he disclosed the abuse.

"Greenfield is reading off a lot of accurate information though," I tell myself.

"The children were encouraged to do acts of sex between themselves.... When I speak of the children, I'm only referring to the two eldest boys and the girl. Apparently, there were no acts involving the youngest, Erik.... The accused then threatened them personally if they told their mother that he would do a number of things, amongst which would cause him to leave and therefore the family would be destroyed; or...that he would have to kill them or do some violence to them."

I am dumbfounded. "No acts involving the youngest!" He must be talking about another Erik. If an adult asking a five year old child to manipulate his penis is not an 'act', I don't know what is.

"Sorry to interrupt you, but I'm not clear on one point, and that is whether or not these acts took place involving two children at the same time," Bannister asks.

"On occasions, it was two children at one time.... The daughter was concerned that the accused might cause the mother some harm. The accused indicated to her that the mother did not like to play with him in this manner, and that's why he had the children.... He would put his penis between her legs but not penetrate the vagina in any way.... He would have her undress, and he would attempt to masturbate her or perform cunnilingus on her.... On one occasion in the motor vehicle, when the youngest brother was present, and in order to try and protect Erik from any sexual contact with the accused, she sent him out of the truck and masturbated her father in the truck.

"On one occasion when the mother was at home, the youngest, in the kitchen with Donald and Marina and the youngest child, came downstairs and indicated that he had been in the attic with his father, and that his father had wanted him to manipulate his penis. The youngster, not knowing anything like this had happened to the others, came down immediately and told his mother, at which time she began to cry and they had quite a family discussion about it. That would have been in late 1971 or '72."

Greenfield obviously has not studied his notes. He said a one-, possibly two-year-old, came down three floors down from the attic to disclose the abuse to his mother. Marina wasn't in the kitchen with

Mother. She was in the attic with Daniel and Erik who was five years old at the time, not one or two.

Because Greenfield fails to say Daniel left moments after the disclosure, the implication is that he was involved in the "family discussion." To label any communication Daniel had with us in all the years we lived with him "a family discussion" is misleading and foreign to my experience. It appears the truth is wasted on Greenfield.

"As a result of the mother finding out, there was a period of time where the accused was able to sort of patch things up in the family; promised his wife it would not happen any further and the family continued on as a family. There was period of time when the accused did not—a short period of time—when he did have no sexual contact with the children. It was in 1971 when Erik was five."

Make up your mind, Greenfield! First, Erik was born in '70, now he is five in '71! The Crown's blunders continue.

"After a short while, the same conduct continued.... The accused taught the daughter to masturbate herself, encouraged her and the brothers in doing this when each was in the presence of the other. He began to substantially affect the emotional growth of the older children, especially the daughter, who became infatuated with herself and with her dolls, and, in fact, the accused encouraged her to masturbate with a doll or dolls that she had....

"In 1976, a religious sect to which the family belonged at that time became aware—because of the difficulties in the family—became aware of the sexual conduct which had been taking place between the accused and his children. He went so far as on one occasion to actually sleep in the nude with the children...when the mother was in the hospital."

Where did Greenfield acquire his information and dates? Did someone forget to provide him our statements? It was in 1973 that the Elders found out about the abuse, not 1976. They also did not become aware of the abuse because of "difficulties in the family." We had those from day one. It was Ronny who first broke the silence. The Elders had no idea anything like that had been going on. Why didn't the Crown interview us in this case? Did he interview Daniel? Had Greenfield interviewed the Elders, he would have realized there was enough evidence to pursue all the charges against Daniel.

"In the fall of 1976, the family split up.... In 1978, the divorce was granted.... During that period of time as well, there was some meeting or hearing of the religious elders...the Jehovah's Witness sect excommunicated—or perhaps that's incorrect—disfellowship is the correct word—the accused from that church because of his sexual acts with his children, and at this fellowship meeting, the accused admitted to three of the church officials...."

"What year was that?" asks the judge.

"1976, in the fall, probably November..."

It is a good question. I just wish the judge would let me answer it. The correct answer is: November, 1973.

"... Admitted that he had committed homosexual acts with his two sons—two elder sons—and as well, had sexual relations with his daughter, Marina; although those relations, as I understand the evidence, did not include intercourse.... Not until after that period of time as the elder children grew up and became teenagers and young men and lady that they began to have some psychological problems; problems with their identity in relation to their peers or other school children. Marina was not able to have any sort of a normal female childhood, which would have included dating or anything like that, but began to have tendencies or feelings that she was a lesbian. As well, Donald began to exhibit homosexual tendencies.

"Donald and the daughter presently are being treated by, I believe, a psychologist in an effort to, I suppose, try and live with what they had as children, trying to get over the difficult time that they had as children. Both of those children are in their twenties, as I indicated, receiving some treatment in an effort to alter their sexual tendencies to those of a heterosexual relationship. This caused them considerable difficulties over the years because of the conduct at home. They weren't able to take part in school activities, normal school activities so they all became rather withdrawn, introverted. Marina, in particular is very distrustful of male figures. They feel that they have been robbed of a normal childhood, and they're hoping that with further and continued treatment, that they themselves can take on a more normal family type life in the future.

"Subsequent to the divorce, the children went to live with the mother. At present, I believe all of them reside on their own—not the youngest, but the ones that are involved in these charges, all are in their twenties now. I'm sorry, Ronald is on his own. Donald and Marina still reside with the mother. The accused since that time has remarried, as I understand it, another person. One of the perhaps more serious factors is the psychological damage that the acts have caused to the children and require their subsequent counselling—probably a better word than treatment. Those are the facts."

"Mr. Greenfield, I wonder if there's any explanation of all this material. It seems all along the way certain people knew that this was going on. Why has it not come to light before? Is there an answer for that?" asks the judge.

Thinking Donald wonders too. Bannister hears so many cases, perhaps he forgot he presided over my mother's divorce case. This time Bannister is face to face with my abuser. Why didn't he ask me then, "Why is this man not behind bars?" I assume it was because I hadn't asked him first. If he had asked me, my stunned reply would have been, "You mean it's against the law?"

"The initial finding out by the mother in 19—I think it was 73—it was kept as a family matter. The accused promised to her that he would seek out some form of treatment and it would not occur anymore..."

I feel lightheaded.

The applause is deafening. The bright lights and cameras distract me. The smarmy host with a microphone asks, "Mr. Harold Greenfield, for $500, when did the mother find out about the abuse?" "I, uh, I believe it was in 1972. No wait, oh, can I change my answer? These things were discovered in 1973. I think I read it somewhere." "Nice try, Harold. Unfortunately, there is only one correct answer: 1971. But we do have some nice parting gifts."

"...The mother was totally dependent upon...the accused for food and any income, and the family was totally dependent on him. They didn't realize that there were facilities that could help them, and the mother really wanted to believe, and did believe, in 1973, that sort of thing would stop."

Because of Greenfield's uncertainty on dates and points, I know it will reflect negatively on the accuracy of other evidence. His presentation cries out for correction and organization. Of course, Thinking Donald knows, if you start speculating, you have to be consistent.

"1976...was an eventful year. Mary split up the children when—so they were rid of their father at that point."

Or not! I was almost getting used to the predictability of the blunders, but this one is ridiculous. My mother's name is Jeannette. Daniel and Feinstein must be enjoying this.

"The children were old enough to sort of assist in maintaining the family. It was during this same period of time as his fellowship from the church at the hearing; moreover, the church reported this outside their church. That's my understanding at that time. Those persons, three committee members who met and conducted the disfellowship hearing were subsequently spoken to by the investigating officers, but that was not until 1981. There was no report made by that group to the Children's Aid or any society such as that, nor was any report made to any persons in authority—the police or anything else. It apparently was kept as an in-church matter. The accused vacated his fellowship, he left the church and about a year, or year and a half after that, he attempted to return to the church, but he was not so allowed to return."

What in the hell is Greenfield talking about? Where did he get his information? Did he even bother to read our statements? In 1976, we children were not old enough to support the family—I was fifteen, Ronny eighteen, Marina thirteen, and Erik ten.

Obviously, Greenfield has rehearsed none of his delivery. First he says, "the church reported this outside the church." Then he says, "no report was made...to any persons in authority—the police or anything else." The Elders had nothing to do with the family splitting up, Mom's divorce, or my going to the authorities. The only thing they did was meet with the family upon Ronny's disclosure, take down evidence, and disfellowship Daniel. They never "reported this outside the church." Daniel didn't "vacate his fellowship." He had no choice—he was kicked out.

"Matters were, I suppose to some extent public when the divorce proceedings took place. I believe, apparently, the proceedings in the divorce, papers and documents in '76 and '77 and '78 when the divorce took place, referred to, I believe, formed some partial basis for the divorce hearing, that the accused had entered into sexual relationships with his three children. So at this time there would have been, I suppose, the original petition in '77—'76—'77, I think that's what there would have been, the petition would have outlined some of those factors, but at that time he did not come—it was not made aware or known to the police."

Will Judge Bannister recognize Mother and me? Will he clue into the fact that officers of the Court, including himself, were aware of the abuse as far back as '78, during the divorce proceedings?

Greenfield's referral to our father's molestation of his children as "sexual relationships with his three children," while acknowledging some degree of psychological abuse, downplays the nature of the offenses.

A detrimental aspect of Greenfield's presentation was the uncertainty, evident in his use of, "I suppose," "I believe," "apparently," and "I think." This was not the language of a crown attorney confident of his facts, working toward building the strongest possible case. Where was the righteous indignation and the hatred for these acts? Wilf was right. This is worse than anything I've seen on television.

"The mother at that time, she was interested in mostly getting a divorce. That was her primary concern and looking after her children. She indicated when questioned about that, there were a couple of problems after the first thing in 1973, the family sort of got back together and she continued to have sex with him between '73 and '76 and because of that, apparently that removed, in their religion, the right of divorce that she had over that period of time. It was sort of forgiveness, therefore you can't proceed with a divorce, according to that religion so it was not until '76 when there were further matters which arose subsequent to their getting back again in 1973 and also some other occasions that anything came of it, she finally, after the break-up, did contact a lawyer or counsel and commenced divorce proceedings."

Unbelievable! The "further matter which arose" is the revelation that Daniel had performed an act of bestiality. Mother wouldn't have left Daniel without that piece of information. Yet here we are in court six years later, and the truth can't be referred to because that particular charge was dropped earlier! Greenfield's presentation would make a "keystone cop" proud.

Greenfield's portrayal of my mother is utterly misleading. He doesn't know our mother. She isn't an educated woman. She has been isolated and unaware of the world outside her home. If we hadn't moved her out, she would still be living with her captor. She never had a desire to divorce Daniel.

Greenfield fumbles onward: "The lawyer advised at that time not to say anything to the accused. Perhaps it was that they took that caution from the lawyer not to say anything to anybody. In any event, she never did call the police about it."

I feel a chill in the courtroom.

Other Donald is placed under arrest, escorted to a cell and brutally shackled to a cold, musty wall. From within his solitary confinement, he screams, "Why didn't the lawyer call the police? As an officer of the Court, did he not have an obligation to report a crime? Did he need Mother's permission to do so? Is this the voice of reason? His cries go unanswered.

"She always thought in her own mind that it was morally wrong, the conduct was wrong, it was against the church doctrine but she was not aware, apparently, that there was some remedy available to her by way of telling the police. She as well was not aware at that time perhaps because the children were still at a younger age, that she was aware of the impact that it had psychologically onto her children."

"Perhaps might not have shown up until later," interjects Bannister.

"That's right. I think it became very much more apparent when they got older. By that time the damage had been done. At that time it was difficult for her and the children to do, and they were more concerned with keeping the family together. I'm sure that each sort of hid as much as they could from the mother."

"How did the matter finally come to light in 1981?"

"The children, I believe it was Donald—it was Donald who, as part of the counselling programme that he was undertaking, was brought about that he had to deal with that matter. He couldn't leave it in the back of his mind and it was as a result of that, that he then made arrangements and went to see the police and then as well, Marina did and then subsequent to that, Ronald did and then it was then in the open. The police began an investigation at that time. There apparently had been some contact between the police and an investigation totally unrelated to this one, between the police and the Jehovah's Witnesses and they then sort of followed it up and somehow got together. I really don't know how it actually happened, but it was Donald who sort of initiated the proceedings."

More weak statements from the Crown: "after the first thing in 1973," "there apparently," "sort of followed up," "somehow got together," "I really don't know how it actually happened," and "sort of initiated the proceedings." The truth is less confusing than Mr. Greenfield's address would suggest: I disclosed the abuse to Detective Rhiness. It is possible that Daniel wouldn't have been charged at all had I not been interviewed concerning the Jackson case. In fact, events proceeded quickly on Rhiness' side. Daniel was arrested before Rhiness even suggested therapy, a crucial point totally wasted on Greenfield. The Court has been misinformed yet again. Where is Detective Rhiness? He can verify these facts for Greenfield.

"In the period of 1962 to 1976, fourteen years, they lived in eight communities either in Elgin or Middlesex and there were also things — there was as well an order made with respect to the divorce proceedings for some form of—I may have the wrong word—maintenance for the wife and children. Although there were not regular payments made as late as June, 1981—the accused was some $9,000.00 in arrears for his wife and children—some form of wage attachment or something that they do was implemented at that time. I don't know what the up-date status of that is."

Wage attachment? We never knew Daniel was in arrears as far as making payments. His wages were never garnisheed. After receiving no monies from my father back in 1977, we considered the whole process a joke. We didn't know we had recourse to obtain the unpaid amount.

Had Greenfield interviewed us, he would have known about the two one-dollar checks Daniel mailed us, along with the box of his old clothes. That certainly would have shed some light on the actions of the "born again" accused.

"As far as I'm aware, the accused never did receive a fellowship back into that church and has not. There was correspondence continued between the Jehovah's Witness and the accused for some years when he attempted to get back into the church in '76—'77. Apparently there was no—although there was no correspondence between the congregation and Jehovah's Witness and the accused, there was never any publication or notification outside that area."

"Before calling on you, Mr. Feinstein, I think I'll have a fifteen minute recess," says the judge.

This is theater of the absurd. Within two sentences, Greenfield says, "there was correspondence" and "there was no correspondence" between the Witnesses and the accused. Not surprisingly, during the intermission, the Witnesses express outrage at what they view as inaccurate references to The Watchtower Society and the Elders.

"We have to do something about this," says one Witness.

"Donald, you have to do something about this," adds his wife.

Thinking Donald is furious but can't express his outrage by any display of emotion.

While Mandy hugs Marina, Wilf puts his arm around my shoulder.

"How are you doing? Are you okay?"

Thinking Donald "knows" that he can trust this embrace in all its sincerity. He just can't feel it.

"Oh, I'm fine."

Our therapists realize that the inaccuracies, the fact that we are not called to testify, and the Crown's lack of communication with us will likely influence the outcome of our trial. They also consider how Marina and I must be feeling, listening to our story read to strangers.

Even though I recognize Wilf's and Mandy's concern as genuine, Erik's situation is too fresh in my memory to consider returning to therapy, but I open up to Wilf.

"How could I be so stupid? Trusting the judicial system, Nort Rhiness, the Crown Attorney. Not only has Greenfield had other people do the leg work in this case—Rhiness, Petz, myself—he obviously didn't study the evidence that was given to him. We couldn't foresee this possibility. What a farce! Why didn't Greenfield involve us in his case? He doesn't even mention the detective's name!"

"Donald, I know it's difficult not to take Greenfield's lack of preparation and interest personally, but don't blame yourself. You did the right thing."

"I'm not going to disrupt the proceedings and shout, 'Who's side are you on? Get your facts straight.' No, I'm the one who plays by the rules." As Wilf listens, I recite all the hopes I see being dashed before us. I didn't break rules of protocol. I naïvely believed in the justice system. All of the energy I have put into this process seems to be for nothing.

"Were the Witnesses right when they told me not to use the worldly court system?" Wilf is silent. What is there left to say?

Chapter Forty-Four

"Think of the hours upon hours I put into our statements, psyching myself up to testify, and the energy it took defending and explaining our decision to charge Daniel, only to get let down by Greenfield."

"That's an understatement. I can't imagine how you felt. I think a case could be made to view the Crown's presentation as a crime in itself."

* * * * * * * * * *

During recess, a stranger's voice calls my name.

"Yes?"

An officer approaches me.

"Mr. Greenfield would like me to verify a point. Was it because of The Watchtower Society's pressuring you that you brought these charges to light? Why did you bring these charges forward?"

How much can I say in two minutes? I am disappointed that Greenfield doesn't speak with me directly, but I answer the officer's questions calmly and clearly. He is gone in a flash.

Upon resuming, Feinstein advises the Court that Daniel has no prior record, that the facts Greenfield presented are substantially correct, but makes the following correction: "The accused was actually disfellowshipped from The Watchtower Society, Aylmer Fellowship in 1973, in November, and thereafter in 1974 he did, indeed, make efforts to rejoin the congregation which efforts were futile. Finally, in 1976, in September, he embraced the Christian church and that, I am advised, was what caused the matrimonial split rather than the disfellowship that had occurred some years earlier or the incidents involving the children."

Feinstein correcting Greenfield's dates might appear superfluous at first glance, but it set the tone of his presentation. He said he would present the facts of this case truthfully and clearly. But "truth" as told by a serial pedophile to his lawyer makes for great fiction. The truth is that Daniel's attempts at rejoining the congregation were futile, not because they were personally punishing him, but because we reported new incidents of sexual abuse. Furthermore, Jehovah's Witnesses are a Christian organization so it would have been more accurate for Feinstein to state that Daniel had embraced *another* Christian church. Feinstein's suggestion that Daniel had only joined a Christian church in '76 was a clever choice of words and unfortunately went unchallenged by Greenfield. The three faiths of Daniel D'Haene's life all profess to be Christian in their origins. Daniel's conversion was as convenient then as it is now.

Mother did not leave Daniel because he had changed denominations. In their twenty years together, Daniel had been a Catholic, a Jehovah's Witness, and a born-again Christian. The immediate cause of the matrimonial split was an Elder's disclosure to us in the fall of 1976 of a previously unknown perverse act, bestiality.

Feinstein elaborates: "I am not in a position to make any judgments with respect to The Watchtower Society....I do have many things that were relayed to me, on instructions from my client, that he feels Your Honour should be made aware of. On that basis, I would like to get into a little bit of the background concerning the Society itself and my client's involvement with them."

"Ronny and I have spoken. He indicates that he certainly has no love for his father. He is unforgiving about what happened in the past, but he confirms that it certainly is his impression that the family break-up was caused by his father embracing a Christian sect."

The beauty of Feinstein's rhetoric, spun to perfection, makes me forget this trial is about sexual abuse, not religion. Almost. Why is it that Ronny, who is not here today, is the only family member Feinstein contacted? No doubt Daniel had informed his lawyer Ronny was more accepting of his new faith than we have been.

Twenty years hence, Ronny told me: "There is no way I told Feinstein I believed, 'the family break-up was caused by Daniel embracing a Christian sect. Had I known my words would be distorted, I would have been there in court. I didn't go because I was certain you would never get justice. We were going to leave him whatever religion he professed to be a member of!"

Even Judge Bannister is getting confused. He asks, "Sorry, is the family break-up because the accused left The Watchtower Society or was ejected from it?"

Feinstein provides a factual response informing the Court "there was no question" Daniel had been disfellowshipped in 1973, that we had continued our involvement in The Watchtower Society while Daniel had not, and that Daniel embraced a new faith in September of 1976.

I can't help but note that there is a stark contrast between Feinstein's and Greenfield's presentations. Feinstein is focused, clear on his part and makes good eye contact with the judge, while Greenfield shuffles through his notes and bungles the facts as if he were reading them for the first time.

Even statements such as, "the problems really started with the family" when Daniel "embraced a new faith," and "he and his wife...continued sexual relations up until then," a version of events entirely concocted from his client's viewpoint, are presented with such strong terminology and forceful delivery, that it adds credibility to Daniel's defense. To imply that the family problems arose when his client embraced a new faith is beyond reason, but seems plausible when stated by Feinstein.

As I sit and listen to Feinstein, I wonder, *why have I bothered going through this ordeal?*

Who other than Daniel, through his lawyer, could possibly suggest we would rather have lived with a molester who was a Witness than a molester who was a born-again Christian? If Daniel had become an atheist, agnostic, or a Buddhist Monk, it wouldn't have changed the fact that he was guilty of a crime.

Will this not go unchallenged by Greenfield?

Feinstein did not refute or discuss any of the evidence Greenfield presented regarding the offenses themselves. Instead he focuses on Daniel's career as an anti-Witness crusader, citing numerous "books, pamphlets, tape recordings" that his client has published, "preaching against the teachings of The Watchtower Society." Then he trots out the claim that it was Daniel who was the one being persecuted.

This distorted view of events has been engineered by Daniel to make him look better to his peers, to his critics, and finally to the Court. Four years earlier, Daniel had not contested the divorce because of the possibility of public disclosure. Now the stakes are much higher. He pulls out all the stops, as he knows he is facing possible incarceration. With no opportunity to address this misinformation in court, we struggle with our frustration in silence.

"It is incorrect to say that his wife did not realize that she had recourse…December of 1976…she sent him a letter with a…a Toronto newspaper…article commenting on a sentence involving a charge of sexual perversion and sexual acts with children. The letter says, 'Be very careful because more people know what you have done against your children and this could happen to you.'"

What "letter?" "A Toronto newspaper clipping?" Where is it? Daniel has never received any communication from us warning, threatening or informing him of our intent to lay charges. In fact, I told Mother in '76, "never acknowledge Daniel in word or deed for the rest of your life." She listened to me. It was Daniel who had tried to control us psychologically, sending hundreds of letters condemning us *for not writing to him*!

How sad to hear both the Crown and Daniel's lawyer misrepresent my mother. God forgive me for wanting to wipe Marsha's and Daniel's smug expressions off their faces!

Even in court, Daniel is able to preach his propaganda through his lawyer. Feinstein's submission focuses on everything but what is germane. Although he pled guilty to the lesser charges, as yet, there is no sign of remorse, no acknowledgement of personal responsibility, so typical of sexual predators. Wilf had warned me the trial could take all sorts of unpredictable twists. I now know it's true.

"Mr. D'Haene, himself, wrote a letter to his wife and his son, Ronald, advising them that their request was blackmail. They requested that he do two things: that he stop associating with his church and that he stop his vocal opposition to The Watchtower Society, and in particular, his lecturing and publishing of articles and books with respect to The Watchtower Society or everything would become known and he would face these types of problems; that is, the charges that have been made, or at least the behavior that he had exhibited would be brought to the attention of the authorities. That is, in fact, what finally happened in 1981, and that, in my respectful submission, based on the instructions I have, is a more accurate representation as to why it took so long to bring it to the authorities."

Again, why is Greenfield not requesting that this letter be produced as evidence?"

I give clever Feinstein full marks for quality of presentation. His controlled delivery of his client's version of events is given without the hesitations Greenfield displays. Confidently, he states, "That is, in fact, what finally happened." Whether based on lies or deception, his argument sounds convincing. Listening to the distortion of facts, I feel abused all over again. My worst fears have come true. Daniel uses the Court to persecute Jehovah's Witnesses. He's turning a sex abuse trial into a star ex-Jehovah's Witness, "born-again" event.

In fact, the Witness organization in no way harassed Daniel as he claims. On the contrary, they unwittingly protected him from the Court system by handling the case internally. Daniel should have been thanking them instead of using them as the scapegoat for his crimes. If there ever was a man persecuted in this life, it certainly isn't Daniel D'Haene.

Feinstein pulls out a folder from his briefcase.

"I would ask, sir, that the report of Dr. Wickware be made exhibit one to these proceedings. That accurately sets out the background of Mr. D'Haene of sufficient detail that I do not need to repeat it. Your Honour will note from the report that Mr. D'Haene did have a very substantial problem with alcohol for many years and in addition to that, sir, he suffered a great deal of traumatic emotional upset which he found unable to resolve while he was a member of The Watchtower Society. He suffered five nervous breakdowns during the years of his involvement with The Watchtower Society."

Mom and I look at each other in disbelief, helplessly rolling our eyes. I only saw him drunk once in my life and that was after the first time I said, "No!" to sex with him, after he had been partying with that loose woman. Daniel uses the scapegoat of all scapegoats: conjuring up an alcohol problem to explain his repellent behavior. Will the judge buy into these excuses? I really believe our case is up shit creek.

Bannister asks why the nervous breakdowns are not mentioned in the report.

"No sir, there are letters, sir, that he sent to The Watchtower Society after they became aware of the involvement that he had with his children and before he was disfellowshipped that amount to very obvious apologies, shame on his part, and cries for help, but he advises me that during the years that he was involved with the Society, the teaching was that psychiatrists were of the devil and that he was to have nothing to do with them.... I'm convinced his real belief is that during the years he was with the Society he felt very much brainwashed. There were changes in the doctrine of the Society that he simply could not reconcile in his own mind. He had always been a religious scholar, had studied all religions and still was, and he just could not reconcile the problems that he was experiencing in the change of doctrine in the Society."

Although it is true that Witnesses do not approve of therapy, my sister and I sought counselling without asking "permission" and received no retribution for this independent act. Here was an opportunity for Greenfield to point out, "Why is it that the victims of the accused who belong to the Witness faith could visit a psychiatrist and the perpetrator had not because he believed, 'psychiatrists were of the devil?'" On some level, our molester is presented as weaker than his victims!

More importantly, why is a psychiatric report presented on the molester and not on the victims? Our therapists were asked to write assessments. They submitted them. Where are they?

As with each traumatic experience in my life, I leave myself. This drama becomes a black and white movie in real time.

Other Donald shouts across the room. "Heh, Greenfield! Why don't you ask Daniel why he didn't see a psychiatrist while his children could?" Greenfield does not hear him. No one does. His voice is trapped within, frozen in the silence.

Outwardly, Thinking Donald is calm and detached. I observe objectively that Feinstein is presenting his client's case brilliantly.

"I wish I had had enough money to hire Feinstein myself," I whisper to Wilf.

Feinstein refers to the abuse as the "involvement he had with his children." Talk about a safe description—technically correct, yet purposefully vague. Daniel's sob story is more than anyone could take. Or is it just me?

Feinstein continues to describe the martyrdom of his client.

"He was constantly afraid of disfellowship because he had been taught, and he believed, that disfellowship meant his total destruction, an eternity of horror, as he describes it to me. So during this time, sir, he became extremely despondent. He had suicidal intentions but he never took steps in that regard. He simply got to the point where he was virtually unable to cope with his life."

Was Daniel more afraid of destruction or disclosure? His fear of the "eternity of horror" was not reason enough to stop having sex with his children. And I don't recall Daniel exhibiting signs of depression. He certainly didn't appear depressed during the thousands of sexual assaults on me!

Why is the Court given a detailed analysis of "the life and times of Daniel D'Haene" when only superficial, inaccurate mention is made of our individual trauma? Who's on trial here?

"He did, as he describes to me on September 12, 1976, experience something in the nature of a revelation. He is convinced that he communed with God and ever since that time, he has become a devout Christian, has had nothing to do with the Society, except, of course, for his involvement in the lecturing and the writing about the teachings of The Watchtower Society."

Considering his behavior and mistreatment of us the last months we lived with Daniel, a "revelation" would have been a welcome occurrence. But why is it that after this alleged "historic" event,

Daniel's actions did not reflect Christ-like qualities? Instead, he spent every waking hour from that moment on monitoring our every move. One form of abuse was replaced by another. And about a month after his becoming, "a devout Christian," I experienced the worst beating I ever had at his hands.

"I am advised by Mr. D'Haene, sir, that while he was involved in The Watchtower Society, he felt that their doctrine was extremely restrictive about sexual contact with his wife. He felt very restrained in that way. As I did mention, he had a very severe drinking problem, but it appears to be a fact that he's had nothing of an alcoholic nature since September 12, 1976."

Feinstein's reasoning is not only an insult to The Watchtower Society, but to us as well. Even if Daniel believed the Society's doctrine restricted sex with his wife, which it did not, how could that translate into his being less responsible for sexually abusing his children?

What is lost in this trial is the fact that Daniel is casting blame on a faith to which he professed allegiance, but in which he was a member in name only. The Witnesses condemn sexual acts outside of the marriage bond. Had the Elders learned of our abuse at any point between '63 and '73, he would have been disfellowshipped immediately upon disclosure.

It appears that the Elders not reporting our abuse to the authorities is working in Daniel's favor.

Feinstein again refers to Dr. Wickware's report.

"Your Honour will also note...that he feels and has felt in the past, that he's completely ashamed of his past behavior. He did tell the police that he has nothing to be ashamed of in his present life and from all accounts appears since September 12, 1976—he has been living a completely normal and religious and Christian life in every sense of that word and in every aspect of his day-to-day life. You will note from the report he feels that he does not require at this time any psychiatric or psychological intervention."

How is it possible, I wonder, that my recovery process may involve years of therapy to deal with ongoing issues, such as sexual confusion and flashbacks, whereas my abuser can be deemed in no need of rehabilitation at all?

"Dr. Wickware really doesn't comment any more on that, other than to say that obviously he wouldn't be of any assistance if he does not willingly participate in some sort of programme. In fact, whether or not, in my respectful submission, what he experienced on September 12, 1976 was genuine, or whether that is something that he embraced simply to pull himself up from the depths to which he had sunk, the fact remains that he has for now five and a half years lived a Christian life, as he puts it, and has become a lifelong member of the community. He is very actively involved in the church."

"He and his second wife were married in 1979, and who is in court today, met in the church. What initially attracted her to him was his religious devotion. She, sir, is unable to work. She obtains disability pension. She suffers from cerebral palsy and some other medical problems. Mr. D'Haene has been the sole supporter of the family. He has, as you will note, a steady employment history, and he has managed to support his wife and him since their marriage since 1979."

Feinstein is describing my abuser as benevolent! Disability. Religious devotion. Cerebral palsy. Sole Supporter. *Maybe it was just a game.*

Judge Bannister interjects, "I take it he hasn't supported the family, the former family?"

"Apparently not. They have absolutely no communication. He doesn't know whether she is remarried or she hasn't. Apparently she is self-supporting. There has been not one word for many, many years. He doesn't even know where she is currently. They simply severed all contact. That is also the case with the children. Ronald and he have spoken in the past couple of years but it has been brief and it has never been friendly.

"The Court of Appeal, sir, has consistently, in cases of this kind, particularly cases involving multiple occurrences over a lengthy period of time, indicated that a period of incarceration is absolutely necessary particularly to reflect Society's abhorrence towards this type of conduct. My submission, sir, is that there's nothing in the circumstances in this case which make it so exceptional that any other penalty ought to be imposed.

"I think clearly he's facing a period of incarceration. The question becomes on the length. In that regard, I ask you to consider several things, sir. The fact that he has entered a plea of guilty. There is some genuine remorse and some genuine shame about the life that he led up until 1976. The fact that by waiving the preliminary hearing on these charges and pleading guilty at trial, he has obviated the necessity of his children having to give evidence about what clearly must be extremely traumatic incidents and very bad memories for them."

Thinking Donald "knows". These statements are classic in abuse cases. Clearly a strategic move on Daniel's part. By removing the necessity of our giving testimony, he removes the danger that we could provide convincing, first-hand accounts that would contradict his lawyer's submission.

Feinstein's acknowledgement of our trauma, although still referring to the abuse in such abstract terms as "incidents," "bad memories," appears more sincere than Greenfield's questionable presentation and scattered delivery.

"I'd ask you to consider he has a good work record, that during the last five and a half years there appears to be a complete reformation, a complete rehabilitation. He certainly has not been accused of any criminal activity during that time. There are no convictions, nothing to suggest that he is anything but a law-abiding citizen now. He indicated to the police that he has a high respect for law and order and it appears that since his revelation, his change in 1976, that such is the case.

"Of course, sir, I ask you to consider that we are dealing in this case with old offences. That doesn't make them any less heinous, but nonetheless, you're sentencing a man now for incidents that stopped five and a half years ago, and continued—or began many years before that. I don't for a moment, sir, try to minimize the seriousness of these offences. As I have reviewed the matter with Mr. D'Haene, there is really nothing that can be said in vindication of the facts. I don't minimize it, nor does Mr. D'Haene. He realizes the seriousness of it.

"With respect to the principles of sentencing, sir, the lifestyle that he has adopted; his involvement in the church; his absolute conquering of his problem with alcohol for the last five and half years, in my respectful submission do not indicate a need for rehabilitation or reformation is indicated. He and his wife cannot have children. They do not plan to have children, and there is nothing to suggest anything in the nature of that sort of activity continuing beyond 1976. Likewise, sir, my respectful submission is there is nothing to indicate that he is a danger to the public at this stage.

"Mr. Greenfield and I have had discussions and I believe that we submit jointly, sir, that a period of incarceration is required in the circumstances of this case and that Your Honour consider that period to be in an Ontario reformatory length rather than penitentiary."

Finally, I understand Greenfield's bizarre behavior. The Crown and Defense have agreed on a plea-bargain. Doesn't anyone care what *we* think?

"My respectful submission is that a member of the public who became apprised of all of the facts in this case, all of the background material, while that person would be shocked and would be horrified by the nature of the circumstances and events that led to these charges, on turning his attention to Mr. D'Haene, the particular offender, would have to be impressed by the fact that there have been considerable changes in his life in the last five and a half years. He's a religious man about whom there has been no concern during that time. It is a version of what took place with the Society and if what took place afterwards is correct, and I submit it is, that he suffered the trauma and the anxiousness of this hanging over his head for some considerable period until it finally came home to roost and the time he was detected by the authorities and apprehended with respect to these charges. I think sir, that a member of the community, having considered the facts and then having considered the particular circumstances of Mr. D'Haene, would not lose faith in the judicial system if the sentence imposed were one of reformatory length, bearing in mind all the circumstances of this case."

The picture Feinstein paints has no resemblance to my black and white movies. Mother is portrayed as a strong, vindictive character. A woman who blackmailed her ex-husband. I am portrayed as a little boy—a body without a voice, a Witness puppet. And Daniel, he's a long-suffering, modern-day Job—godlike and innocent.

I don't know what I'm doing here. I want to run, but my silence and calmness prevent me. As I look into the faces of those surrounding me, I see disgust and disbelief, four words planted firmly on the tips of their tongues: "I told you so."

"Is Greenfield like me?" Other Donald wonders. *"Will he object to nothing?"*

"Mr. Greenfield," states the judge.

"Sir, I might indicate at the outset, before my friend's comments, the accused has no previous record. With respect to the submissions made by my friend on behalf of his client, my submission would be that this type of case is not the type of case where rehabilitation is of primary concern. My submissions would be that of primary concern is protection of the public, that the public sees that the judicial system abhors this type of conduct and that those factors must, by far, outweigh the factors of rehabilitation which we all heard since the 1978 divorce or '76 split-up.

"My submission will be that we must not lose sight of the offence. As my friend indicated, his submissions were by way of submissions that the accused wish him to make. My concern is that we not lose sight of what it is that the accused has been charged with and that he is here in relation to those charges because of them, not because of any religious belief that he held. Certainly the Crown's position is not that if he had some quarrel with the Jehovah's Witness sect, it arose because of their abhorrence for the acts that he had been committing. I have some concern on the comments made that the accused felt brainwashed by the Society. Certainly it is not my understanding, nor is it the position of the Crown that if it was called brainwashing that it had anything to do with these offences. There is nothing in the doctrines as I understand it, that would condone this type of activity and that the accused quarrel with the Society is a religious one. It has, perhaps, some foundation in his own beliefs, but is not relevant, in my submission, to the offence before the Court.

"Information that I received with respect to how the matter arose is that the victim, Donald, was the one who complained and as I understand it, I had the officer check with him on the recess, it was not because of any pressure which was put on him by the Society. His concern was his own, it was his own well-being, that he had been so deprived of a normal upbringing that he found himself in this sexual identity crisis. What the counselling and his own research into the problem indicated made him want to come forth so it could be out in the open and it could be dealt with once and for all, and he could get on with the rest of his life. He talked it over with his sister before he actually took the step of reporting it. As I understand, he has talked it over with his brother Ronald. He has indicated that it was not for any religious motives or any motive other than the psychological damage which had been caused to him in an effort to lessen the psychological blow or to remove the identity problem that he has told me and that he has, as I indicated, he continued counselling and talked over the matter of reporting it with his counsel who are, as well, here today."

I don't know what happened to Greenfield, but he seems to have kicked into gear after listening to Feinstein's submission. I am hopeful.

Greenfield refers the Court to a number of cases. First, *R and Tomago*, a decision of the Ontario Court of Appeal which states that, "Parents who...engage in sexual activities with their children must realize that it is dealt with very severely." Second, Greenfield cites *R and Scheiber* from the Saskatchewan Court of Appeal: "Psychological trauma suffered by the victims...[is] a significant factor in considering sentence." Then he refers to *R and C* from the Newfoundland District Court which held that regarding the issue of consent in gross indecency matters, "Consent to an act of gross indecency is not a defence and not relevant. It is a relevant circumstance only in determining the grossness or the indecency and that any acts between males and females or one of the parties under the age of twenty-one certainly would be an act of gross indecency and that type of fact which might not be gross indecency amongst adults is with children."

Greenfield also notes cases which suggest sentences are required for this type of offence: The *R and Petrovich* decision of Saskatchewan Court of Appeal, "stated that in imparting the eighteen month sentence the Court must maintain public confidence in the judiciary in respect of charges involving children.... The three victims involved were prostitutes, the age of fourteen; so that even in dealing with known prostitutes which was before the Court, the Court imposed significant sentences.... In speaking to the element of deterrence, *R and Moore* found in *22 Criminal Law Quarterly, 157* a decision of the Nova Scotia Supreme Court as the Appellate Division...stated it was imposing [a] sentence because of the necessity for general deterrence to be shown to like-minded parents."

"In summation, as my friend indicated, I think we are in agreement, certainly that this type of offence calls for a custodial sentence. My submission would be that the minimum sentence ought to be for the maximum reformatory term. Many of the cases speak in terms of first offenders, initial periods of incarceration in penitentiary."

"Why in this case, Mr. Greenfield, do you feel a penitentiary term is not appropriate?" asks Judge Bannister.

"I think for two reasons: firstly, there does not appear to have been any continuation of this sort of conduct since about 1976-77 when the family split up. There is no indication of a continuing course of conduct approaching the period of time and trial. So I think that is a relevant factor and further, I think I had the same concerns as Your Honour had initially, I don't know, there's just something—there's something about a situation where there are purportedly reasonable responsible people in the community who know about the commission of an offence involving children, young children, who are aware of that in their professional capacity as fellows or brothers of a religious society who, knowing that in 1973, do nothing in respect of the law of the land about that knowledge. I think that no one reporting that known conduct allows some credence, perhaps, to the submissions made by my friend that the accused may well feel that he is being persecuted for religious matters because of his change or present religious beliefs. Had this matter come before the courts in 1973 or '74, my position would have been much different, but my feeling when I speak of feeling—I'm directly referring to those persons in this church who were independent and objective out of the family, who did nothing to see that the laws of the land are somehow enforced to protect these children and that, in fact, doing nothing in 1973—and again I'm speaking of doing nothing vis-à-vis the law, as opposed to whatever actions they took vis-à-vis their own church, but by doing nothing vis-à-vis the law, they then allowed the accused to continue this type of conduct until '76—that's three years of terror and traumatic experience for the children."

"How does that benefit the accused in terms of sentence?" queries Bannister.

Greenfield replies: "I always concern myself with trying to deal with the matter of sentence when you're sometime removed from the offence and when it's not—where the time span in between is not due to the accused running away or something like that. We know the accused was there. He certainly made statements to the senior persons in the church in early 1973 admitting his guilt in relation to these—to this conduct and had they acted at that time, then I think there would not—we wouldn't be in a situation where anyone might even think that it was because of religious persecution of the matters before the Court. I'm not suggesting that is the case, what I am saying is that the non doing anything about it allows for this feeling that perhaps it is persecution for the wrong reason.

"I am satisfied that in the present case the prosecution came about as a direct result of the counselling treatment programmes undertaken by the children and my belief is that those counselling treatment programs had nothing to do, they were totally outside of the church, so to speak, and that it is as a result of that counselling and treatment that the complaints were made."

Judge Bannister responds, "I suppose my concern is the point you're making is a mitigating factor. Had he went to the authorities of his church on the basis of Mr. Feinstein's thoughts of help at that time...."

Had Daniel gone to the Elders for help? He was summoned before a judicial committee composed of Elders. He never disclosed the assaults. Ronny did. Daniel did not seek help! At that point, he didn't know the Elders would not go to the police. He was caught between a rock and a hard place.

"At that time, because there was nothing done other then disfellowshipping him, he must have, in some fashion, probably thought in his own mind and chose not to receive any outside help. I assume what my friend has said is that the accused received all the necessary help that he needed right directly from God."

"That was sometime later," Judge Bannister interjects.

"Sometime later, yes. I think there was really nothing different in 1973 than there was in 1976. For some reason, between '73 and '76 the accused, almost without exception, continued the conduct. It may be the stopping of conduct obviously, he would stop, you know, with his family moving away but maybe it was the public nature of it, the knowledge by the accused that many of these acts now formed part of the divorce proceedings which were in the courts of the land, and to some extent, public as opposed to what he was able to do in '73 and that was keep it within the church, and the church condoned that."

Not only does Greenfield not correct the judge's confusion, he obliges the Defense by providing speculative mitigation for Daniel.

"Perhaps the psychological damage that was attributed by these acts to the victims would not have been so severe had the accused actions stopped in 1973. I think one who has knowledge of the commission of a crime in his community and who does nothing about —a person who is reportedly responsible, concerned in the community who does nothing about it, should bear some of the responsibility for the subsequent acts, so that there's a mixed end.

"It would be my suggestion that the fault not lie only with the accused from '73 to '76, but he was allowed, to some extent, allowed to continue that kind of conduct."

Am I hearing correctly? Greenfield is suggesting Daniel is less culpable because others share the responsibility.

Judge Bannister seems unconvinced.

"I'm just wondering, my impression is that many cases of this nature, penitentiary term is imposed. I'm wondering what sets this apart from that?"

"I agree with Your Honour. There are probably more cases in which penitentiary sentences are imposed than not. It seems to me that the length of time involved, which is really not attributable to the accused before the matters come to prosecution, my primary feeling for not suggesting to the Court a substantial penitentiary term for the length of time before the matter, you know, came before the courts, that there were opportunities by persons other than the children. You can't expect children to know that, you know, they can go to a police, or they can go to somebody, some group of persons who will be able to assist them when they have some problem outside of the family. Children can't be expected to know that, especially children who have been abused as these ones have through the very formative years of their life and who received a continuing abuse even after elders and adults became aware of what had been going on. I mean, what must the children have thought in 1973 and '74 when that conduct which they didn't wish to participate in was then continued after persons became aware of it."

If no one else is listening, at least Judge Bannister seems to be paying attention to detail.

"By 1973, it appears that according to the indictment, with respect to the son these matters had been going on since sometime in or about 1965, eight years. My concern is that there was a course of conduct over a substantial period of time before 1973, and that the quality and nature of the acts is really not diminished by the passing of time between the time he ceased and the time matters were brought to trial. That period of time to me would seem irrelevant in going to the issue of rehabilitation in the nature and quality of the acts."

"I agree with Your Honour, there's no doubt the acts started in 1965 with the other son and around '70 with the daughter."

"I'd like to make a response sir," interjects Feinstein. "I agree with Your Honour's concern over the length of time it's taken to bring these matters to court in no way mitigates the seriousness; however, I do feel, sir, that the Court must take into consideration the fact it is now punishing a man for offences that ceased five years ago. His life since then, that must be worth something. If, and I think it clearly is the issue, is whether or not penitentiary or the maximum reformatory sentence is indicated, my respectful submission is at that time, once we have reached that point, Your Honour is certainly entitled to take into account the life that this man has led for the last five and a half years, and you add that to the equation and to balance that against the seriousness of the offences, while it is clear that had it not been for the fact that he appears to have straightened his life around over the past several years, that he would be a prime candidate for penitentiary. My feeling is Your Honour must give some consideration in determining whether or not circumstances of this case dictate penitentiary.

"I also ask you to consider, sir, that regardless of exactly how the matter came to the authorities or what prompted it—and I don't disagree with Mr. Greenfield—that certainly his indication is that one of the sons took it upon himself to report it in the course of his therapy may well be the case—I do suggest to you, though, sir, that a considerable period of time after this conduct ceased, after the involvement with his family ceased, and after he had embraced a new faith, was under some considerable strain and anxiety, by the fact the matters were not just forgotten for five and half years, but held over his head as a threat for some considerable time. I have disclosure which I have received, the Elders of the church brought letters to the investigating officer, I gather, became part of the Crown's brief, two letters, sir, from 1976 to his son: 'You are continually rubbing it in and using threats. Stop blackmailing me.' A letter to his son, Ronny: 'Stop blackmailing me. Either carry out your threats or shut up.' That was at a time, sir, when as I indicate earlier, he was being pressured to stop his denunciation of The Watchtower Society by having the threat of detection and prosecution with respect to these matters held over his head. And now, five and a half years later for whatever reason, finally he must face these charges. It appears to me, sir, that is something Your Honour ought to take into consideration and adopt, perhaps, keeping in mind his lifestyle a sentence to a reformatory as opposed to penitentiary.

"Those are my submissions."

"We'll have a short recess and I'll pass sentence on the accused."

Chapter Forty-Five

I want to scream. It's like we just got started and it's almost over! People are talking to me and I don't want to respond. I'm embarrassed I wasted everyone's time.

We look at each other in disbelief, wondering what case is being tried.

Daniel's rationalization skills have been perfected to the point that he could fool a psychologist. Can he fool the judge? Obviously on some level he has succeeded because Bannister never once asked for any documentation to be submitted as evidence.

Daniel's lawyer condemns the Aylmer Elders for their silence in 1973, and at the same time praises Daniel for being "saved" for five and a half years and demonstrating exemplary behavior. Greenfield submits that The Watchtower Society should bear some part of the blame. Whose side is Greenfield on anyway?

What a circus! It's like Daniel is a neighborhood brat, and he just needs a good spanking. If only Greenfield had gone over our story with us, this would be a different scenario altogether. I think I shall go mad myself.

"Talk about an anti-climax. Trials certainly aren't like they are in the movies, are they, Wilf?"

"No, Donald. Although, this one is relatively short.'

"Yeah, four hours. I thought trials build up to the dramatic sentencing."

"Unfortunately, plea bargaining is part of today's justice system."

"Thanks for not telling me, 'I told you so.'"

"Well, I'm surprised how things went myself."

"I guess we should go back in. This shouldn't take long," I predict.

"Please rise...."

"Before I pass sentence on this accused, I want to express the Court's thanks to both counsel in this case for the submissions which were made. I thought they were, to be expected, frank and open and helpful to the Court. I appreciate the canvassing of the various alternatives open to the Court and the reasoning behind submissions of both counsel.

"In this case, the accused has pleaded guilty to certain counts contained in the indictment relating to acts of gross indecency with three of his children. In summary, this accused forced his children to participate in a variety of indescribably vile acts with the accused and among themselves. These acts were accompanied by threats of physical harm or the break-up of the family. These activities were not confined to the home.

"Once the older children became aware that this conduct in which they were engaging was wrong, they began to shelter the youngest child of the family, a son, and submitted themselves to the accused's sexual demands in order to protect him from becoming involved in this type of activity.

"A young child is part of a defenseless class in our society. Such a person looks to a parent as an example, and for guidance, and in normal circumstances has complete trust in his parents. Here the trust was abused abominably, in my opinion, to meet the needs of the parent with a complete disregard for the welfare of the children or the effect that these activities might have upon them. The result is that at least two of the children have sustained psychological damage to such a nature and degree as to require psychological counselling. They apparently have some type of identity conflict and they were certainly deprived of any semblance of a normal childhood.

"Their childhood at home must have been hell on earth and the harm that was done to them was probably impossible to calculate.

"One of the primary functions of a parent in our society is to instruct a child as to socially acceptable behavior and to protect the child from harm, nurturing it and encouraging it to an independent maturity with values that will allow it to function as a useful and contributing member of society.

"This accused, by his example, instructed these children in a way which can only be described as violating the standards of morality held by any normal decent person in our community. Rather than protecting his children, he exposed them to incalculable harm for his own perverted pleasures.

"In passing sentence in these circumstances, the Court must express the absolute loathing of the community for reprehensible acts of this nature and reflect society's revulsion and condemnation of this accused's conduct. It must also make known to the community, and particularly to the parents of young children, that those parents who subvert the trust of children in their care will be dealt with severely by the Court.

"Mr. Feinstein and Mr. Greenfield have jointly submitted that a reformatory rather than a penitentiary term is appropriate. Mr. Greenfield submits that it should be a maximum reformatory term. Submissions of counsel are obviously not binding on the Court since it is the Court's sole function to determine proper sentence in any individual case. I respect the submissions of experienced counsel, as it is in this case. However, the final decision is the Court's alone.

"Mr. Feinstein, concedes, and properly so, that there is no reasonable, logical alternative in this case but to impose a period of incarceration. The real issue becomes the length of that period and as a result, the type of institution in which it will be served.

"Mr. Feinstein then points to certain areas for consideration: First, and I think importantly, these acts ceased approximately five and a half years ago and there has been no repetition of these acts or anything resembling them during the intervening time period. The accused is divorced from his prior wife, the mother of the children in question. He has remarried. There are no children of his remarriage and it is submitted that there are none planned, so that there is no threat that these acts might be repeated with children of a second marriage.

"The accused is described as being a good worker, with an excellent work record and as the sole support of his present wife and himself. His wife suffers from some medical disabilities and is unable to secure employment. This accused supports her and himself. The accused has had a life which has followed religious principles for some period of time. During the course of his first marriage, he was a member of The Watchtower Society. The submission is, and I have no alternative to accept, or hesitation in accepting, the submission, that since he embraced his new faith in 1976, he has been an exemplary member of the community.

"The psychiatric report, which has been filed with the Court, shows clearly that there is no overt sign of mental illness which was revealed by the assessment. The accused has expressed shame for the conduct in question and has conquered a previous problem which he had with alcoholic beverages and I am advised that he has not consumed anything of an alcoholic nature since 1976. He is not now therefore, in my opinion, in need of rehabilitation or reformation and is not now a danger to any member of the public. His children are now more mature and he has no contact with them at the present time, except perhaps of a brief and unpleasant nature, nor does he have any relation or communication with his former wife from whom he obtained a divorce in 1978.

"The accused has no previous criminal record of any nature at all. He entered a plea of guilty to the offences before the Court. He also waived the preliminary hearing, thus sparing the complainants from the difficult task of appearing and giving evidence and reviewing these unpleasant memories from the past. He has spared them this. Although there were threats of violence towards the complainants, the children, there was no actual physical violence visited upon any of them according to the submissions relayed to me and I note particularly that the acts involving the daughter did not include sexual intercourse and stopped short of that type of activity.

"There was a submission made by Mr. Feinstein as well that the accused once was a member, with the rest of his family, his first family, of The Watchtower Society and that when the Society became aware of his activities, he was disfellowshipped in November of 1973. He indicated that in 1976 he joined another church and it was in that year apparently that the family unit disintegrated. The children went to live with their mother at that time.

"It was submitted that there was pressure brought to bear upon the accused by family members to give up his new religious faith and to stop denouncing the old one, (which he in fact had been doing, after unsuccessful attempts to return to it), or they would expose him and his activities. The submission is that he was being, in effect, blackmailed which caused him a great deal of anxiety and stress and that this is a factor which the Court should consider in terms of punishment which has already been visited upon the accused, although not through the instrumentality of the judicial system.

"It appears, as well, that although the church officials at The Watchtower Society knew in 1973 of these activities, they were not reported. As a result, the family reconciled upon the accused giving a promise to his wife that he would cease such activities in the future. Apparently these activities ceased for a short period of time and then they began again. It has been suggested, if I understand the submissions of Mr. Greenfield properly, that perhaps the Society should bear some part of the blame for the continuation of these activities after 1973 since these activities at the time were known, or made known, to responsible members of the community who failed to act upon that information.

"I pass no judgment on that Society, which is not before the Court and has not made any representations. I have merely reviewed the submission which was made by Mr. Greenfield as a factor which he feels the Court ought to take into account.

"The fact remains that the matter came to light because one of the sons reported these matters to the police as a result of the psychological counselling process which he underwent and, as I understand it, not from the pressure brought upon him by The Watchtower Society.

"The primary concern of the Court in this case must be to deter others and to express society's revulsion regarding the acts of this accused. I do not believe it is necessary on the evidence before me to deter this accused in order to protect the public and particularly young children from him nor to effect the rehabilitation of this accused. Had it not been for the elapse of five and a half years from the ceasing of these events during which time this accused not only ceased this type of activity but has apparently changed his life around and has lived during that period of time an exemplary and productive life—had it not been for these factors, I would have sentenced him to penitentiary.

"I believe, however, that the accused is entitled to some credit for the last five and a half years of his life notwithstanding the gross and shocking activities in which he was engaged with his children over those years preceding that time. I am hopeful and I believe the sentence I shall impose in these circumstances will adequately reflect the Court's attitude to these offences and deter other like-minded persons, and that in this particular case it is not necessary to incarcerate the accused in the penitentiary to achieve that end.

"Would you please stand?

"You are sentenced to two years less one day in reformatory. That will be the sentence on each of the counts and the sentences will be served concurrently."

My movie reels grind to a halt: only two years in a reformatory!

Standing in the prisoner's docket tightly clutching a small red Bible, Daniel weeps. He looks to Bannister, then turns to those in attendance.

"Please forgive me. I'm ashamed of my past, but I think the Lord Jesus Christ has helped me in many ways."

As Daniel is led away, I somehow manage to find my way out of the courtroom. I am in Jehovah's Witness mode. I tune out my real feelings. If I did not have this escape, how could I handle the gut-wrenching events that just transpired?

I thank those who have driven down to support us. People are amazed that I handle myself so well. Have I? I hear comments such as: "Now you can get on with your life" and "It's too bad the Witnesses were given such a bad representation." I sense we have bothered everyone with this trial. Considering how things turned out, I am left with the same feeling. Something didn't happen.

Looking upward from the courthouse steps, I imagine not a rabbit in the clouds this time, but rather a large banner draped across the sky: "THIS IS THE BEGINNING OF THE REST OF YOUR LIFE!"

Other Donald screams: "We are NOT GUILTY!"

A few years after our day in court, I requested a transcript of the Reasons for Sentencing. A decade later, I made another request for the Sentencing Proceedings. Each time I only glanced at the cover page. I delayed reading the transcript until nineteen years after my court appearance. I had not thought about anything that had transpired during those four hours until I read the record. I had blocked from memory that day in court.

This trial proved to be an education, all right—for me more than anyone. Even though a conviction was achieved, I learned that justice is a relative term.

Why is it that no Jehovah's Witnesses from Aylmer attended the trial? Witnesses believe that energy should not be wasted on worldly endeavors. Marina, Mother, and I certainly felt insignificant that spring day so many years ago. In many ways, it was a familiar road we'd often traveled.

Who could blame me for wanting to protect my baby brother, Erik, from this experience? Yet the experience of testifying could hardly have been more traumatic than witnessing this debacle.

The judge had nothing but what counsel presented on which to base his decision. He expressed indignation at the abuse, acknowledged the hell we lived through, but why did he not request evidence regarding our experience?

Things could have been so different. Because the incident of abuse with Corey in 1969 had taken place in another county, and Daniel was not recharged in that county, evidence from that molestation could not be presented. Had I been called to testify, I certainly would have brought up that Daniel had asked us to recruit victims for him. This glaring omission enabled Feinstein to paint a picture of a "family" situation. The fact that he had molested outside of his family would have altered the proceedings in that Daniel posed a threat to the public at large. It's a sad commentary that the incident involving Corey would have been judged more harshly than our years of abuse.

Had Greenfield understood the psychological abuse we endured at the hands of Daniel D'Haene after 1976 when the sexual abuse stopped, I believe he would have handled this case differently.

Back in 1982, education on sexual abuse of girls was minimal, of boys, almost non-existent. Unfortunately, at that time, rape of males was viewed quite differently from rape of females. It was stressed Daniel had stopped short of intercourse with my sister. Because Greenfield did not pursue the charge of buggery against me, no evidence was presented concerning my rape by Daniel at the age of twelve.

What would have happened had Greenfield informed the judge that he had presided over the divorce case back in 1978? Would Judge Bannister have asked for a transcript of that hearing and my testimony? Would Greenfield and Feinstein have been less harsh on the Witnesses had they realized how many officials outside of The Watchtower Society were aware of the abuse and failed to report it to the proper authorities?

Feinstein submitted a psychiatrist's report on Daniel. Why did Greenfield not call on experts to give testimony regarding the effects we suffered at the hands of Daniel D'Haene? There were two therapists in the courtroom who had treated Marina and me for seven months. Why didn't Greenfield interview them? Greenfield was familiar with the legal aspects of sexual abuse, but his presentation of our history of abuse betrayed a gross lack of understanding and empathy for our feelings.

Exposing this trial to the public is important, in that it shows how victims can be re-victimized by an imperfect system of law. Untruthful evidence can be entered in court unchallenged. A molester can misrepresent himself. Victims might not be called to testify. A Crown Attorney may choose not to present documented evidence. A psychologist's report can be entered as evidence unchallenged. A judge can only weigh the evidence that is before him.

The fact that the assaults on us had ended five and a half years earlier was stressed. Studies show that a high percentage of molesters abuse several children over a period of years. The fact that the abuse stopped only because we physically left the family home was lost in the presentation. My father was an intelligent man who had kept us from the real world. He was not a blind follower of the Witness philosophy, as he tried to project, and he certainly was aware that his abuse of us was criminal.

Feinstein stressed the fact that Daniel was the sole supporter of his disabled wife and was living a life following religious principles. Greenfield failed to stress that Daniel was the sole supporter of his first wife and four children during the years of abuse. Purporting to live a life following religious principles during those years had not prevented him from committing the criminal acts for which he was then charged.

There were other matters of interest. First, court witnesses who are subpoenaed do not always appear in court. My older brother, Ronny, refused to comply with his subpoena. More to the point, subpoenaed witnesses aren't necessarily called to testify. Second, obtaining a reputable lawyer may be costly but legal aid is always an option. Third, plea bargains may be made without a victim's knowledge. Finally, in the normal course of a trial, it is deemed bad practice to interrupt other counsel's submission. There is one exception, and that is where there is an egregious factual error. In that case, counsel stands until he is recognized by the judge, then he presents his correction. If it is a matter that can be effectively addressed in his response, then that would be the place to do so. It is a matter of judgment. If Greenfield had interrupted opposing counsel's address for a minor point, or if he was wrong in his factual correction, he may have incurred the judge's wrath. Because Greenfield wasn't properly prepared, he had no prior knowledge that there were errors to correct.

But protocol, at the very least, should dictate that the Crown introduce himself to the key witnesses. Greenfield never spoke to my family. We were not called as witnesses on the sentencing because the lawyers had previously agreed on a sentence. To call on us may have resulted in the judge not accepting their joint submission. The same explanation may apply to the psychiatric reports. I would like to believe the Crown wanted to spare us the discomfort of disclosing our personal history, but I cannot since Greenfield made no effort to make us feel comfortable before, during, or after his presentation. Nor did he keep us informed of what was happening.

I couldn't help asking myself, "Was it worth it?" If I had known what was going to happen I may never have embarked on this journey—at least not without my own lawyer. Even though Daniel would definitely spend time in a reformatory, it seemed a Pyrrhic victory at best. I put our privacy, our souls in the public domain, to what end and at what cost? Was there anything of me left? What was to become of me? Us?

Would I have had my father charged if I had never met Nort Rhiness? The mid and late 1980s saw an explosion in cases of children who disclosed their abuse. I most certainly would have been influenced by the publicity. On the other hand, I might have been discouraged by the negative experiences other victims have faced. Perhaps not knowing how the court system really treats victims worked in my favor.

What would the future hold for us? How would the press respond to the trial? Would they even notice? What would happen to Erik in the foster home? Would he get himself straightened out? Would Marina and I go back to therapy? Would we discover our true sexual orientation?

Would this trial be the last reminder of Father's touch?

* * * * * * * * * *

"Take me home, Maurice."

"I thought we were going to stop off at your Mom's and say hi."

"No, I'm tired. Besides, I've done twenty years of remembering in one day. That's more than enough. We can review the next two decades on another day. Thanks for...you know, being there."

"You're right, I think you need a break from all this. I just have to stop by my office to do a few things. You can work on your column while I'm doing that."

During the car ride back to London, impulsively I pull down the visor to look at myself in the mirror. I don't recognize that face. Physically I have aged twenty years, but emotionally I am frozen in time.

But what a wonderful gift it is to be able to turn off the film projector, the movie reels, the picture stills, the side view mirror...all in a blink of an eye. At least I can change reels. What about those poor souls who have no such relief?

Nevertheless, sometimes I feel trapped inside a body the outside world defines me by. As the aging process continues, everything seems out of whack. Because my physical, mental, and emotional selves all progressed at different rates, in any single day, I feel at turns ancient, childlike, and adolescent.

The outer and inner selves are still out of sync and rarely intertwine, but their connection is closer than it ever has been before. I perfected a mask in order that I could survive, and now I must remove the mask in order that I may be truly be free. *Objects ARE closer than they appear.*

Today's trip has convinced me that I should at least consider returning to therapy. It's time for a "tune up." I'll think about that tomorrow.

So many memories—so long ago. I find it difficult to believe my life is based on a true story.

I'm almost forty. There's no midlife crisis. I'm loved by a caring partner, and my life is rich with family and friends. Professionally, I write a regular column for an arts magazine, film a regular segment for a local television station, and I have an excellent agent for my acting career in Toronto. I'm a happy, thriving adult survivor. Life has never been better. Isn't that the most important thing?

Chapter Forty-Six

Turning the key signals our return home. Two felines greet us at the door.

"Can you believe Max and Garfield were just kittens when you were in St. Thomas for the trial in '82?"

"My goodness. They are that old." *I'm just glad they're cats and not bunnies,* I say under my breath.

"Yes, you've had a long, good life, haven't you?" says Maurice as he pets his nineteen-year-old cats.

"It's so long ago, like a dream I've long forgotten."

"Do you want something to drink?"

"Sure."

On my way to the kitchen, I notice the answering machine light blinking.

"Hey, Maurice, you didn't check the messages."

I push "play" as I walk by.

"*12:30 A. M. You have one message:* This is the father of Donald D'Haene. Hello, Donald. Your sister has died in a car accident...."

Epilogue

Clearly, my story does not end here. I am now working on a follow-up memoir.

Dealing with incest involves looking at how present behavior and past circumstances are interconnected. Recovery is an infinitely complex process.

Each victim in my family is different—we have nothing in common, yet we have everything in common—nevertheless, every one of us experienced abuse by the same man who unwittingly united us as comrades in battle. Our armor and weapons are as individual as we are. I have discovered that armor protects you from the world but does not protect you from yourself.

If in one family the individual paths are so completely unique, how can one outline a map for a successful recovery? There is no map. There is no blueprint for survival. One can only recount experiences, choices, and trial-and-error decisions. How empowering the revelation of these events is—their echoes can never be silenced. Letters, syllables, words put in ink leave an indelible mark in the world of reality. Hidden, they are meaningless. Visible, they are not erasable: they equal power.

I was one of the first males in Canada to come forward and speak openly about being sexually abused, thereby breaking the barrier of silence.

The truth is that chosen path is one of the reasons that I am alive today. I found my way of surviving. I want to continue my journey of self-discovery, but there is no graduation class, no point where the past means nothing. My experiences and choices have molded and shaped a character that is truly unique. I believe that if every human were to experience the awakening I have, he would find the world is not such a bad place to inhabit. I have an awareness, a sixth sense that cannot be bought, taught, or taken away from me.

Survival has been defined as a continuation of a life beyond that of another. In my case, I survived a horrific childhood and became a healthy adult. That's right. People who meet the adult Donald I am today do not see a victim—they meet a survivor. Yes, it takes a strong person to survive years of abuse. But forging your own way is something survivors discover as essential, for no two victims experience abuse the same way. No two recoveries are identical.

While individual history is important, pain is pain, so detailing the specifics of my experience is not as important as what I did to survive it. But I think it will help victims to realize they weren't meant to be abused! We just happen to fall into the path of a perpetrator. Understanding the abuser's process will not only remove our "guilt" feelings, but also diminish the "why me" dialogue.

There have been many men who were sexually abused before me. I personally know several men who have experienced unspeakable acts of abuse and torture, but who will never disclose their abuse to the authorities, their church, their families. I hope they will find strength and courage in my story.

Writing this book has become a catharsis. Now I understand that the reason I waited nearly twenty years before starting is because I didn't want to go into that emotional vortex of the past. For the first time in my life, I wept about my experience. At the age of forty, that emotional breakthrough signaled a major milestone. It proves the psychological damage that sexual abuse creates is life-long. Band-aid solutions to complex problems are only temporarily effective.

Although I have distanced myself from my childhood experiences, in this new millennium, my quest for inner peace continues. Me, myself, and I have found relative success. I'm well liked. I'm outgoing, I get people to open up, share experiences. When I met my relatives in Belgium for the first time at twenty-three, I was warmly received. Now my life is infinitely better.

When I was going through the public humiliation, I had no core, no self-esteem. I was a blank slate on which people drew and colored me in their own interpretations.

My metamorphosis has taken decades of hard work, in and out of therapy. People I've met along the way sometimes refused to accept the changes in me. They wanted me to stay who I was.

Epilogue

I have been more childlike in my thirties than I ever was as a child or teenager. Sometimes I see the innocent sparkle I had as a child. Other times, I discover an innocence I never had.

If it is because of a God that I exist, and because of my parents that I was born, it is also true that many people visiting my space have helped me to survive and choose life. Foremost among them have been my therapists. They taught me there is no true recovery unless there is risk, openness, love and loss, hurt and acceptance. But even their couch was not the last stop in my story, for surviving is a lifelong journey, not a destination.

I feel fortunate I have people in my life who care about me, love me, and support me. On good days, such love envelops me. Fortunately the good days are many, the bad few.

I've always felt different, sometimes even special. I think that's because I am.

Acknowledgements

I would like to thank the following people who provided criticism on the early drafts of this work: novelists Joan Barfoot and Charlotte Vale Allen; Lesleigh Turner; Linda and Alan Nagata; Beth Ashford. To all others who were so generous with their help, I extend sincere thanks.

I also wish to acknowledge the Ontario Arts Council for their Writer's Reserve Grant, which helped in the initial stages of this book.

Special thanks to Sue Parkinson, for her unfailing encouragement and grammar skills; Jim Cotton for his editing suggestions; Wilf Graham, for seeing goodness and strengths through a tortured façade; and especially my partner in life, Maurice Ambeault, who loves all the 'Donalds'.

Professional and Personal Reactions to *Father's Touch*

An amazing and deeply moving testimony of survival, faith and courage, *Father's Touch* reinscribes in positive, empowering ways, the meaning of human relationships and social responsibility.

Kalpana Kannabiran, *Biblio: A Review of Books*, New Delhi, India; Co-author, *De-Eroticizing Assault: Essays on Modesty, Honour and Power*, Calcutta: Stree, 2002

****

This well written and fluent book should be required reading for all engaged in the protection of children and the victims of today. A triumph of talent and the will over adversity.

Dione M. Coumbe, LL.B. (Hons.) Editor & Reviewer for www.DoverWeb.co.uk; Managing Director of Book Publicity Ltd., UK, www.BookPublicity.co.uk; Dover, England

****

Told with unusual candor and its message of survival—spiritual and psychological—under almost impossible conditions is one of hope for all of us.

Peter Desbarats, author, journalist, and educator, London, Canada (*Somalia Cover-Up: A Commissioner's Journal*)

****

A memoir that should be required reading for every adult in every community. A testament to the importance of public education and prevention programs to eliminate sexual abuse.

Peter G. Jaffe, Ph.D., Clinical Psychologist; Executive Director, Center for Children & Families in the Justice System of the London Family Court Clinic, Inc.; Adjunct Professor, Dept. of Psychology, Part Time Professor, Dept. of Psychiatry, University of Western Ontario

****

A compelling read. The book contains much that is unexpectedly enjoyable, thanks to D'Haene's ironic, but not bitter sense of humor, lively writing style, and the upbeat outlook on life he has achieved in recent years. D'Haene has many cards up his sleeves with which he tantalizes the reader away from putting this book down.

The relevance and educational value of *Father's Touch* are heightened by its dissimilarity to the customary dark and often self-absorbed exposes in the writing genre of personal revelation. And for all who have experienced sexual abuse, directly or indirectly, *Father's Touch* offers a gift of encouragement, faith, and hope.

Patricia Black, Arts Reviewer, *Scene Magazine*, London, Canada.

****

The generosity of D'Haene's treatment of all his subjects is profoundly moving.

Herman Goodden, columnist, *The London Free Press*

****

Donald D'Haene's *Father's Touch* is not only a cry from the heart of boyhood itself, but also the outraged testimony of an adult survivor bearing witness. His voice is direct, powerful, and important.

Richard Hoffman, author, *Half the House: a Memoir*

****

An important story, honestly and inspiringly told. It will open many eyes, and touch many hearts.

Dan Woog, author of *School's Out: The Impact of Gay and Lesbian Issues on America's Schools*

****

An evocative tale that cuts to the quick of human existence. Despite the horror of his upbringing, Donald D'Haene infuses moments of great light, and even humor, into his narrative. There isn't anyone who won't be able to relate to this powerful and compelling tale, which combines great insights with a natural story-telling ability.

Judy Liebner, columnist, *The London Free Press,* Ontario, Canada

****

Unsettling and cinematic.

Eric Bunnell, columnist, *The St. Thomas Times Journal*, Canada

****

A very well written memoir. D'Haene presents his story with dignity and honesty.

Denise M. Clark, Author (*A Man's War*)

****

D'Haene has produced a most remarkable and moving book. By this telling memoir, those involved in the administration of the justice system can hopefully be more sensitized to the needs of those who legitimately turn to the Courts for help.

Scott Ritchie, LL. B. QC, London, Canada

****

Stunningly intimate yet objective in the telling. It is several first persons—complex and compelling—interwoven yet explicit. A must read. A stunning read!

Richard Murray, Superintendent of Human Resource Services, Thames Valley District School Board, London, Ontario, Canada

****

Father's Touch is a story of surviving at a cost. This is an amazing story. We cannot escape our ghosts; they follow us at every turn in our lives, like fate.

Wilf Graham, London, Ontario, Canada

****

A powerful, very well written book. As a fellow victim, I am proud a male survivor had the guts to write his story.

Herb Walsh, survivor of sexual abuse, Ontario, Canada

****

A brave account of a life's journey. A definite must for all sexual abuse survivors to read.

Glen Nisbett, sexual abuse survivor, Niagara Falls, Ontario, Canada